THE INCARNATION OF LOVE

THE DIVINE WORLD-TEACHER AND TRUE HEART-MASTER,
DA AVABHASA (THE "BRIGHT")
Sri Love-Anandashram, Fiji, 1993

THE
INCARNATION
OF LOVE

"Radical" Spiritual Wisdom and Practical Instruction
on self-Transcending Love and Service
in All Relationships

Compiled from the Wisdom-Teaching
of
The Divine World-Teacher and True Heart-Master,

Da Avabhasa
(The "Bright")

THE DAWN HORSE PRESS
CLEARLAKE, CALIFORNIA

NOTE TO THE READER

The devotional, Spiritual, functional, practical, relational, cultural, and formal community practices and disciplines referred to in this book are appropriate and natural practices that are voluntarily and progressively adopted by each student-novice and member of the Free Daist Avabhasan Communion and adapted to his or her personal circumstance. Although anyone may find them useful and beneficial, they are not presented as advice or recommendations to the general reader or to anyone who is not a participant in Da Avabhasa International or a member of the Free Daist Avabhasan Communion. And nothing in this book is intended as a diagnosis, prescription, or recommended treatment or cure for any specific "problem", whether medical, emotional, psychological, social, or Spiritual. One should apply a particular program of treatment, prevention, cure, or general health only in consultation with a licensed physician or other qualified professional.

First edition October 1993
Second printing May 1994
Third printing October 1994
Printed in the United States of America

Produced by the Free Daist Avabhasan Communion
in cooperation with the Dawn Horse Press

International Standard Book Number: 0-918801-86-9
Library of Congress Catalog Card Number: 93-74170

CONTENTS

INTRODUCTION: Moved to All by Heart   ix
            by the Free Daist Writers Guild

PART I: **THE DISCIPLINE OF LOVE IN THE WAY OF THE HEART**
    1 Love Without Expectation   2
    2 The Heart Is in Bondage Until Love Is
           Incarnated in the World   10
    3 Enter Fully into the Spiritual Life-Sphere of Love   17
    4 The Great Purpose of self-Transcendence   23
    5 You Must Become Human Before You Can
           Become Spiritual   31
    6 Serve All Others   35
    7 Love Is a Great Discipline   39

PART II: **TRANSCENDING REACTIVITY**
    8 No One Is the Beloved of God   44
    9 I Call You to Transcend Your Reactivity   51
   10 Rather Than Struggling, Turn to Me   63
   11 Do Not Be Concerned   75
   12 Your Relationship to Me Is Sufficient to Overcome
           All Reactive Patterning   80
   13 Transcend Reactivity, but Do Not Lose the Virtue
           of Your Emotion   87

PART III: **THE HUMOR OF LOVING WHEN IT IS MOST DIFFICULT**
   14 You Are Not the Guilty Party   94
   15 Assume Relationship   104
   16 Do Not Blame   106
   17 Be Wounded, Not Insulted   111
   18 Serve the Person Who Makes You Angry   114
   19 Forgive   116
   20 Be Served   122
   21 Release Guilt   123

PART IV: **BASIC PRACTICAL INSTRUCTIONS**

22 Do Your Relations Some Good   126
23 Know My Love and Grant It to All Others   131
24 Say the Words of Love   135
25 The Wound of Love   140
26 Undermine the Tendency to Create
      Emotional Dissociation   145
27 Giving and Receiving   149
28 The Mother-Force and the Father-Force   151
29 Equanimity and Feeling   154
30 Do Not Become Bound Up in the Search for
      Dominance and Power   159
31 The True Politics of Human Relationships   163
32 Honor Your Agreements and Obligations   170
33 Transform Your Speech   172
34 Compassion and Tolerance   176
35 Bless All Others   181

PART V: **COOPERATIVE COMMUNITY**

36 You Are My Gift to You: Cooperative
      Community in the Way of the Heart   186
37 A Visit to the Optometrist   201

PART VI: **BECOME A RENUNCIATE BY HANDLING YOUR LIFE-BUSINESS**

38 Letting Go   206
39 The Undying Beloved   214
40 No Fish Is to Die   224
41 The "Cave" of Relationship   228

PART VII: **MY GIFT OF HEART-VISION**

42 The Beatitude of Perfect Surrender to Me   234
43 For the Love   241
44 Love Is a Puja   250

About Da Avabhasa: The Giver of "Brightness"   257

An Invitation   263

About the Way of the Heart   268

The Seven Stages of Life   274

An Invitation to Support the Way of the Heart   284

Further Notes to the Reader   286

A Selection of the Sacred Literature of Da Avabhasa   290

Glossary   298

Index   304

DA AVABHASA (THE "BRIGHT")
SRI LOVE-ANANDASHRAM, FIJI, 1993

Moved to All by Heart

by the Free Daist Writers Guild

D uring the years of 1975 and 1976, Da Avabhasa Sat every weekend with the entire community of His devotees (which, at that time, was still localized in northern California). There were several hundred of us—many drove from jobs and homes in San Francisco—and we treasured the opportunity to see Him. Most often, we would sit with Him in meditation in one of the large meditation halls on the Mountain Of Attention Sanctuary in Lake County.

I had never meditated before becoming Da Avabhasa's devotee, and I was not as well prepared to be there as I should have been. I had only the most rudimentary sense of being able to participate in a meditative process with Him, but I was very aware that He was doing a Great Work with me and with everyone else in the room as we sat. I would feel His tremendous Blessing-Energy, sometimes felt even as a pleasurable physical pressure, but more fundamentally as a feeling that His Love was being directly Communicated to me.

Sometimes I would feel that I was being opened up emotionally, and I was often aware of great psychic forces in the room and especially around Sri Da Avabhasa. His face would often change into what appeared to be archetypal images of oriental Spiritual Masters of the past, and it was very common to see a golden-white Light Radiating from His Body. But there were other occasions when I struggled mightily with myself—sometimes it took every ounce of will that I could muster just to stay in the room and remain seated. But the content of my experience seemed beside the point—I was always so grateful and excited to be able to participate with Sri Da Avabhasa and to feel the Mystery of how He Works with His devotees.

After these occasions were over and Sri Da Avabhasa had left, we would mill about on the large, covered porch in the front of the meditation hall. These were very special moments to me, second only to being in the room with Sri Da Avabhasa. We would talk with one another in very soft and sensitive tones—the rough edges of conventional speech *were gone and the conversations always felt so intimate. If you looked around the crowd, you would always see at least a half a dozen people hugging one another—men embracing men, women embracing women, intimates and friends embracing one another. Laughter could always be heard. And even though the quality of the group seemed vulnerable and open, it was very high energy and did not feel twinky at all. I could literally see Sri Da Avabhasa's "Brightness" shining out of the eyes of my friends.*

Many years later, I was visiting an old friend from high school, someone I had not seen in a long time. At the end of our visit, we stood up to hug one another goodbye. In the middle of our hug, my friend exclaimed, "You give such good hugs! They are so heartfelt." Tears of gratitude to Sri Da Avabhasa welled up in my eyes—the Love He has Communicated to me so unfailingly for so many years shows itself in many ways, but one of the ways I treasure most is the way His Example, His Love, His Giving to me sets me free to love and to give to others.

A devotee

How does a community of ordinary people—bus drivers and secretaries, nurses, artists, dropouts, salesmen, businessmen, teachers, librarians, and lawyers (not saints, Yogis, or great humanitarians)—learn to be like this?

There is one reason: They receive a Gift of Love so great that it compels them to celebrate and shine, to give, to see themselves and others differently.

What is that Gift of Love? Da Avabhasa's devotees will tell you: It is Sri Da Avabhasa Himself.

Perhaps the best way to explain why His devotees are so convinced of His Love and so transported by It is to recount another story.

In 1988, I was about to leave the Great Hermitage Ashram in Fiji where Sri Da Avabhasa now lives to go and serve elsewhere. There is nothing that means more to me than being able to see Sri Da Avabhasa and be near Him, so I was racked with emotion about my impending departure as I walked into the small thatched building where He was Sitting.

As I entered the room, I had a fleeting concern that I would not be able to release my sorrow enough to really participate in this parting occasion. But as I took my place in the cluster of devotees seated near Him, I felt the characteristic Force of His Love begin to fill me. I felt the blissful Force of Sri Da Avabhasa's Love penetrating me at the heart, as though He had placed a giant, warm, healing hand on my heart and was gently pressing Love Itself into my body. I felt how strong Sri Da Avabhasa's Spiritual Love is, and how that Love is implicitly Wise. I knew that I could completely trust Him, and my concern and my sorrow dissolved.

I sat near Him and simply gazed at Him for some time, all the while feeling the tremendous Force of His Love pressing Itself into me like the most unspeakably potent and wonderful Healing Balm. As I let go and allowed this Feeling to penetrate more and more deeply, I was moved to close my eyes. I felt swooned by Sri Da Avabhasa's Love-Blissfulness. I felt Him showing me that I am more than the body, more than the mind, more than emotion. I felt His Love for me so strongly that I knew, more certainly than I have ever known anything in my life, that His Love is the Most Perfect Force that exists. I knew that nothing can touch or diminish the Power of His Love, the Power of Who He Is. And my sense of "me", the one who is afraid and alone and struggling, began to dissolve in His Radiant Divine Love like butter melting in the heat of the sun.

Some time later, as the meditative occasion came to a close and I "came to", opening my eyes to see the human Form of my Heart-Master Seated before me, I was overcome with gratitude. He had shown me that the Love-relationship He Lives to me, and that I enjoy in loving response to Him, cannot be affected by geographical distance or any temporal factor. He had shown me that He would always be with me, and I began to sob with love and gratitude. Truly, the months of my service elsewhere proved to be a time of necessary lessons and growth, and I always felt His Love available to Help and Guide me at every turn.

Meg McDonnell

The Love that Sri Da Avabhasa Radiates is Powerful beyond description. It is as tangible as the feeling of water coursing down your skin would be if you were standing under a waterfall, as real as the sense of wind buffeting you in a tropical gale. But even though the Force of Da Avabhasa's Love is just as real and noticeable as any natural phenomenon, it is much more deeply compelling than any of these external causes, because It touches the very heart, or essential core, of existence.

AN ENTIRELY NEW UNDERSTANDING OF LOVE AND RELATIONSHIP

To understand why Sri Da Avabhasa's Love has such a dramatic effect on people, it is helpful to study His use of the Greek myth about Narcissus. Since the beginning of His Blessing Work more than twenty years ago, Sri Da Avabhasa has used this myth as a metaphor for egoity, and this is why: Narcissus turns away from the lady Echo, who calls out to him in love. Narcissus thinks he is engaging in a grand contemplation of something much more real and meaningful than Echo's offer of relationship—but he is only looking at his own reflection. He is enamored of an illusion! Narcissus is (as Sri Da Avabhasa has described we are all in our egoity) "avoiding relationship".

For centuries, this myth has held a compelling force for human beings—Narcissus' plight has seemed disturbingly familiar to people of many different cultures, in many different times. But Sri Da Avabhasa is the first to Reveal the real, practical, and ultimate meaning of the myth and of human egoity—and He has shown that the entire history and the collected written works of our common religious, Spiritual, philosophical, and psychological history as a human race (and everything that we tend to do on a personal scale) are just like the ruminations of Narcissus at the edge of his pond, nothing more than a complex meditation on an illusion, on a self that does not exist.

What is that illusion?

Each of us experiences a continual, subtle (sometimes not so subtle) sense of suffering, discomfort—at any rate a sense that we are less than ecstatically happy. This fundamental sense of suffering often registers as the feeling that we are not as close to others as we would like to be, as conflicts or failures in our intimate relationships and in society at large, as a sense that we are not loved as fully as we would like to be. But this nagging, painful sense of incompleteness that we suffer is not caused by something that happens to us or by psychologically disturbing events that may have happened in the past. It is not caused by events outside us. It is, Da Avabhasa points out, the result of our own activity of <u>contraction</u>. And He uses yet another metaphor to describe how this contraction generates the illusory sense of "me":

All ordinary suffering is only a cramp. It is this contraction. Wherever there is this contraction, there is obstruction to the flow of the life-force. There is also the tendency in the living consciousness for there to be the sense of separate existence. If you cramp the hand together in a fist, there is a sensation in the hand, as the hand, that is different from the space around it. When the vital itself is contracted in this manner, the center of the "hand" is the ego, the "me", the separate self sense. The mind of this "me", like its form, is separate, separative, compulsively differentiating. So the whole drama of seeking that is a reaction to this contraction, or reaction to life, always begins with this "me". "Me" is the core of this experience. It is the center of the "fist". Every person seeks by every means to be relieved of his or her suffering, but the suffering cannot be relieved, this contraction cannot be uncoiled, without the "me", which is its center, dissolving.

The Method of the Siddhas

Once "me" is presumed, there are inevitably "others", different from and apart from "me"—thus the entire course of human history, of human conflict and suffering, is set in motion. Da Avabhasa has repeatedly reminded His devotees of a passage from an ancient Indian scripture, the *Brihadaranyaka Upanishad,* that states very pointedly, "Wherever there is an 'other', fear arises." Human beings spend most, if not all, of their lives trying to overcome the difficulty in loving others, and all the other chronic conflicts and forms of unhappiness that spring from that one simple but deadly error in consciousness—the sense of separation, difference, and "otherness" that springs from the self-contraction.

In fact, every single one of the pursuits of humankind, from psychology to sports to the arts to cooking to religion, has been a search to overcome this sense of suffering as though it were a real thing. Da Avabhasa is the first to penetrate this illusion and to call us to understand the very <u>action</u> that is the ego. He says:

Your suffering is your own activity. It is something that you are doing moment to moment. It is a completely voluntary activity. You cognize it in the form of symptoms, which are the sense of separate existence, the mind of endless qualities, of differentiation, and the whole form of motion, of desire. You are always already living in these things, but their root, the source of it all, the thing whose form they are all reflecting, is this contraction, this separative act, this avoidance of relationship, which constantly "creates" the form in your living consciousness that you cognize as suffering. Where it is re-cognized, known again, this activity and its symptoms cease to be the form of the living consciousness. Then what is always prevented by the usual state becomes the form of the living consciousness. Where there is unqualified relationship, where there is no contraction, where there is no separation, no avoidance, there is no differentiation, no necessary mind, no necessary desire, no identification with separate movement. Then the living consciousness falls into its own form, without effort. . . .

Then, prior to effort, motivation, or attention, there is only the Divine Self, Reality, the Heart.

The Method of the Siddhas

We are so habituated to the activity of self-contraction that we ordinarily do not even notice we are doing it. But everything changes when we really become aware of our act:

SRI DA AVABHASA: When you can see the self-contraction directly, it is even a laughing moment. Suddenly there is a resource that you always have and that is always usable. You must then live that understanding, of course, but it gives you the greatest arms there are, the greatest source of power or release or freedom. You are associated, then, with this moment of existence and every possible moment of existence in a uniquely free manner that has nothing to do with the ego.

Taken to its ultimate consequences, this understanding shatters all boundaries of the current "self-help" movements and psychotherapeutic methods that try to tell us how to improve our relations. It even draws us beyond religious notions about love, charity, and self-giving—because it penetrates the very sense of independent self that underlies conventional religious notions of doing good unto "others".

Until the self-contraction (or the sense of separate self that generates the apparent need to return to intimacy, to love, to God) has been penetrated, the futile search for intimacy, for relationship, for re-union with God inevitably continues. Da Avabhasa addresses the whole method of search for re-union:

*How could you pursue union if you did not already feel sepa-
rate? A feeling of separation always instigates the motive to union. If
you did not feel separate from the thing you want to get, you would
not have to seek it, would you? What you must find out is that this
feeling of separateness is your own activity, one that you are always
doing. That discovery is self-understanding. That is the Way of the
Heart.*

CONTEMPLATE THE ONE WHO STANDS FREE
OF THE SELF-CONTRACTION

For all those who are moved by Da Avabhasa's Wisdom and His
Blessing, Da Avabhasa offers the Way of the Heart—a transformative
Spiritual relationship to Him that touches every aspect of life, including human relationships. In Sri Da Avabhasa's Way of the Heart, the
obligation to love and serve all others is fundamental—but it is not a
conventional, social, humanistic matter. It is not about "me" being
nicer, or more meaningfully related, to "you". It is a matter, literally,
of receiving and then incarnating Sri Da Avabhasa's Divine Love.

His devotees have literally countless numbers of Stories to tell
that bear testimony to the transforming power of Sri Da Avabhasa's
Great and Boundless Love.

Sri Da Avabhasa is the Living Incarnation of Love. He was born
in this world, as He Says, "for the sake of Love", and His Divine
Intention is to bring the Gift of His Divine Love-Bliss into the
human world. He is the Bearer of a unique Realization—a
Realization that, for the first time in history, utterly and entirely penetrates the illusion of the self-contraction.

What does it mean that Sri Da Avabhasa has penetrated the
myth of the ego, and that He Stands before us, fully Alive as That
Which is prior to the self-contraction?

With the Appearance of Sri Da Avabhasa, a unique Process has
appeared in this world, and an unprecedented opportunity is being
Offered. Sri Da Avabhasa invites all who are sensitive to the suffering of life and the failure of conventional relations, all who are
inspired by His Words and His Silent Communication of the Heart,
to turn to Him for Spiritual Guidance and Great Help. He Offers a
transformative Spiritual relationship to everyone who will choose

it—and the potency of the Spiritual relationship that He Offers can be summarized in one simple sentence: "You become what you meditate on."

Narcissus stares at himself in the water, and the destructive results are obvious. Those who turn their feeling and attention to Sri Da Avabhasa, who Contemplate Him and call upon His Grace through real practice of the Way of the Heart, realize an entirely different result.

He Declares:

> *I __Am__ Love-Bliss Itself, the Truth and the Reality of Non-separateness.*
> The Da Love-Ananda Gita

> *I Am the Radiant Heart of Love, Eternally Free of fear.*
> The Hymn Of The True Heart-Master,
> *"I Am Grace Itself" section*

All the while that Da Avabhasa Calls us to transcend the self-contraction and <u>be</u> love, as He does in this book, by Offering us the practice of feeling and Contemplating Him, He provides the Wellspring of Love and Grace whereby we become moved to incarnate love in our relations and become capable of doing so. And His Help is always available to all. Da Avabhasa Promises:

> *I Have Come For all beings.*
> *Each one Is My Beloved.*
> *Therefore, Because Of Love, I Always Serve You With Great Humor, Tolerance, Forgiveness, and Blessing Power.*
> The Dawn Horse Testament

SELF-UNDERSTANDING IS THE PASSAGEWAY TO LOVE

Da Avabhasa has summarized His unique Wisdom about life, relations, and Ultimate Realization in many ways, but in simple terms He has Said that it is the complete undoing of the tendency to contract rather than to shine. It is not Realized by an effort to radiate love as one's separate self or return to God by any means that He might recommend—but by the reception of His "radical" understanding that penetrates the action of the self-contraction itself and by reception of His Graceful Transmission of the State of non-separateness, or "inherently pleasurable Unity" itself.

Sri Da Avabhasa's Wisdom-Teaching on the nature of egoic sep-arativeness and His Offering of the relationship to Him make possi-ble a "radically" new way of relating to others. But the passageway to that relational capability is not easy. It is painful to observe the ego in action, and it is perhaps for that reason that human beings are so universally reluctant to do so. Truly, it is only because Sri Da Avabhasa so clearly Reveals what it is to Stand Free of the ego that we can, in contrast, begin to notice the self-contraction in its vari-ous levels of operation.

A friend of mine had died, and I was sitting in the room of the funeral parlor where her body lay. As Sri Da Avabhasa Instructs us to do, I was feelingly-Contemplating Him to help align her to the Divine in order to serve her transition. I very much wanted to do this, for she was very dear to me.

Suddenly my attention went to a woman in the room whose seemingly superior attitude had recently irritated me. I could feel my anger arising in the moment, and I said to myself, "Oh no, you just cannot be distracted now—not while you are trying to serve your friend this last time!" But my attention kept returning to this woman. I felt so petty and full of remorse about this, and I turned to Da Avabhasa with great need.

Then, through Grace, a thought came to me: "This woman with whom I am upset is one of Sri Da Avabhasa's 'babies' (as He at times has called His devotees). She is one of the five billion He Loves so much!" In that instant, I felt a powerful Love-Force pour down through the top of my head and saturate my whole body. All of the cells of my heart were being wrung by the most poignant love-feeling I had ever known. It reached out to all beings, easily including this woman with whom I had been upset moments ago. I wept freely, knowing that such Love had nothing to do with me but was an Invasion of Sri Da Avabhasa's Divine Force.

In such moments, Sri Da Avabhasa has Revealed to me how small my egoic love is and that it does not matter, for a far Greater Love is available than I ever dreamt possible, if I will only turn to Da Avabhasa, Who is the Perfect Agent of Divine Love.

Barbara Knoblock

THE CIRCUMSTANCE OF DEVOTION

The essence of the Way of the Heart is feeling-Contemplation of Sri Da Avabhasa—and it is through that Contemplation that all Happiness, all Realization, and all necessary self-understanding flow. In order to support our feeling-Contemplation of Him, Da Avabhasa has also Given the Gift of self-discipline, which includes all the means whereby all the functions of our human life can be conformed to support that feeling, that Contemplation, that celebration of Sri Da Avabhasa's Divine Love.

All the forms of self-discipline in the Way of the Heart are intended only to create a circumstance of support in the chemical and biological nature of the body-mind for your submission to Me, your alignment to Me, your attunement with me, your Happiness in My Blessing Company. They create a biochemical basis for God-love. That is their only import. They are not difficult disciplines. They are circumstances of God-love, of love of Me, of devotion to Me, of Love-Bliss Itself, Happiness Itself, Divine Communion, Mystery, Delight.

The forms of self-discipline that Sri Da Avabhasa has Given His devotees touch every area of life—because only discipline applied to <u>every</u> area of life can provide the stable foundation for the primary practice of feeling-Contemplation of Him.

Practice of the Way of the Heart is not only Contemplation of Me, but it is Contemplation of Me in the context of functional, practical, relational, and cultural disciplines.* Contemplation and self-discipline—the two go together, <u>necessarily</u>.

The Da Love-Ananda Gita,
"I <u>Am</u> (My Self) What you Require" section

---

* Functional self-discipline includes disciplines governing diet, health, exercise, sexuality, etc.—in other words, the full range of bodily <u>functioning</u>.

Practical self-discipline includes a broad range of agreements—from the common financial responsibilities assumed by practitioners of the Way of the Heart, to specific legal agreements addressing practical areas, such as intimate partnership agreements and the disposition of one's body at death, and including other practical aspects of life in the community of Da Avabhasa's devotees—in other words, all aspects of the <u>practical</u> arrangements involved in the life of practice.

Cultural disciplines include all the sacred, sacramental, and meditative practices (including study of Da Avabhasa's Wisdom-Teaching, which is the foundation of meditative discipline, and also at least a basic discriminative study of the Great Tradition of religion and Spirituality that is the Wisdom-inheritance of humankind), and regular participation in the "form", or schedule of daily, weekly, monthly, and annual devotional activities.

The four forms of self-discipline could be likened to four cornerstones that support the practice of feeling-Contemplation of and Communion with Sri Da Avabhasa. Relational discipline in the Way of the Heart is the practical, living demonstration of one's self-transcendence and one's real resort to Sri Da Avabhasa as it is enacted in relation to others.

In His Summary Source-Text, *The Dawn Horse Testament*, Da Avabhasa defines relational discipline in the Way of the Heart as

The Progressive Incarnation Of self-Transcending Love, In all relationships, Beginning With, and Always Founded Upon, The Great and Tradition-Honored and <u>Constantly</u> To Be Demonstrated Devotional and Service Relationship To Me, . . . At First Embraced In My Foundation Function As Adept Heart-Teacher, and Then Fully In My Function As True Heart-Master, and This Expressed Through All Kinds Of Service, Including Service In Cooperative, and Formal Community, Association or Affiliation With Other, and Even All Other, Practitioners Of The Way Of The Heart, and Including Sacred, or Sacramental, Ceremonial, and General Cultural, Activities, and, Eventually, All The Kinds Of Spiritual Activities, All Of Which Kinds Of Service and Activity Are, Because They Radiate Love, Ultimately Of Benefit To all conditionally Manifested beings

In the Way of the Heart, the discipline of relationship, of loving service to all beings, is not about trying to be more loving or trying to get more love, from Sri Da Avabhasa or anyone else. Because of Sri Da Avabhasa's unique Realization of the egoless Condition, an entirely different process is now available—one that is about observing and understanding (and thus transcending) what you are doing right now to undermine Love, to separate yourself from the Force of Divine Love that is already the substance of your very being and of the entire universe. And that process can now take place because Sri Da Avabhasa Himself is here. His "Egoless Embodiment of the Divine Reality" and His Steady Communication of Inherently Perfect Love-That-Is (when the ego is no longer enacted and presumed) make it possible for us, by feeling and Contemplating Him, to come alive in that same Realization. By embracing the practice of the Way of the Heart, by persistently feeling and receiving Sri Da Avabhasa's Grace and thereby growing in the discriminative ability to observe and stand free of the ego, we are Blessed to duplicate His Great and True and Complete Realization.

It would mock Sri Da Avabhasa's Greatness to suggest that one could duplicate His Realization in a weekend or on the basis of taking up an exercise of feeling for a few hours a day here and there. No—the Way that He Offers requires a tremendous investment of time, energy, commitment, passion. It requires tremendous devotion and persistence—for, ultimately, the practice in Sri Da Avabhasa's Company addresses egoity on every level at which it exists, in every fraction of our potential experience as human and Spiritual beings. It is a comprehensive Way of life that, if you will invest yourself in it, will bring Blessings that are greater than all imagining.

If You Steadily and Really Feel (and Thereby Contemplate) all beings, things, circumstances, and conditions (Including Your Own body-mind) In Me (and, Thus and Thereby, In The Divine Person), You Will (By Grace) Discover That The Spiritual, Transcendental, and Divine Qualities Are Pervading them all, and, Most Ultimately, You Will (By Grace, In That Feeling-Contemplation) Realize The Transcendental (and Inherently Spiritual) Divine Self-Condition and Self-Domain.

The Spiritual, Transcendental, and Divine Qualities Pervade whatever You Behold In and As The Divine Person. Therefore, If You Will Listen To Me and Hear Me and See Me, and (Thus and Thereby) Heart-Turn To Me As The Divine Person, and If You Will (With The Heart-Deep and self-Transcending Feeling-Submission Of Your Total body-mind In Me) Contemplate The Divine Self-Condition Revealed In My Mere and Blessing Presence, You Will (By Grace) Realize My Very (and Inherently Perfect) State (That Is Also <u>Who</u> You <u>Are</u>).

This Inevitable Process Of Duplication Is The Single Principle (or Universal and, Ultimately, Divine Law) That Accounts For Both The Necessity Of individual or personal Responsibility (or The Real Progressive Practice Of self-Transcending, or Counter-egoic, Submission Of body, mind, and attention) and The Necessary Free Gift (or Grace) Of Spiritual, Transcendental, and Divine Help and Realization (To Which Free Gift Of Grace individual or personal Responsibility Is The Necessary Response). You Must "Consider" and Realize and Demonstrate This Principle, and You Must Receive and

Respond To The Inevitable and Inherently Perfect Gifts Of This Divine and Universal Law.

The Dawn Horse Testament

The greater the vessel, the greater the investment, the more one can receive of the Gift. But it is not just in the advanced practice of the Way of the Heart that you will realize the Happiness of responding to Sri Da Avabhasa. On the contrary—you will receive the Touch of Sri Da Avabhasa's Complete Divine Love at the very beginning—and that Gift of His Love will make your heart break with gratitude, It will carry you beyond your present limitations and motivate your further persistence and growth. It will give you strength and purpose. It will become the Source of great feeling in all your relationships. And It will Grant you wisdom and the ability to discriminate between What is True, What is Love, and what is not. Ultimately, His Divine Love will Reveal Itself as the only meaning of your life or of anyone else's—and you will celebrate all your relationships, all your experience, in that Light.

But always, no matter how humble or sophisticated one may be (or become), Sri Da Avabhasa's Divine Love, in His Words, is "the only cure for the loveless heart". Sri Da Avabhasa is, in Person and as Extended to us through His Words in this book, the very One we have all been waiting for—all five billion on the planet Earth, all the noble and worthy men and women who have practiced in all the religious and Spiritual traditions to date, struggling to be free of the ego and to Realize Love Most Perfectly. Sri Da Avabhasa is, as He Himself has Confessed and as His devotees freely profess, the answer to the heart-cry of all humankind, the Completing answer to human prayers.

Sri Da Avabhasa is the very Incarnation of Love—and He passionately Calls us all to incarnate that same Love through Him and to magnify It throughout the human world. May we be humbled by His Words in these pages to accept our need for His Love. May we be moved, by the wounds of lovelessness that can be seen everywhere in our world, to cooperate Spiritually with Sri Da Avabhasa and, by that Spiritual cooperation, bring the world a new Sign, the Sign that heals the hearts of all, the Sign of the One Who Is Love, and Whose Love is reflected in the lives of all who touch His Heart and draw upon His Wisdom.

NOTE TO THE READER

The Instructions included in this book have been selected from Sri Da Avabhasa's Writings and Discourses from the beginning of His Work until the present day. In 1986, Sri Da Avabhasa began to summarize His Instruction in six books, which He Calls the "Source Texts" for practice of the Way of the Heart. These are *The Dawn Horse Testament, The Da Love-Ananda Gita, The Da Avabhasa Upanishad, The Basket of Tolerance, The Hymn Of The True Heart-Master,* and *The Perfect Practice.* (Even now, Sri Da Avabhasa continues His great and passionate Work to revise, update, and expand His Source Literature.)

The selections in this book that have been taken from those definitive Texts have been referenced for your further study. Other titles that are not Source Texts but that have been published in new editions since 1986 have also been referenced—*The Knee of Listening, The Method of the Siddhas,* and *Easy Death.*

Sri Da Avabhasa's Talks and Writings before the establishment of His Source Literature in 1986 have been updated, under His direction, so that they are consistent with His definitive and summary Wisdom in the Source Texts. *The Incarnation of Love* is thus the current reference of origin, and earlier publications have not been cited.

PART I

The Discipline of Love in the Way of the Heart

CHAPTER 1

Love Without Expectation

A Conversation with Sri Da Avabhasa

SRI DA AVABHASA: [to a woman] Are you still dwelling on your mother? She was a movie star?

TONI VIDOR: Yes, she was a star. She was very beautiful but totally unattainable.

SRI DA AVABHASA: Did she play at being a star with everybody, including her family?

TONI: It was obvious that up to the moment of her death she was acting. I think that is the reason I go in the other direction and do not dramatize anything. I under-dramatize.

SRI DA AVABHASA: It is your way of dramatizing. [Laughter.]

TONI: I think I was always angry at her. Toward the end of her life, I transcended it, though. I took care of her, but she kicked me out of the house . . .

SRI DA AVABHASA: Turned on you and kicked you out of the house! There was a great deal of anger even now as you said it.

TONI: It hurt me greatly.

SRI DA AVABHASA: So no matter what you did, she still would not love you.

TONI: That is right. Then she died. I was not there when she died, but she psychically contacted a friend of mine after her death and she told my friend that I had to forgive her. Apparently she could not move on without my forgiving her. It was very difficult. I could not <u>really</u> let myself forgive her.

SRI DA AVABHASA: You haven't yet! You are still talking angrily about her turning on you and throwing you out of the house. You went through the process of her death in a kind of ritual fashion. You did not deal with yourself, your reasons for not wanting to forgive her, your expectation that she would approach you and ask for forgiveness and somehow make you feel her need for your love. That did not happen, so you did not really go through the process of forgiving her. Your process of forgiving or letting go is still waiting to happen.

TONI: I ask to really forgive her and let her go.

SRI DA AVABHASA: Well, yes, that is easy to say. But what must happen in you so that you can do so? It is not enough to admit that you must perform the ritual of forgiveness. You must be in a position to let your mother go. You have based your relationship with her on her loving you. She did not give you that satisfaction, so you are not about to give her any satisfaction now. It is the attachment game again, not the discipline of love. The discipline of love has absolutely nothing to do with whether or not you got what you wanted from her.

TONI: To love her in spite of everything.

SRI DA AVABHASA: Yes. But you will not do that yet because you expect a gesture from her that fulfills the expectations you have had all of your life—that she not be the star, remote, unattainable, but that she mother you, love you, forgive you, nourish you. She did not do so. And because she did not, there was conflict between you the whole time she was alive. Now that she has passed, you are still making it a source of conflict. You are not letting her go because your expectations have not been fulfilled. You think somehow she must fulfill your expectations before you can let her go. Even the word "forgiveness" seems somehow false, as if some sort of justice must be done.

The discipline of love is not about justice. It transcends justice. Love is greater than justice. You never had exactly a love relationship with your mother. Your relationship with her was based on

3

attachment and on expectation that was frustrated. You are still holding to that position. You must understand yourself, how you work, how you worked all your life with her, how you work even now, not only in relation to her but in relation to others. Your practice is not a matter of forgiving her. It is not a matter of her fulfilling your expectations. It is a matter of love.

TONI: Simply being in relationship?

SRI DA AVABHASA: [slamming His hand on the table near Him] Love! No justice, no expectations, no forgiveness. Love! Love is its own forgiveness. Even to think in terms of having to forgive is about the attachment game. You have never been able to love your mother, simply, straightforwardly—or anyone else for that matter. To you, love is based on conditions, expectations, and you always feel in the frustrated position, relatively unloved. You are always doing things for others that are love-expressions from your point of view, but there is no glow on you. There is no energy in you with all this service to others that you call "love". If you are truly loving others, it shows all over your body. You yourself have always done healing service—if that service is about love, it shows all over your body. What you are doing is not about love.

TONI: I do it so I can get love from others.

SRI DA AVABHASA: That is it! You are always doing all kinds of service because you expect to be loved. Somehow you think that you have not been loved all your life, even though you are doing all of this service. You served your mother, you serve everybody else, and you are not being loved for it. Your life is basically all about a frustrated expectation, and you yourself are not practicing the discipline of love. You are living on the basis of expectation rather than loving, simply, uncontaminated, not contracted, not being frustrated because others do not give you the love you expect, released in the full feeling gesture, no withholding, no contraction, no reasons not to love, none!

Your mother was the way she was. She never changed, and that is the way it is. Why should that retard your heart?

TONI: There is no reason.

SRI DA AVABHASA: Your relationship to your mother seems to characterize your life altogether. It seems to be the paradigm, the symbol, in which you have fixed your entire life. You are always serving and doing what is good, and expecting love in return. Love never fully happens to you, so you can never fully receive it. It is always the same dramatization. You never live on the basis of self-understanding and practice the discipline of love yourself. You think you are loving, but you are dramatizing. You think your service is about love, but it is something you are doing to serve yourself. It is a dramatization of your problem.

You will let your mother go not when she approaches you and asks for forgiveness, not when you decide to forgive her, but when you become love. To become love takes real self-understanding, real practice, real discipline, and the giving up of your psychology of expectation. Stop making your expectation the bargaining point of whether you will love or not. Just give it up entirely.

To do that requires real self-understanding, a change of life, a change of disposition altogether.

Some months ago, you were suggesting that you had heard Me. You said that when you were travelling in India this past year, you got the reality picture of life and that some kind of detachment came over you as a result, as if that were hearing, or most fundamental self-understanding. What we are discussing now, not detachment, is is what hearing is about in your case. Your detachment is just another way of immunizing yourself against your frustrated expectations.

TONI: The celibacy that I chose at the time was about the same thing.

SRI DA AVABHASA: Yes. Look at the details of your life and see how they are associated with this principal dramatization—the frustrated expectation of love. You deal with it in various ways, through your healing services, through your choice of celibacy. But these are all aspects of the one dramatization. This dramatization is what you must "consider" in yourself, and you must begin to change your life. There is no true hearing until you do. This is what hearing is about in your case.

You look like a child in some ways. You have a fixed expression of a kind that communicates this frustrated expectation. There are other relationships in your life, to your father and other people, that have the same limits, but your relationship to your mother was a very important one, perhaps the key one. Nevertheless, the many other relationships were about the same thing. You must see how you developed this particular character game and how you dramatized it in all your relationships and all your choices and all the aspects of your appearance and all the aspects of your doing. It is all the same dramatization.

What else about it? Anything?

TONI: Thank you.

SRI DA AVABHASA: Tcha.
What else then?

JERRY SHEINFELD: Beloved Master, I am sure it is different in every case, but is it basically true that this complication about love is one of the primary areas of limitation in all beings?

SRI DA AVABHASA: Absolutely. The Heart is the great Principle of life. It is Inherently Free. It is never damaged. Many things are superimposed on It, however, and presumptions of un-love are made. The Heart is feeling without limitation. In the context of daily ordinary human living, the Heart is expressed as love, or feeling in relationship. Why is "Avoiding relationship?" the principal form of self-Enquiry I have Given to My devotees? Because of your heart-suppression, your suppression of the feeling process.

You are crippled because you live as the ego, self-contracted, with the heart contracted, therefore, or seeming to be. This contraction is shown in the dramatization of a fundamentally loveless life. Even though you say you experience feelings, you experience them through the mechanisms of egoity, the games of attachment, the games of suppression, the games of avoidance. Therefore, love, or the Heart, does not become the context of your life.

The great "Consideration" that is the Way of the Heart is not just about the human exchanges of love in social relationships. It is about the Awakening of the heart. It is about proceeding from the heart-foundation to Awaken fundamentally and altogether and then Absolutely. The beginnings of understanding have everything to do with the observation of what you are doing in the terms of your ordinary life. And you are suppressing the feeling dimension of life.

You live as self-contraction. Therefore, you dramatize self-contraction in all relations. Yet all the while you are this knot, you say you are loving. How can it be so? You are really suppressing love, withholding love, not being animated by love altogether. A little of it leaks out, perhaps, when you are associated with something that pleases you, that fulfills your expectations, or that you want to fulfill your expectations. That is why you use the word "love" to describe your feelings for almost everything—"I love ice cream, I love going to the movies, I love my girlfriend, I love my boyfriend." You are playing the games of attachment to things that please you, that fulfill your expectations or your desires. If anything does not please you or fulfill you, you do not love it, you do not love that one, you are not happy with that one, you are contracted, you are dramatizing, you are independent, you are separate.

Therefore, you carry around with you the presumption of love, or the heart-principle, but because you live by self-contraction you adhere to an agreement in yourself that you will not practice the discipline of love, you will not manifest free feeling, unless you are pleased, unless your expectations are fulfilled. When anything or anyone does not fulfill your expectations, the knot is dramatized everywhere in your feeling. It comes all over your body, all over your face. And what are you doing? The dramatization of "I don't love you".

How much of your life do you spend doing this? Basically you are doing this almost all the time. When now and then your expectations are fulfilled, suddenly you are the love boy or the love girl.

JERRY: But is that love, Sri Gurudev? Is that authentic love in those moments when we feel fulfilled?

SRI DA AVABHASA: Of course it is not authentic love. It is feeling come to the front, fine, but it is based on the egoically "self-possessed"‡ (or self-absorbed), self-contracted notion of how to live. You will manifest such feeling only if you are pleasurized, only if your expectations are fulfilled, only if you get what you want from another. You are not free to exercise free feeling unless your expectations are fulfilled. And, as a matter of fact, the moments of such fulfillment are rather rare! You build up so many expectations over a

---

‡ In conventional usage, the word "self-possessed" means possessed of oneself—or with full control (calmness, or composure) of one's feelings, impulses, habits, and actions. Da Avabhasa uses the term to indicate the state of being possessed by one's egoic self, or controlled by chronically self-referring (or egoic) tendencies of attention, feeling, thought, desire, and action.

lifetime that there is hardly any room for the expression of free feeling. Free feeling rarely occurs.

In moments now and then, on special days, on special occasions, at special events in your life, all of a sudden you are full of feeling. Everybody gets together in December, for example, especially Christians and Jews, who have special holidays at that time, but the December holiday is a ritual that is fairly common all over the Earth. People give one another gifts and show in their faces and on their bodies how pleasurable they find one another's company. This lasts for a few hours, and then everybody goes through the ritual of the New Year, when they separate from one another once again and return to business as usual.

In certain ritual moments of life, like everyone else you manifest free feeling, but basically you have founded your life on expectation and you will not express free feeling unless your expectation is fulfilled. "Consider" it. This is exactly how you operate. This is why your expressions of free feeling are so rare, because you base your life on the expectation of pleasure from others rather than on the discipline of love founded on self-understanding. If you founded yourself on self-understanding and the discipline of love, the manifestation of free feeling would characterize your life no matter what happened. You would uncover more and more impediments to free feeling and go beyond them.

To do that is to grow. To do that is to mature. To do that is truly to be a human being instead of a subhuman ego.

JERRY: One of my strategies has been to avoid what I really have to deal with in life.

SRI DA AVABHASA: As if everything is okay, and you are really practicing, living the Divine life. What you are really doing is dramatizing the self-contraction through the loveless order of the first three stages of life‡ and a little bit of the fourth. You say you are practicing devotion to Me. Is it love? Or am I just another party to your lovelessness? The Way of the Heart is not about mere observances, it is not about consolation, it is not about indulging in the stimulation of seeking. It is about self-understanding and the transcendence of the self-contraction through real devotion to Me.

‡ Here and elsewhere in this book, Sri Da Avabhasa refers to His unique and complete description of the seven stages of human and Spiritual development. Please see the "The Seven Stages of Life", pages 274-83, for a summary of this key aspect of His Wisdom-Teaching.

You must equip yourself, then, with these arms of self-understanding and authenticate your practice and not reduce your practice of the Way of the Heart to mere observances. It is not by mere association with Me that you Awaken and grow. It is by right practice in relationship to Me that Awakening and growth are potential.

You want to rattle around here and call yourself My devotee and not deal with this dramatization. You want to talk about subject matter, talk about love in an intellectual sense, perhaps, make pronouncements about it. I am talking about the real sadhana that cuts through your drama. I am talking about real content that must be dealt with. The Way of the Heart is a "reality consideration". You must really deal with yourself, really deal with your dramatization, or you are an amateur at the Way of the Heart.

I practice the discipline of it! I do not have to look one way or the other. I just do it for real. That is why I do many things, act in many ways, not just "kissy-kissy, I love you". I act in all kinds of ways to serve your Awakening, your responsibility, your real practice of the Way of the Heart, your Realization. Therefore, when love is really exercised, it appears in many forms.

CHAPTER 2

The Heart Is in Bondage Until Love Is Incarnated in the World

SRI DA AVABHASA: The import of My Appearance here is not that I have Come into the world and that I Am Love, or that God independent of human beings is Love. The import of My Appearance here and of My Communication is that you, and every being, must <u>be</u> Love.

* * *

The heart is in bondage until love is incarnated in the world. Therefore, you must incarnate love. You must make room for Me in life.

* * *

The first principle of Spiritual life is God-Love, submission to the Divine Being. First you must love Me, and then you are able to love everyone. Your practice of the Way of the Heart is thus a paradox. It is not exclusive withdrawal into an orientation to the Divine Reality. There must be that orientation, yes, but your Realization of the Divine must be incarnated in the plane of relations.

* * *

The relationship to Me, the True Heart-Master, is the epitome and the primary form of relationship. And that relationship contains hidden within it the whole Mystery and Form of Truth. But it cannot be enjoyed or understood apart from the practical or sacrificial application of your life to the whole condition of relationship as it everywhere and every moment appears.

Therefore, practice of the Way of the Heart is the practice of relationship to Me, but also the practice of the condition of relationship itself. That is why I Give practical Instruction in the form of life-demands. The Spiritual Master must be the Master of actual conditions. Thus, I am always bringing My devotee into appropriate conditions, to test and mature him or her. In every circumstance, My devotee will either function in relationship openly, effectively, wisely, and with love, or My devotee will observe his or her own resistance, understand, and gradually restore himself or herself to the relational condition in that area of his or her functional life.

The practical living of the conditions of relationship is of fundamental importance, and it is a fundamental expression of the process of true practice at every developmental stage of the Way of the Heart.

* * *

Love all your friends. Love all beings. Through devotional submission to Me as your True Heart-Master, be Liberated from all otherness, which is painful, a form of suffering, something to be Liberated from entirely. How can you be Liberated from otherness? Only through feeling-Contemplation of Me.

* * *

You must become responsible as love in all relations, under all conditions, and as early in your life as possible, so that you can transcend the repetitive destiny of the ego, of separation, of the avoidance of relationship, of un-love, of "you don't love me", that keeps you out by the pond, meditating on yourself like Narcissus. Then you can go on to fulfill the Destiny of Divine Self-Realization while alive.

* * *

Every being must fulfill the Law, regardless of his or her past. It does not make any difference how difficult it is for you. The Law remains the Law. The Law is unobstructed feeling-attention, or love, under all conditions and in all relations until Divine Translation. If you are obstructed in feeling and attention, you fail to fulfill the Law. That is why you suffer, and why you stop growing.

* * *

If you understand My Wisdom-Teaching of the Way of the Heart, you understand that the ego that is to be transcended exists only in the context of relations. The ego is the body-mind in the state of contraction. Therefore, it is effective as contraction in the field of relations. And, therefore, among the primary disciplines in the Way of the Heart, among the most fundamental disciplines, are those in the domain of relations.

* * *

Those who Fail To Practice The Sadhana Of Love In their intimate emotional-sexual relationships, and In human relationships Generally, Will, By That Failure, Turn Away (or Contract) From God (or The Great Condition That Is Reality Itself).

The Dawn Horse Testament

* * *

Practice of the Way of the Heart is always demonstrated functionally and in the plane of relations. Therefore, it is always obvious whether or not you are practicing the Way of the Heart. If you are Contemplating Me with feeling-devotion, your practice is obvious. If you are not Contemplating Me, that is also obvious. You know whether a person is transcending the ego-bond by how he or she appears in life, in the moment of relations. Of course, the Way of the Heart is not about relations. It is simply lived in the context of relations. The Way of the Heart is about feeling-Contemplation of Me, or Divine Communion. But it cannot be lived except in the plane of relations.

* * *

Among the fruits of the life of understanding are human ones. Your functional humanity, your ability to love and live in relationship, is a real test of your self-understanding. To live in relationship is simply a process of unobstructed energy, fullness, happiness. Until you become happy with others, your Spirituality is garbage. It serves no purpose whatsoever.

Self-transcendence is consequential for humanity. It is not an experience of phenomena that transcend humanity. When the quality of unreasonable Happiness, prior Fullness, or genuine life and love is present in an individual, you are certain of that person. You are healed by that person's presence.

* * *

If you are about Spirituality and you are not about love, then you are only deluded. To live without love has nothing whatever to do with Spiritual life. I have known many people who were very Spiritual, so-called, and who did not know the first thing about love, had no interest in it, had no capability for it. They could shine out a little love selectively here and there, but anyone can do that—any libertine does that. I have known many people who claimed to be involved in Spiritual life who could not grasp this principle of love. They could not incarnate it, could not live with it, could not make humanity out of it, could not make human life out of it.

Such people want to be celibate and wear all the trappings of religion, but they cannot love. There they stand in their ridiculous costumes, their eyes rolling up in their heads, swooning in the Yogic perfume, and they are nothing but self-obsessed egos. They cannot love, they cannot submit to love, they cannot accept being loved, and they cannot love others consistently. They cannot bring Spirituality into life, into relationship. Therefore, they are dramatizing the same problems that all egos suffer and at the same time they are calling themselves "Spiritual".

I have "Considered" this with you on many, many occasions. There is no true Spiritual life without incarnate love that is demonstrated in very practical terms.

*   *   *

The true test and proof of a human being is not whether or not he or she can attain mystical experiences, or "out-of-body" experiences, or even sophisticated scientific knowledge and power over the world. The true test is whether or not any individual human being will exist as love and persist as love, transcending himself or herself in the midst of all experience and all knowledge, even when all experience and all knowledge press upon the individual to be less than love.

*   *   *

You may fantasize that Spiritual life is about living in caves, wearing your robes, and renouncing everything. Such a notion is just a dream. It is nonsense. True renunciation is <u>here</u>, in the body, suffering it, becoming Illumined by submitting to be a human being. The practice of such true renunciation is the agony of self-knowledge and knowledge of another.

13

That practice uses you up, burns you out, and kills you eventually. But it is better to die from that than from bacteria or old age or a rotting liver or something to do with your intestines. Die from the heart-stress. Die from love. That is what I am Doing. And anybody who follows or fulfills the Way of the Heart must do the same.

*   *   *

You literally depend on other beings for your continuing existence in this form—not your ultimate existence, or even your mere vital existence (except that you do depend on the sexual play of others for your birth), but your human existence. You cannot exist as a human being for one more moment without participation in the life that other beings give to you, and that the whole grand affair of the manifested world gives to you.

When you realize your dependence on the conscious communication of life from others, then you see the reasonableness—or, rather, the unreasonableness—of love. Then, in spite of what the other person seems to be, you bring your life to him or her in the form of real energy, real intensity, real attention. The person is enlivened, then, literally. The person is fed.

The food that you take through the mouth is gross and secondary. The food that you take through the nose is gross and secondary. These are also necessary forms of food, generally, but they support a lower organic form of existence. Many people eat well enough and breathe well enough, but they are depressed and insane because they do not communicate through the eyes and through the heart. They do not enjoy the life-process in its subtle form. To be present with life to other beings, and to expect their presence to you, is merely intelligent, not moralistic, not even a matter of Yoga. You are present to other beings in the form of a righteous demand for life. You should absolutely demand life from other people. And you should finally discover what it is you are demanding of them. It is life, intensity, love, conscious energy. You absolutely need it to survive.

Therefore, you should cut through all the garbage that you tend to give other people and absolutely demand that exchange of love. Settle for nothing less, and settle for nothing less in yourself. And submit to that righteous demand from others. To bring your own presence as life to other beings and to demand it from them is simply an appropriate discipline, just as it is appropriate to take meals every day.

14

But you tend to settle for less than life. A smile, a bit of sex, or a cigarette is sufficient. You do not really require life from others, yet that is what you need. You cannot survive in your truly human functions without it. If all of you here were busy truly loving one another, truly being present to one another without complication, without making any assumptions about one another or yourself, you could live for a long time. Even if you lived for only 20 years, you would be happy, at least on the ordinary human levels. You would be feeding one another, and you could die happy—if some day you happen to have to die—because everybody would be with you. Everybody would be holding your hand and shooting you full of conscious life. You would be loved, free, not prevented from Truth. And who cares about death then?

*   *   *

To love is to share principal food, to share the energy of manifested being. The mind is simply a modification of the conscious elemental, and it does not move down into life. Only in loving do you permit the life-force, the life-energy, principal food, to manifest on the functional human level.

Therefore, you can think all you like, but until you love you do not make the life-force available, you do not feed others. If your common life, your social life, is unsatisfactory, it is because there is no communicated life-force, you are starving, you do not love. Loving is not just a psychological and personal affair. It is not just good for psychological health and society. Loving is absolutely essential for life itself, because it is the functional manifestation of the life-force, or principal food.

There cannot be any withholding, for any reason whatsoever, without violating the fundamental functional demand of human life. Love is not a petty affair. It is not just better if you love others. It is an absolute demand and responsibility to love and be free. Only thus do you make available in human terms the Divine process, and only thus is anything like the realization of truly human existence possible. Such true existence depends on love. Then human life can become elemental and alive. Then the bodies can be improved and all the rest. But until love is established as the communicated theatre of human life, there is no evolution of humanity.

*   *   *

15

Do not just live a moral life. Live a life of love.

* * *

Love is Unqualified Divine Self-Radiance, without center or bounds. Since it is without center (ego-self) or bounds (body, thought-conception-perception, world), Love may not be willfully presumed or generated. It is a Process Realized by Grace, progressively, until it is altogether True.

The Hymn Of The True Heart-Master,
"I Am Grace Itself" section

* * *

CHAPTER 3

Enter Fully into the Spiritual Life-Sphere of Love

SRI DA AVABHASA: Love is feeling-Contemplation of Me, and that is the summary of the Way of the Heart. Live it under all conditions.

* * *

Simply to give Me your regard, simply to feelingly Contemplate Me, should be the moment of ecstasy that draws you naturally into feeling-response to Me, the mood of love, devotion, freedom from mental bondage, physical bondage, relational bondage. Thus ecstatic, you are naturally capable of incarnating this love, through all the forms of practice I Give you, including your love-relations and friendships.

The Hymn Of The True Heart-Master,
"I Am Grace Itself" section

* * *

What Is Necessary (and Also Possible) Is To Enter Fully Into The Spiritual Life-Sphere Of Love. In The Way Of The Heart, This Is Done By First Entering (By Heart) Into My Company (and, Thus and Thereby, Into The Company Of The Divine Person), and (Therein) To Submit To The Divine Embrace Of Love, Wherein Not Only Are You Loved, but You Are Love Itself. Then You Must Magnify That Love-Radiance In the world of human relationships.

The Dawn Horse Testament

* * *

When the contraction does not take place, when it is not meditated upon, when it is no longer a matter of concern, when there is simply this unobstructed relationship, there is no dilemma. Then there is no one superior to the other, no problem, no jealousy, no distinction. There is only enjoyment. And where life is constant as that enjoyment, there is the Infinity of Liberation, the Perfect Consciousness of Truth, the Siddhi of the Real. But it is always simply that basic enjoyment, that unobstructed, spontaneous, moment to moment existence as relationship. It is what is called "love". It is simply the Force of the Heart, the Real, which is unobstructed, unqualified existence. When there is no resistance, no contraction, no separation, there is just this ease of pleasure in one another. And where there is that ease of pleasure, there is no problem. Give it a name, if you like. It is simply your natural state.

The Method of the Siddhas

* * *

"Love" is perhaps the most abused word in at least the Westernized world. The ego wants to call lust "love". Lust is not love. Attachment is not love. Liking what somebody does to you is not love. Do you not know this? True love is an expression of going beyond your separate and separative self, going beyond what consoles you. Ultimately such love is magnified universally. It goes beyond your house, your castle, your egoic "self-possession", your underwear. Do you know this?

You do not love someone because you are attached to the person and like what the person does for you. That is not love! Do you not know this? All such consolation must be understood and gone beyond. Then there is love. Then you serve another's sacrifice, another's Realization—and that is "true intimacy" in the Way of the Heart.

* * *

Positive socializing is what you call "love". But that is not love. That is just lust and vital energy, congeniality, satisfying the vital personality and its purposes and desires. Love is a sacrifice of the ego in feeling-Contemplation of Me in all relations and under all conditions. Therefore, the primary manifestation of love is Ishta-Guru-Bhakti Yoga.

* * *

Love is not mere attachment, or any kind of fascination with objects or others that represent the possibility of self-fulfillment. Love itself is <u>renunciation</u> of separate and separative self, in relationship to another.

The Da Love-Ananda Gita,
"I Am (My Self) What you Require" section

* * *

Love is the disposition of uncaused Happiness in the moment. You always are natively certain of what it would be to look, and feel, and be, and act completely Happy in this very moment. Love is to do just that, and to do it effectively toward all relations, whether apparently within or apparently without, so there is no recoil, no separation, no self-definition, but only the Divine Self-Condition Which precedes these.

* * *

To love requires a great transformation. It requires your absolute Realization of the fundamental Nature of your True Condition, Which is not this separate one.

* * *

Love is relational action rather than the action of one who is egoically "self-possessed"—but love is <u>action</u>, or real availability, not a merely subjective attitude of mind and emotion.

* * *

What you call loving people very much does not amount to much. Real loving changes your life. It changes your action. It eliminates your patterning, your egoic tendencies, your game.

And you cannot avoid pain. The avoidance of pain is a primary part of the motive to be superficial and mediocre. You do not want to feel the difficulty, so you will never address it. Therefore, you just smile and say [Sri Da Avabhasa speaks in a very squeaky, superficial voice and forces a superficial smile] "I love you." Devotion must be suffered. Intimacy must be suffered. A unique kind of suffering Awakens you. It is joyous if you suffer it most profoundly. If your life is to be transformed by it, then you must go beyond pain.

Love has a wall of pain in it. If you do not endure that pain, then you make love into a social convention and your so-called loving does not amount to anything. Everybody is smiling at one another and shaking hands and speaking pleasantries. That is not love. Love is very serious, even when it laughs.

Divine Self-Realization is not the avoidance of the pain of life but it is to suffer it to the nth degree, to the point of Awakening, to the point of Freedom, to the point of being utterly transformed, in effect, by love, to murder the murderer, to be Free of limitations—but not by evading them.

*   *   *

The ego-transcending point of view actively acknowledges the principle of love. My devotee who is functioning in an ego-transcending fashion—even to the degree of Divine Enlightenment—presumes himself or herself to live in a world of love. In the world of relations, that one is alive in the Domain of Love.

Love is the principle of human functioning. It is the principle of relationship. Love is what is to be Realized and expressed. You must overcome all limits upon it. Spiritual life is many things, but at the level of human relations, its essence is love.

*   *   *

Love is what you are all struggling with, you see. You would sit in meditation in a cave for twelve hours a day long before you would begin to get serious about the matter of love. You do all you can to see that you are pleasurably situated in your sexual relationship, in your work, in your household, or in your automobile. You work very hard to study and read about and think about and imagine and even perform meditative exercises. Yet love is the most profound, and the most difficult, activity to do. And love is the one single act that you are most reluctant to perform—whether in public or in private.

*   *   *

All My devotees should be able to bring the principle of love into active manifestation in daily life and eliminate all the rituals of un-love, all the mediocre versions of love, all the ceremonial affirmations of love. Actually live love in feeling-Contemplation of Me.

Express love all day. Do not allow the conventions of egoic worldliness to suppress love's expression. Contemplate Me with your feeling-devotion, and make your love of Me the principle of all your acts, and change everything. Take a look at all the ceremonies of un-love you have built into your life and eliminate them. Change them however you must, so that you manifest actual love, its real, verbal, physical, human expression, and its practice altogether, Spiritually, ultimately.

* * *

You can never truly be anyone's friend, or lover, or husband, or wife, or father, or mother, and you can never be My devotee, until you decide to surrender to Me. Until that time, you are wandering in your attention, and you cannot really be trusted. You cannot be faithful, you cannot make agreements, you cannot love, you cannot persist as love.

* * *

If, as My devotee, you would transcend the ego, you must deal with the emotional gesture of the feeling-being from moment to moment. Transcendence of the ego is entirely an emotional matter. Thus, there is no transcendence of the ego until love appears, until there is self-transcendence via emotional sacrifice of the body-mind in feeling-Contemplation of Me, the Incarnate Divine Person, the Adept of the Living One, Who is Expressed as everything and Who absolutely Transcends everything.

As My devotee, you must choose this sacrifice, this loving gesture. If you will choose it, if you will make this emotional commitment, then all experience becomes Divine Revelation to the point of Ecstasy and the Transcendence of everything in Self-Existing Divine Being and Self-Radiant Love-Bliss.

* * *

You cannot idealize this great Love-feeling and say that from now on this is how you are going to live. You will discover, as you have discovered on countless occasions previously, that you do not do that. You cannot merely make love an ideal, in other words. You must first become involved in love by finding That Which Is Love, Which Comes to you as Love, and Which Is Supremely Attractive.

21

Acknowledge That One, know That One, and allow yourself to respond to That One in love.

The Way of Truth, then, is not merely to love. The Way of Truth is to be the devotee of the One Who <u>Is</u> Love.

* * *

The Great Purpose of self-Transcendence

SRI DA AVABHASA: Always be purposed in response to Me and to My Wisdom-Teaching.

*   *   *

You must become associated with the Divine Purpose from the beginning of your practice of the Way of the Heart, so that when all of the lesser offshoots of that Purpose appear they will not suddenly become your "great purpose". They will be the simple demonstrations of your practice as you mature in the Way of the Heart.

*   *   *

You must observe, understand, and overcome your conventional vision—the vision made of conditional existence—and instead Realize the Vision of the Heart Itself, so that you can become consistently purposed to transcend conditional existence in Communion with Me. To do otherwise is to fall into separateness and self-indulgence.

Even at the beginning of your practice of the Way of the Heart, all of your involvement in "money, food, and sex" must always be associated with the Great Vision, the Heart-Vision, and the purpose of self-transcendence. Therefore, you cannot casually indulge in the modest designs of "money, food, and sex" and practice the Way of the Heart. Whatever those designs are for you personally, they must be animated in the context of the real process of self-transcendence as it is demonstrated even at the beginning of the Way of the Heart, when the disciplines are minimal. Nonetheless, whatever the forms of self-discipline at your developmental stage of practice of the Way of the Heart, they should always be demonstrations of the process of self-transcendence. They should not be expressions of the illusion that conditional existence is purposed for its own sake, or that conditional existence can fulfill itself on its own terms, by consolation, self-pleasure, and self-fulfillment.

As My devotee, you must eventually realize true self-discipline through true listening, true hearing (or most-fundamental self-understanding), and true seeing (or the Awakening of Heart-Vision), so that you are purposed to transcend every fraction of conditional existence in Communion with Me. Then you will assume self-discipline as it is in the Way of the Heart.

* * *

I Give you the Divine Vision of existence a piece at a time, and the piece I am Giving you now is the matter of human loving. But do not ever imagine that this is all there is to it.

* * *

You are not being asked to love and be radiant as an answer to your dilemma.

* * *

In every moment of manifested existence, there is the mechanical tendency of self-contraction, or the creation of the illusion of difference between egoic self and all objects. This very mechanism is the cause of the perception and conception of manifested existence as a "problem", or the apparent separation from and non-Identification with the Divine Being. When this tendency is presently understood and transcended, it is Realized that there is only the Self-Existing and Self-Radiant Divine Being, Apparent as all "subjects" and all "objects". On this basis, manifested existence can be lived as Happiness, in Freedom, spontaneously and creatively.

* * *

The purpose of the Way of the Heart is to devote energy and attention to the observation, understanding, and transcendence of the self-contraction and to Realize That Which Is at the root, or Source, of that contraction. This "radical" orientation to transcendence of the egoic self at its root, or in its fundamental form, through feeling-Contemplation of Me, is the Way of the Heart.

* * *

24

The first form of the conditional "I"-activity that is observed and felt beyond is the bodily, emotional, and lower mental display of the avoidance of relationship (in the ordinary context of human exchanges). When the freedom of no-contraction, unqualified relatedness, or love is basically restored in the ordinary human sphere through Spiritual Communion with That Which Is (Always and Already, before the self-contraction is apparently added to What Is), then the conditional "I"-activity begins to be observed and transcended most directly, as contraction itself, even in the subtlest forms of mind. Finally, the self-contraction is observed and transcended in its essence, root-form, or first form.

The Da Avabhasa Upanishad

* * *

Human responsibility, whereby people serve survival mutually, is not to be laughed at, not to be dismissed, not to be taken lightly, but it is an easy course to bondage. It is an easy argument for relinquishing That Which Is Great. It is not a Yogic argument. It is not a God-Realizing argument. It is an argument of your own conceiving, based on self-contraction, defined by objects, obsessed with bodily based messages.

* * *

Now you are looking for the cause of your suffering. You are seeking to be relieved by examining the phenomena of experience. You are seeking to create an arrangement in the body-mind itself that is satisfying. But the body-mind is a limitation. The body-mind is mortal. There is no way to be Divinely Ecstatic and at the same time to be identified with something mortal.

"Ecstasy" by definition means "standing outside oneself". To be Divinely Ecstatic is to stand outside what is mortal, to transcend it, to be greater than it, but also to include it and to realize it as a superficial aspect of What you Are Ultimately. If you cannot find a way to Realize this Ecstasy, there is no way that you can be Happy. You will simply be obsessed, obsessively pursuing pleasure in this life and obsessively identifying with this mortal body-mind. You will be obsessively thinking, obsessively complaining, obsessively reacting, obsessively desiring. You will be obsessively depressed. Your capability to love, to communicate Happiness in the world, will be profoundly limited. Life will always be problematic.

* * *

As soon as there are two rather than One, the great fear arises.

*   *   *

Wherever there is another, fear arises. Where there is the slightest sense of another—in other words, wherever there is separateness, wherever there is self-contraction—there is fear.

*   *   *

In The Way and Manner Of The Heart, Understand Your Separate and Separative self (As Un-Love) and Transcend Your Separate and Separative self (By Love). And This Is Perfected (Progressively, In The Way and Manner Of The Heart) By Devotional (or self-Transcending and self-Forgetting) Heart-Surrender Of the conditional body-mind To My Bodily (Human) Form, and My Spiritual (and Always Blessing) Presence, and My Very (and Inherently Perfect) State, and, Thus and Thereby, To The Person and The Forms or Characteristics Of The Spiritual, and Transcendental, and Divine, Self.

The Dawn Horse Testament

*   *   *

The emotional-sexual ego Constantly Hunts For an other. The ego-"I" (or self-Contraction) Hunts (or Seeks) an other (Even all others and The Total Objective Cosmos) In Order To Be Gratified, Consoled, and Protected. The Compulsive Hunting (or Search) For an other Is Generated By The Feelings Of Un-Happiness, Emptiness, and Separateness That Possess and Characterize the self-Contracted being.

Once an other Is Found, the ego-"I" Clings To the other, At First pleasurably, and Then Aggressively. The ego-"I" Depends On the other For Happiness, and, Over time, the ego-"I" Makes Greater and Greater Demands On the other For Fulfillment Of itself (In all of its desires). Often, In time, the other Becomes Depressed and Exhausted By This Demand (and Thus Leaves, or Dies). Just As Likely, the ego-"I" Discovers, Over time, That the other Cannot or Will Not Satisfy The Absolute Demand For attention and Consolation. In That Case, the ego-"I" Feels Betrayed, and the ego-"I" Begins The Strategy Of Punishing, Rejecting, and Abandoning the other.

Every conditionally Manifested being Has (In time) Often Been The Proposed Victim Of This Strategy Of Separate and Separative selves. Even More, Until The Heart Gives Way To Divine Love-Bliss,

26

every conditionally living being Is The Original Genius and Grand Performer Of This Strategy Of Separate and Separative selves. It Is The Strategy Of Narcissus, and It Is The Dreadful Work Of all conditionally living beings who Are Not Awake To The Truth Beyond the ego-"I".

The Dawn Horse Testament

* * *

The avoidance of relationship . . . is the primary act of identification and differentiation. When understanding begins to arise, the individual is consciously relieved of many patterns of avoidance, including all kinds of un-love, incapability, and obsessive habits. Such a one becomes more relational, communicative, and positive. But when understanding is attained in its radical and inclusive form, there is also a primary transformation of experience.

At first understanding promotes a healing of effectiveness and freedom within the "I-that" structure of awareness, where "that" signifies all forces in opposition or contact, high or low. But at last that very structure dissolves in understanding. The whole complex of identification with a "personality", an arbitrary center of memory and experience that the mind rigs up as an entity, ceases. And thus also the objects seen over against that "I" cease to be differentiated— because there is no concrete "I" from which to differentiate them.

Perception and consciousness, then, are loosed and unqualified, and this unqualified consciousness remains as the known and realized form of being, even under the usual conditions of natural life. All of this is the truth of understanding, wherein identification and differentiation are seen to be the avoidance of relationship in its most prior and primary sense.

The Knee of Listening

* * *

The Avoidance Of Relationship Is The Method Of psycho-physical egoity, but The Feeling Of Relatedness (or The Primal Illusion Of "Difference") Is Itself The (Original and Originating) Fault. Therefore, Divine Enlightenment Is Not A Matter Of The Perfection Of Apparent Relationship (or The "Curing" Of The Avoidance Of Relationship By The Apparent Perfection Of Relatedness). Rather, Most Ultimately (or Most Perfectly), Divine Enlightenment Is A Matter Of The Most Perfect Transcendence Of Relationship (or Relatedness, or All "Difference") In What Is Always

Already (Inherently and Perfectly) The Case (Which Is Being, Itself, Consciousness, Itself, and Love-Bliss, Itself).

The Dawn Horse Testament

* * *

The contents of the ego, or the body-mind, or self-contraction, are reduced, broken up, and in one or another way eliminated by My Divine Work. This is literally, and not merely figuratively, so.

When I spend time with you, or sit with you to Grant you My Darshan, I Magnify My Spiritual Heart-Transmission to you, and It Combines with the various contents of your conditional being. My Transmission is Self-Radiant Energy and Self-Existing Consciousness. In Satsang with Me, this is what you confront in your life and meditation. This is the character of My Divine Siddhi. And It spontaneously Works to stimulate the contents of your conditional self, in life, in meditation, and in moments of repose. That Siddhi also breaks them up and eliminates them in a process that is not possible by any other means. Ultimately these contents are eliminated by My Transmission Work, and they are returned to the Primal Energy-Condition, or the Ultimate Condition of Divine Being.

The Hymn Of The True Heart-Master,
"I Am Grace Itself" section

* * *

My Spiritual Heart-Transmission is the Transmission of Non-Separateness! In *The Da Love-Ananda Gita*, I Speak of the Wisdom of Non-Separateness. My Spiritual Heart-Transmission is Non-Separateness Itself.

* * *

By this right feeling-Contemplation of Me, by surrendering and forgetting the separate and separative self, you are able to stand in the natural position of being able to observe the act of self-contraction, the knot itself, the obsessions that fall from it, the perceptions that fall from it, and all the rest. In the Way of the Heart, that is the only right position in which to do sadhana. To be already in the position obsessed with objects and others, already self-contracted, unable to view the self-contraction, is fruitless. No real sadhana can be done there. You can only manipulate your behavior.

* * *

There are two ways to engage Spiritual life: the Way of Satsang and the way of egoic struggle in response to instruction. I do Give you My Instruction, but only in the context of Satsang, only in relationship to you. Therefore, practice of the Way of the Heart is realized in relationship to Me. I do not merely Instruct you and then leave you on your own to fulfill My Instruction. I am steady in My Transmission of My Spiritual Heart-Presence. I am always Available to you. I will always be Available to you, even after My physical Lifetime. I have promised it in Writing in My Source-Literature. It is literally so, and it will always be so. Now you and all My devotees must create a culture based on your practice and your realization of the Way of the Heart. Only on the basis of perpetual Satsang with Me will the community of My devotees serve My Work in the world. Satsang with Me, My Grace Transmitted to you in My Company, makes it so and makes you My devotee.

Therefore, understand this principle and practice it moment to moment under all the difficult, ordinary, and nonsensical experiences of conditional life, under all the conditions of the body-mind. Instead of being astonished by the painful qualities of limitation and mortality, Find Me and enter into Divine Communion with Me.

The Hymn Of The True Heart-Master,
"I Am Grace Itself" section

*   *   *

The confession of Love-Bliss is the confession of devotion to Me, not the confession of struggle and apology. Of course, the Way of the Heart is associated with self-discipline and the transcendence of egoity. Nevertheless, My true devotee does not practice self-discipline and the transcendence of egoity through struggle with the ego-self, but through feeling-Contemplation of Me in every moment.

The Hymn Of The True Heart-Master,
"I Am Grace Itself" section

*   *   *

The practice in My Company is a "reality consideration". It is about locating the action for which you must become responsible. This is absolutely essential if Divine Self-Realization is to be the case.

*   *   *

Your practice of the Way of the Heart, when it is fruitful, is based on present self-understanding, present awareness of the activity of self-contraction and the relinquishment of it in Communion with Me. That true practice is what I am moving you toward and what all of your practice altogether in the Way of the Heart should be moving you toward.

*　*　*

CHAPTER 5

You Must Become Human Before You Can Become Spiritual

SRI DA AVABHASA: Be willing to straighten out your life and handle your life-business as the basis for receiving Me. This is what it takes.

* * *

People think that the first thing they are supposed to do when they enter into the Way of the Heart is to become Spiritual, so-called. This is absurd. People who are full of suffering and fundamental misunderstanding about themselves one day, think they are "Yogis" the next. What is first required of an individual is not to become Spiritual and manifest Spiritual phenomena, but to become human.

* * *

Your social presentation of yourself, or your manner of participating in relationships, is to be "considered" at the beginning of your practice because the Way of the Heart begins not in the context of the larger Process of Wisdom but, rather, in the ordinary context of the first three stages of life. The beginner's practice, therefore, has very much to do fundamentally with social relationships. The social personality must be observed and understood and disciplined, even from the very beginning.

* * *

The Spiritual process rests upon the moral foundation of responsibility for the egoic action of un-love, or the avoidance of relationship. Only through responsibility for the disposition of

"I love you" may you continue to grow in the ordinary, evolutionary way and at the same time be God-Realizing in your disposition.

*   *   *

There cannot be a beginning to life in Satsang with Me and to the Spiritual process in My Company until you are fundamentally responsible for the strategies of your childishness. Deal with one another openly, simply, with humor and love, and do not dramatize any strategy at all.

What if you did not do that any more? Really, even that would amount to nothing. It seems like a giant step for mankind, like the first footstep on the moon, as if it were so profound. But truly it is only a paper route!

*   *   *

As long as you have a problem with the incarnation of the Divine Principle in Satsang with Me, you will have problems with sexual intimacy, problems with friendships, problems with community, and problems with living sanely and happily every day. You have such problems primarily because you do not acknowledge the Divine Reality, Who I Am and Whom I Reveal, and you do not submit yourself to Me. Secondly, problems arise for you because you do not incarnate That Which is Realized in Satsang with Me humanly, and you do not allow your devotion to Me to humanize you through love.

But as soon as you Realize this Principle, as soon as you are submitted to It, as soon as you allow yourself to incarnate your devotion to Me and allow it to humanize you, your life gets straight.

*   *   *

In every moment you are obliged first to handle things with your neighbor, that is, to establish stable, ordinary conditions in this body-mind and its relations. Only then are you prepared to go to the holy place, to enter into sacred occasion (such as meditation or My physical Company)—even to realize this moment in Truth. Therefore, the natural and obligatory life-conditions of the Way of the Heart are primary and necessary in every moment. Otherwise, even though the moment itself is Only-God, your own face will hide the Truth of it.

*   *   *

I do not Call you, as My devotee, to conform to the world. I Call you to conform to Me. The entire purpose of Divine Enlightenment is that you conform all your parts, all your moments, the whole display of your limitations, to the Divine Reality. That is how I did it. Of course, I did not take so long at it as all of you, because you are justifying your reluctance and I did not. I was just as aware of reluctance as you, but I did the sadhana—not just sometimes but moment by moment. I did not refuse it. I dedicated My entire Life to it.

That is what it takes to make the course as brief as possible. Then soon—as soon as you can manage it—your practice of the Way of the Heart exists on a different plane, in the domain of Spiritual life with real Spiritual responsibility.

It cannot be so without your handling your life-business. It just cannot be so. You can get a taste of such mature sadhana here and there, but it cannot be so steadily and responsibly until you handle your life-business and endure the original sadhana of being purified in the context of ordinary life.

* * *

Notice what is affecting you. In one fashion or another, through the Grace of Truth Itself, you must handle business—even after the fact, at a later date. You must. You cannot continue to grow, you cannot move on in the Way of the Heart, until you handle your business, until there is nothing left over, nothing unforgiven, nothing unspoken, nothing unthought. You must be physically, emotionally, and mentally purified of memory, of insult, of moments of pain and separation. You must be. You can make great leaps in that process, because Truth is a great Force, but nonetheless you must endure it. You must handle your personal business, the business in your past, the business in your friendships, the business in your blood relations, the business in your intimate relations, the business in your friendly relations, your business with the world.

You are suffering many concrete things in life, and others are also suffering. By the power of Truth erase what you and they are suffering. That is the Way of the Heart, and nothing else, nothing less, at all. You have very real things to do, very real things, very human things, even very ordinary things. You must do these things. There are conversations you must have. There are things you must say and things that must be said to you. Energies must be released, feelings must be exposed, thoughts must be expressed, bodily signs must be given. New society must be generated. The entire culture of My devotees must be changed by this exercise. Do not tell Me I am Free to give you My Native Sign until you do that and give Me your sign.

* * *

You can see what a cave the ordinary life is, what a wilderness it is, what tapas it is, what sannyas it is, what self-mastery it requires, what manliness it requires, male or female. It is in precisely those moments that you must make the great Choice that is the measure of My devotee.

Especially in the beginning of your sadhana in the Way of the Heart there is so much gross, petty nonsense. Because you are only at the beginning, you are dealing with all the ordinary, first-three-stages-of-life stuff. But do the real sadhana and it becomes—I would not say "easier", necessarily, but it becomes more straightforward, subtler, more refined, more profound. You must endure that beginning, the handling of life-business, and be purified of the grossest part, which is there at the beginning.

* * *

Notice everything, notice every insult, be sensitive to everything. This has always been My policy. I have suffered everything. I have relieved My Self of nothing. This Body will not die with unfinished business, absolutely none, for its sake—and I am not even it. One must be sensitive and do the work. You kill your egoic "self" with it—but "you" must die from something. Therefore, die from the sadhana, die from Truth, die from nothing less than the Truth. Invest yourself in the Truth absolutely. Handle all business. Exhaust yourself in the process. It is better than nothing. It is better than failure, and it is at least on the way to Realization.

Handle all business, and set yourself free, by the power of Truth Itself. And let nothing be left over. This is not only how you serve your own Realization. This is how you will serve all beings. Fulfill the Law by handling all business. This is love. To suffer reality is love. And to handle business, you cannot indulge yourself. You simply cannot.

* * *

CHAPTER 6

Serve All Others

SRI DA AVABHASA: The condition or demand of service is the condition or demand of love. Love and service are identical, and they are fulfillment of the Law, which is sacrifice.

* * *

To truly serve is not merely to be nice, or to fulfill conventional moral imperatives, or to develop a conventional social personality, or to try to save the world—or to animate any similar obsession. Rather, service is an expression of the self-transcending disposition, an expression of Ecstasy in feeling-Contemplation of Me. And it is a profound discipline.

* * *

Be truly a servant in the world and be nothing else. Enjoy no other disposition than ecstasy and ecstatic service.

* * *

The Basic Disciplines Relative To Service Involve The Re-Orientation Of social activity, work, money, and, Indeed, Even all activities, To The self-Transcending, Cooperative, Inclusive, and other-Serving Disposition, and, Altogether, To An Intention That Is Characteristically (and Always Positively, Rather Than Insipidly) Harmless and Basically Non-Competitive (and Otherwise Only Most Positively Competitive, or Competitive Without Negative, or Loveless, Intentions, and Competitive Only In circumstances that Either Strictly Demand Or Rightly Expect Competitiveness). And, In The Process Of This Re-Orientation, There Must Also Be The Effective Relinquishment Of The self-Serving, Exclusive, self-Fulfilling, Basically Competitive, and Otherwise Negative, or

Loveless, and (Characteristically) Not Positively Harmless, Disposition. And All Of This Is To Be Accomplished Simply By Engaging all activities (functional, practical, relational, and Cultural) As Sat-Guru-Seva (and, Thus, As self-Surrendering, self-Forgetting, More and More self-Transcending, and Always Directly and Really Felt Devotional, and Truly Me-Contemplating, Service To Me, and, Thus and Thereby, To The Divine Person and Self-Condition That Is Only, all, and All).

The Dawn Horse Testament

* * *

As My devotee, you are not to indulge inner motivations or desires for satisfactions within and without. You are to serve. You are actively, intuitively, and radiantly to bring effective life, energy, or love into the plane of all presently arising relations and conditions.

* * *

In the Way of the Heart, service is the life of Happiness in all relations and under all conditions. (It is the discipline of looking, feeling, being, and acting completely and truly Happy in all relations and under all conditions. And such is not a matter of "seeming", or adopting a conventionally happy face or merely enthusiastic social personality. It is a matter of truly and presently Finding Me, As I Am, and living the Way of the Heart in My Divine Company.)

* * *

True service is a relationship of tolerance, compassion, help, the giving of energy and time to others.

* * *

If service is the principle of your relationship to all beings, including your intimates, you do not have three days to dramatize some event with someone. You do not have a week for anger. You do not have even five minutes, because service is your obligation. The demand for service, then, produces a kind of attention in this moment that makes you see your turning away, your separativeness. It generates spontaneous self-observation.

* * *

Service is an orientation to others. It is not an orientation to oneself in the presence of others. To have some sort of ulterior motive is self-meditation. The obligation of service shows you exactly how your presence with others is a form of self-meditation. It is not that when you are present with others you must always be doing something—such as trimming their toenails! Just be present in a natural way.

The demand for service, because it is a demand for natural attention in the company of others, for functional presence in their company, is a continuous criticism of what you are tending to do in every moment in relationship. Service is an orientation toward relationship, rather than an orientation toward subjectivity. It is in itself a simple condition, but it is a demand, and in every moment its reflection in you is different. There may be times when you are frustrated by the condition of service, when you are very awkward in fulfilling it, or when you are super-active, or super-inactive, or even apparently successful. It is a test in every moment. It is a demand for relationship.

*   *   *

The mature individual in the Way of the Heart is active as love, under all conditions. Such a one always primarily grants love and attention, rather than seeking, or watching for whether or not he or she is being given love and attention. It is not that the mature individual does not enjoy or need the love of others and the Spirit-Blessing of the Divine Being, but the mature individual enjoys such love and Spirit-Blessing as the Happiness that arises in the midst of a life wherein he or she is perpetually responsible to love and to be a personally, morally, and Spiritually responsible sacrifice in God.

*   *   *

All action must become service. All service must be Guru-Seva. All Guru-Seva is Guru-Contemplation. Action, or service, then, is Guru-Contemplation. In the Way of the Heart, Sat-Guru-Seva is to abide in that feeling-Contemplation of Me constantly in the midst of activity. In the Way of the Heart, service, like meditation, is a form of sadhana, and both service and meditation are about feeling-Contemplation of Me, each through a somewhat different apparent design.

The secret of service, and of meditation, is to remain always in feeling-Contemplation of Me.

*   *   *

As a practitioner of the Way of the Heart, you are obliged, by your devotional relationship to Me, to express your commitment to self-transcendence in all your relations and under all conditions. And you are obliged to do so constantly. Such service to Me is practice of the Way of the Heart. Such service to Me is participation in the reception of My Grace. Such service to Me is the God-Realizing Way of life.

*   *   *

CHAPTER 7

Love Is a Great Discipline

A CONVERSATION WITH SRI DA AVABHASA

JOE TAYLOR: I have found in my relationship to people throughout the day that I make judgments on the basis of people's competence. If I see someone with competence, I can demonstrate love to that person. During the recent hurricane, everybody became competent.

SRI DA AVABHASA: Yes, whenever there is an emergency, a threatening situation, people work together. But when the threat passes, everybody is back to competition.

JOE: During that time I was in love with everybody. It was so easy to love them. And during these gatherings when You are here, my heart melts and again I love everyone. During the day when everyone is serving and everything happens marvelously, I am in love with the people who are participating. They are all very competent, and I can surrender myself to the project and take any dramatization that comes up from anybody.

But when a project is not going right, there comes my dramatization. It is in my speech and in my interaction with people. They feel that I am not free, and they do not feel free, and our service does not feel full.

SRI DA AVABHASA: What is the alternative?

JOE: I think I have taken on the alternative, which is to renew myself fully in the service, to not be so sensitive, and to help everyone make it happen.

SRI DA AVABHASA: That is a rather negative alternative! Is there some other disposition or way of functioning that would be wholly right and also more productive?

JOE: I cannot see it.

SRI DA AVABHASA: Is it all right to express displeasure when people are animating themselves minimally? Why isn't that all right?

JOE: I like to see things happen and get done.

SRI DA AVABHASA: That is good. I do, too! Isn't it appropriate to express displeasure when people are not functioning fully, happily, and with great attention? Is this not a time to express displeasure, rather than withdrawing?

JOE: I think that my expression of displeasure is un-love.

SRI DA AVABHASA: Why is it un-love? I express My displeasure. To express displeasure is not inherently loveless. It depends on who is doing it. There are times to express displeasure, and such an expression is not necessarily loveless.

JOE: I feel it as a burden.

SRI DA AVABHASA: Because of how you are doing it, perhaps, because of your intention, your disposition. I express My displeasure for My devotees' sake, and they regard it as just another form of My Blessing. When you express your displeasure, it is felt as pettiness, withdrawal, dissociation, lovelessness—and perhaps it is all those things.

JOE: Obviously it is.

SRI DA AVABHASA: Therefore, the problem is not the expression of displeasure but your failure to deal with yourself.

JOE: Everyone here has shown that they are absolutely competent in certain circumstances.

SRI DA AVABHASA: And everyone here on staff has shown how incompetent they are, as well, under many circumstances. And I have to raise My Voice about it sometimes, don't I?

Generally, you express lovelessness, displeasure, dissociation, a lack of interest in familiarity with anyone, a sort of "hard-nosed" attitude. Expressing displeasure or trying to help people to function more productively can be appropriate enough, but what is your disposition in it? When some people make such a demand, others are happy, even inspired, to straighten themselves out. They feel something positive about such people. The displeasure of such people motivates them. When others—like yourself, apparently—express their displeasure, people run for the hills, become uninterested, and do not want anything to do with such a person. They feel you are dramatizing, even being nasty.

People notice your egoic attitude, your dissociativeness, your egoic "self-possession", your nastiness as an egoically "self-possessed" character, and they do not get the point you are trying to make. They are not motivated. They do not do anything different. They do not feel in you a motive of congeniality, of support, of getting on with it. They just become focused on your nastiness. In that case, your displeasure is not really productive.

JOE: I basically just write them off in my heart.

SRI DA AVABHASA: Sometimes getting people to respond is fundamentally what there is to be done.

In any case, your will to competence and making the "hard-nosed" measure of it in everybody else is obviously part of your pettiness, your lovelessness. The problem is not so much your expressing a managerial intention, or criticizing people, or raising your voice. These things in and of themselves could be all right, but they are being done by someone who has, in some sense, bad intentions, negative intentions, or an egoically "self-possessed" attitude that does not become very productive for everyone.

Is that you?

JOE: It is me. I am the force behind this. It is my expression to people that causes this reaction. It has nothing to do with love.

SRI DA AVABHASA: So you get into the petty attitude without any regard for anything else, is that it? It is just pettiness. You expect people to just do the job at hand. This is just another way of saying that when people fulfill your expectations you feel for them. And when they do not fulfill your expectations, you may deal with them—that is all right—but you withdraw your feeling. And that is not all right.

41

In your circumstance of managing people, there are two ways to do it. The way you are doing it is rather petty, egoically "self-possessed". It is your way of dissociating from people, and that is the wrong way to do it. You could still insist on competence or getting down to the job at hand, but in a different disposition. Regardless of whether or not other people changed very much, <u>you</u> would be in a different disposition. You would be there as My devotee and really practicing the Way of the Heart.

You are just describing the same old fault that is in everyone, the conditional manifestation of feeling. You manifest feeling when your expectations are fulfilled, and you withdraw feeling when they are not. If you did not withdraw your feeling when your expectations were not fulfilled, you might still raise your voice or call for what you regard to be competence but your communication would be entirely different. The outward manifestation is the same, but the character is different.

Instead of practicing the discipline of love, which is a real discipline requiring self-understanding and intention, you avoid that discipline, and you manifest feeling according to whether or not your expectations are fulfilled. That is the ego's game. Your confession, like the confession of others, suggests that this is a universal principle, a universal act, a universal game. Everyone is up to the same thing. You manifest it in various ways through the design of your own character, but it comes down to the same thing in everyone. The feeling dimension of life is manifested by you conditionally when your expectations are fulfilled, and not otherwise. Everyone is doing just that, every single one of you, all the five billion. Everybody is playing this out. This is just how <u>you</u> do it.

When there is real self-understanding, real self-responsibility, when you are no longer playing the heart on the basis of whether your expectations are fulfilled or not but you are manifesting love in any case, love is a great discipline. That is the difference.

PART II

Transcending Reactivity

CHAPTER 8

No One Is the Beloved of God

A CONVERSATION WITH SRI DA AVABHASA

BRUCE BURNHAM: Sri Gurudev, recently I made a decision to move out of the household where I have been living, because my relationship, or lack of it, with one of the people there was not tenable.

SRI DA AVABHASA: Why wasn't it tenable?

BRUCE: Because there was always so much conflict.

SRI DA AVABHASA: Why is conflict not tenable? Why isn't it useful? Why isn't that a creative situation?

BRUCE: For quite a while I felt that it was very useful because of the heat it created for both of us.

SRI DA AVABHASA: It wasn't really Spiritual fire, or heat, because both of you became less and less involved with one another. To love when you are not loved, that is the heat of Spiritual practice. The heat is not to love less and to feel unloved when you are not loved. That is not heat. That is lovelessness. I believe I have called it "the avoidance of relationship".

BRUCE: Several times this person made it very clear that she could not live in the household with me any longer, and her refusal justified my departure.

SRI DA AVABHASA: That is probably the logic that had to appear eventually. The whole episode obviously was a dramatization, the rehearsal of a script. Everything became inevitable, and now you are living alone. You made the emotional choice, not necessarily the intellectual one. You chose by habit to respond to being unloved by not loving. Therefore, the rest of it became inevitable. But if you had done the opposite, then that script could very well have been unnecessary. You might not have become one another's favorite human being, but you could certainly have realized a human relationship.

This is what you do when you are not loved. You separate yourself. And when you get similar metaphysical feelings, so that you are really not certain that you are loved by the Divine either, the script continues to be one of isolation. You go inside to find the "Big Self". You take the inward path in isolation, indulging in meditation for fifteen hours a day and all the rest of it. You choose the loveless life.

Do you think you are loved by Me, the Divine Person? Do you believe that the universe is pervaded by My All-Sustaining, Absolute, Immortal Love?

BRUCE: I feel that in Your Company.

SRI DA AVABHASA: Apart from what you may feel by association with Me in Divine Communion—Satsang with the Realizer of course being the cure for lovelessness recommended since ancient times— and apart from the love that you may feel is coming from any individual specifically, when you are off naked in the universe do you feel connected to the Divine through love? Or are you uncertain of it?

BRUCE: I mainly feel in a state of shock.

SRI DA AVABHASA: Right. In the metaphysics of your existence you are responding to a "Great Woman" or "Great Being" or "Great Condition of existence" by Which you are not loved.

BRUCE: It feels now like a great tension in the heart.

SRI DA AVABHASA: Yes. That is the contraction of the ego, the avoidance of relationship, the collapse from the Divine Reality. At birth, when the human being individuates bodily, the apparent individual feels cut off from the Divine. As a born being you become dependent on the food source, on the sources of love, in your childhood, when you are vulnerable. But those sources are always doubtful. You always come to discover that the love and attention any being can give you is not steady, not absolute. Yet you continue to depend on such gestures. This dependence, however, enforces a sense in you that you are fundamentally disconnected, vulnerable, mortal, unloved. That is the mood of the ego, contracted from the Divine and in fear of annihilation. Independence is the false incident of birth. It is a disposition a human being inherits through psychological individuation. And you must individuate because you are born.

The third stage of life should be the time when you are unparented at last, thrown from the nest, when you are guided to the point of responsibility for that presumption of independent existence, that false incident, so that you can assume your full humanity and enter into Spiritual life, which is not founded on the sense that you are individuated and moving toward annihilation, to be murdered by cosmic Nature. In the third stage of life you are to become responsible for all the adaptation that you have inherited in your incarnation, and to be open-heartedly connected to what sustains you in Truth. It is only on the basis of this responsibility that Spiritual life begins, not on the basis of the agony of your egoic life, struggling to be consoled by some vision, some relationship, some functional pleasure.

BRUCE: I never feel consoled by any kind of vision.

SRI DA AVABHASA: You have been looking for visions, haven't you? Trying to realize some state that is completely pleasurable through meditation, perhaps!

BRUCE: I have always felt that I would realize such a condition only in Spiritual relationship to You.

SRI DA AVABHASA: That is good. But in terms of your position in the midst of things, this reaction to being unloved is what you are all about. And of course the cure is to find Me and enter into Divine Communion. That is the cure: Abandon the incident of the ego and realize the incident of Divine Communion, or reconnection to the Divine Source-Condition That I Reveal to you.

BRUCE: Over time I have felt that realization coming more and more into play.

SRI DA AVABHASA: But you are still dramatizing this loveless lie. You are still dependent on being loved. What you discover is not that love comes to you from Infinity, as from a super-cosmic Parent. You discover in Communion with Me that you are love. That is the Realization.

Divine Self-Realization is not a relationship to some great Something that loves you. No one is the beloved of God, absolutely no one. The Divine is not the kind of Reality that makes beloveds out of individual beings. All beings owe their love to the Divine. You do not Realize the Divine by finding the Divine Being, Truth, and Reality at the end of a great chain but by being wholly one with the Divine so that you yourself are love. If you come to Me only to get loved, expecting the Blossom of My Spiritual Heart-Transmission to be projected at· you, there will be no change because you will remain loveless.

Divine Communion begins when you love. Then not only are you connected to love but you are it. The only way whereby you Commune with the Divine is by being love. Love has great strength. When it is Realized Most Perfectly, Love is Siddhi, the "Bright" Blessing Power of the Divine. It is the fundamental Power, the great Power, when you are It, but not when you dissociate from It in your egoic separation and weakness.

What this "consideration" comes down to in your case is that you are living the usual life of contraction, not just in a relationship here and there but fundamentally. Your infantile reaction to being unloved is not just something that you bring into a certain few relationships. It is your philosophy. It is an interpretation of things as they are. It is an interpretation of the universe: to be loveless because you do not trust love. You are not certain of being loved and, thus, you cannot love. But to love is the Law. You must love, regardless of the circumstance. The essential principle of the Way of the Heart is unobstructed feeling-Contemplation of Me expressed via all functions, in all relations, under all conditions. That principle is to be realized in all the complicated mechanics of your relationships and in all the esoteric developments that may be Given to you as you mature in the Way of the Heart.

Love is the principle, but love is not what you are living. You basically feel unloved, unable to depend on love. You are always reacting to the universe as a great Something in which you are not loved, always protecting yourself from death. This reaction is the essential learning you must undo in order to become a human being.

The Way of the Heart is not a matter of reading signs about yourself and going within, through meditative techniques, trying to find the great absorption. That is the method of Narcissus, whose solution is further isolation. God-Realization is in the moment, yet it has nothing to do with the conditions that are arising in this moment. They are not it. God-Realization is the Awakening to your true Condition, Which is Love-Bliss Itself, and to live It, not just to believe It, not to depend on others for It but to Realize that confidence, that overwhelming Love-Bliss, unthreatened—that is the business of My devotees, not the mediocre drama you are telling us about here.

Because of your emotional adaptation, which comes early in life, you feel greatly justified in your un-love, your weakness. You realize your true manhood, male or female, when you are able to confront that contraction, when you are able not to dramatize it any longer but to grow far beyond it. Everything follows that Awakening. Then you no longer seek Divinity in the form of either your lower functions or your higher functions. All your functions are simply conditions of experience. They are not themselves the Divine or the not-Divine. They are simply conditions of existence that are not other than the Divine. They do not have the force, in other words, to separate you from Me.

The ego finds all kinds of consolation in the lower life, and, if it can, it detaches itself from the lower life. The ego thinks that the visions within the body and above the brows are the Divinity that loves you. That is simply heresy! All this nonsense about so-called Spiritual life is My complaint. I have seen all those visions, and they are not the Divine. You might as well call your intimate partner "God". Your intimate partner is not the Divine. He or she is not other than the Divine, if you Realize Me Most Perfectly, but he or she is not independently the Divine. Your intimate partner is not burdened to fulfill you absolutely, unless you make the egoic demand, which is what you tend to do. You make that demand of all your relations, high and low. "Fulfill me, love me, console me."

Some people feel "close to God" when they go to the mountains on vacation. Some people have to look into their heads to feel that they are in touch with God. Some people must be having an orgasm to feel that they are with God. But none of that, in itself, is God. Those experiences are only the possibilities of human bodily existence altogether, of human adaptation in the most ordinary sense. They are essential to human beings perhaps, but deluding, unless you are Free as the Heart by virtue of Most Perfect Inherence in Me. Only thus can you see these experiences for what they are and become the sacrifice of them. If you are not free from the egoic contraction, then you interpret all experiences as sublimities and you become attached to them as conventional Yogis, or as ordinary lovers, or as whatever form of attention you are animating at the moment.

The key to your existence is at the heart, in feeling-Contemplation of Me—not in the planes of experience above or below the heart but at the heart. The condition of the heart, the profundity of your devotion to Me, determines your disposition, your Realization, your understanding of every experience, high and low. That is the essential Communication of My Wisdom-Teaching.

BRUCE: Yes. I have heard this Argument many times, and yet there is just that contraction, that tension at the heart.

SRI DA AVABHASA: Yes. But you are toying with all the possibilities of experience, high and low, mainly low, perhaps disposed at times to be meditative and to go up. You are dramatizing this contraction, this dilemma of independent consciousness, in the form of your experiences. People look to increase their experiences all the time without being responsible for the fundamental matter. The conventional Yogi in his or her so-called Spiritual strategy is also a loveless individual.

BRUCE: I always feel that it does come back to that dramatizing, and yet it seems that what has to be cut through is this contraction at the heart.

SRI DA AVABHASA: But in your case it is like using a hair to cut through a twenty-foot marble wall! You are not cutting through it. You are busy meditating on the problem, busy being the contraction, and therefore self-transcendence seems to be immensely difficult. But you see that there was no purifying heat of real sadhana at all in the conflict you talked to Me about. It was your dramatization of being unloved and unloving. Such dramatization does not transcend anything. There may be literal heat, but it is not the heat of devotional practice of the Way of the Heart, not the heat of love, of sacrifice. The heat of self-transcendence is the heat that cuts right through self-contraction. Your activity must be the gesture of absolute certainty, not a tentative feel, weakly asking, "Do you love me?"

BRUCE: It is not even a question of that, because I knew she did not!

SRI DA AVABHASA: Nevertheless, you asked the question, and the answer was no. And so you did what seemed necessary—you left. You withdrew. You went into your solitude. That is the very model of Narcissus! And that is the model of your life. That is the way you have done it since childhood. That is the level of your emotional adaptation.

In that case, you are not living in Divine Communion with Me. You are living with yourself. You are meditating on yourself. You are keeping "bad company"! The traditional recommendation is that the primary form of practice, the one thing necessary, the essential of Spiritual life, is to spend your time in the Company of a Realized man or woman. But such practice is not just to be sitting here in the same room with Me. You must pass out of self-meditation and literally enter into Communion with Me.

CHAPTER 9

I Call You to Transcend
Your Reactivity

SRI DA AVABHASA: What is a negative emotion? It is not feeling, it is not relationship, it is not happiness. It is always a recoil from some circumstance, some condition, some state. Therefore, all the forms of emotion other than love, or the natural radiance of emotion, are karmic in nature, forms of contraction, forms of suffering that cause you pain in the body, reinforce the sense of separate self, and cause you to dramatize life in separative ways, as a seeker.

* * *

Birth is separation, or identification with the vulnerable born-condition. It is, in the human case, vital shock, or fear.

When fear becomes self-conscious—when you are seen and known, even by yourself, to be afraid—shame arises.

Shame leads to self-indulgence, or patterns of desire and self-manipulation that enervate the body-mind, spending the available life-force. This includes every kind of activity relative to the great cycle of "money, food, and sex".

When energy, or life, is spent to the point of enervation and loss, feelings of emptiness and sorrow overcome the individual being.

When emptiness and sorrow become self-conscious—when you are seen and known, even by yourself, to have wasted life or failed to master its impulses—guilt arises.

Guilt leads to flight and the sense of being chased or under attack. It may lead to suicidal egoic "self-possession", but when escape is realized to be impossible, then anger arises.

When anger does its aggressive work, murderous in its intent and power—so that you are seen and known, even by yourself, to have become the enemy of life and love—remorse arises.

Remorse repents of separation, fear, shame, self-indulgence, emptiness, sorrow, guilt, flight, anger, and aggressively egoic "self-possession". Therefore, remorse, or repentance, fully and clearly realized, establishes the body-mind in the mood of non-separation and love.

For this reason, men and women are advised since ancient times to repent and to love, to become established in the balanced, feeling center of the being, which is the heart. Therefore, as My devotee, turn to Me with feeling-devotion. Receive My Love, which moves you beyond egoic "self-possession". By these means, enter into Communion with Me, the True Heart-Master, the Divine Person, Who Stands eternally in front of your heart.

* * *

Once there is self-understanding and the Awakening of attention and energy to Me, the will must convert this body-mind, this mound or pillar of "Narcissus", into a true and living temple of God-Communion. Thus, through practice of the Way of the Heart in My Company, fear must be converted into the will to free surrender as bodily existence; sorrow must be converted into the will to present relationship; anger must be converted into the will to forgiveness, compassion, and self-transcendence; the withholding of love must be converted into the will to love; life-depression and negativity must be converted into the will to life-positive feeling, action, breath, and speech; doubt and confinement to fixed ideas and illusions must be converted into understanding and the will to free attention; and bodily separation from the Divine Being, Truth, and Reality must be converted into the will to total psycho-physical surrender to and inherence in Me, the Self-Existing and Self-Radiant Divine Being.

Only when all of this is done have you entered into that disposition and Condition in Which karma, or negative tendency and guilt for past negative activity, can be transcended. Negative tendencies, guilt feelings, and actual guilt are a complex dis-ease of the total structure of the body-mind, and all of that can be released or "forgiven" only in the event of the conversion of the total body-mind from the negative pillar of your egoic "self-possession" to the living temple of surrender to Me and inherence in My Divine Love-Bliss, or Happiness Itself.

*   *   *

Reactivity is basically a ritual you engage all day long, week after week, month after month, year after year, as you cycle through the ritualized demonstrations of mind, emotion, and body. There is no ultimate necessity for it. Your emotional reactivity is an organized form of behavior for which you are not responsible, and your irresponsibility is the problem of life, the "Dreaded Gom-Boo".

This imaginary disease is not merely a little bit of philosophy. It is a ritual life, a prerehearsed, prefigured automaticity you crank out every day of your life in relation to standard events. You are always doing it. You live as if you are diseased. The Dreaded Gom-Boo is a real disease in the sense that you experience it and are animated in it every day of your life, but it is imaginary, or unreal, in the sense that it is not necessary, not based in reality. It is just an automaticity. It has no necessity.

Since the Dreaded Gom-Boo is unnecessary, there is therefore no necessity to devote your life to overcoming it! You should understand it and transcend it directly.

*   *   *

On Fear

Fear Is The Primary Mood Of Separation. Fear Is Especially Associated With The First Stage Of Life and The Vital Shock Of birth. It Is Signalled By the gaping mouth (In Pitiful Awe), As If the mother's teat Were Suddenly Torn From the infant lips.

Fear Is Also The Principal Motivating Mood Of the "Solid" character. Paradoxically, the Obsessively self-Controlling and other-Controlling "Solid" character Is Founded On A Fear Of Being Controlled By others (or By conditions outside the body-mind-self). And That Fear Is Originally Developed In the years of infancy, childhood, and adolescence, Generally In A Passive and Rather infantile Reaction Either To The Feeling Or To the Actual experience Of Being Too Much Controlled and Threatened By others, Especially adults.

The Dawn Horse Testament

* * *

Fear Is the self-Contraction. . . . All Of Fear, egoity, self-Contraction, or Un-Love Is Only Suffering. It Is Only Destructive. And It Is Entirely Un-Necessary.

The Dawn Horse Testament

* * *

I have often "Considered" with you the passage from the *Upanishads* that says, "Wherever there is an other, fear arises." No demons, no bows and arrows, no nuclear war—only an other, only the sense of otherness, need arise to give rise to fear. And how does the sense of otherness develop? Through the self-contraction, whereby one feels separated from what one observes, therefore limited by it, and thus limited to what one can seem to be at this moment. Feel mortal and you feel incapable of flow, or change, or freedom. There is no ultimate metaphysical means for getting rid of fear, no ultimate knowledge. The alternative to fear is not some great answer that will ultimately prevent your being chronically and mortally afraid, which you now are, and which people in general are always. Such knowledge is not even possible. The alternative is to feel Me, Contemplate Me, and understand fear as an ordinary mechanism of the body. You can, and should, in any moment feel and breathe beyond fear through surrender to Me. You should be resting in your natural state, feeling and breathing whole bodily into My Divine Condition in Which you exist. Do not remain full of fear, doubt, contraction, becoming a black hole, another universe unto yourself into which everything is sucked, like Lake Narcissus!

* * *

As soon as there are two rather than One, the great fear arises. And that fear tends to make you crave more fulfillment through the things you desire. Thus, people are obsessed with what they desire. They are angrily at work to be fulfilled, high and low. But at the root of their desiring is despair, pleasurelessness, fear. When people Find Me and enter more and more fully into Divine Communion, which is the Way of the Heart whereby fear and anger are undone, the necessity of all human experience begins to break up and disappear. The "two" of separate self and whatever is not separate self become the One of Divine Love-Bliss.

* * *

Certainly, fear is fundamental to Spiritual life. You must uncover enough of yourself so that you cannot immunize yourself against fear anymore. You do not want to be that vulnerable, do you? So you say, "Forget Spiritual life." It is easier to stay consoled, stay busy, stay sexy. Spiritual life is not merely a matter of being afraid, but it is a matter of transcending fear and not merely immunizing yourself against it all your life.

The Hymn Of The True Heart-Master,
"I Am Grace Itself" section

* * *

To surrender your consolations is to open the door to fear, to the naked reality of your own vulnerable mortality. This mortal fear is the first three stages of life, which are based on identification with the body and elemental existence and which are committed to protecting that identification. The first and foundation and great gesture is to go beyond that impulse to consolation, that refusal of fear.

* * *

What you identify as fear is the natural energy of the individual being contracting upon itself and causing an implosive and unpleasant pressure.

Easy Death

* * *

Fear is your recoil from the gesture of participation.

* * *

Through your self-transcending resort to Me, you can be free of fear in this very moment, in any moment, even in a moment when some degree of fear seems conventionally appropriate. Fear collapses attention. Therefore, even when fear might seem appropriate, it is still better to be without fear, so that you may have complete attention in the moment to deal with the threat. Fear is plainly and simply inappropriate, except in the flash of noticing imminent danger. But even then, in the very next moment you are dealing with the danger rather than with the fear. Fear has only the most minute significance as a practical necessity in your life, and yet you tend to be completely overwhelmed by it!

* * *

Activated as an automaticity by your mood of anxiety, fear releases the subtle chemicals secreted by the hypothalamus and other endocrine glands. Then, as a reflection of this activated mechanism in the body, thoughts of death and bad possibility arise to the mind, and in response to these chronically fearful thoughts, you recondition the bloodstream again with more negative chemistry! The usual man or woman lives always in a chronic state of fear, committed to egoic "self-possession" and meditating on self-contraction.

* * *

As you begin to see how fear works as a mechanical process, you will also feel that it arises without external cause. You will begin to notice how it clicks into and out of operation in a subtle range of mood from anxiety to terror in every moment of your existence, as a reaction to everything that is present to your awareness—as if life were a question you had to answer before attaining the right to be free of fear. Fear is a rolling process in the body, a constant bodily tension, a permanent recoil or flight. As My devotee, you can also observe that through the natural process of feeling-Contemplation of Me, by surrendering to the One That Lives you, fear is transcended in every moment. Thus, it is not by means of a long and complicated process or path, like slaying a dragon, that fear is overcome, but through natural, tacit surrender to Me, the Living Divine.

On Sorrow

Sorrow Is The Primary Mood Of the Rejected individual. Sorrow Is Especially Associated With The Second Stage Of Life, The Loss Of self-Security, and The Loss Of Power Over others On whom one Depends. It Is Signalled By the grimace, the downturned and puckered mouth, As In the eliminative anal grunt, The End-Game Of oral Dependency.

Sorrow Is Also The Principal Motivating Mood Of the "Peculiar" character. The Alternately Idealistically (and Thus mentally) self-Controlled and Chaotically self-Indulgent "Peculiar" character Is Founded On A Basic and Sorrowful Feeling Of Being Neglected. The Chronic Sorrow Of the "Peculiar" character Is A Yearning To Be Effectively Touched, or Loved. It Is A Call and Even An Hysterical Need (or Search) To Be Controlled, or Restored To Balance By A Positive Controlling Influence. And That Sorrowful Need Is Originally Developed In the years of infancy, childhood, and adolescence, Generally In An <u>Hysterical</u> and Rather childish Reaction Either To The Feeling Or To the Actual experience Of Being Neglected, Denied Love, and Denied A Positive Controlling Influence.

The Dawn Horse Testament

* * *

Sorrow is ego-based. It is your way of dwelling on what you have lost, when someone you love has died, for example. The feeling of sorrow does not really take into account the one who has died except as something from which you are separated. Thus, most of the emotions you indulge when somebody dies are your own problems, reactions you must deal with or overcome.

Even so, it is not altogether inappropriate to be sorrowful when someone dies. But you must find another resource, a greater capability, through which to be free of the vision of death that is pushed in front of you at such a time. The sorrow you feel at someone's death is not just the result of memory. It is ritual, like so much of the rest of what everybody does repetitively, compulsively, constantly, hour after hour, day after day, from birth until death. People generate very few truly appropriate actions in the whole period between birth and death.

Most of the sorrow associated with death, therefore, is totally unnecessary, a self-destructive and other-destructive ritual. Passing through the ritual sorrow and complication relative to the sickness or death of someone with whom you had a very strong emotional connection and daily dependency is perhaps inevitable. You must still overcome your sorrow, but sorrow is at least temporarily appropriate.

On Anger

Anger Is The Primary Mood Of Reaction To All That Seems To Justify Fear and Sorrow. It Is Especially Associated With The Third Stage Of Life, The adolescent Struggle With The Motives Of Dependence and Independence, and The Aggressive Effort Toward genital Victory (Glorifying the Separate and Separative self, egoically Powerful Over all others). It Is Signalled By the tortured mouth with gnashing teeth, The facial Display Of genital Shapes and genital Agony. Everything Of The First Three Stages Of Life Is Displayed In Common egoic Anger. Even egoic sex Is Full Of Rejection and Anger, Threatened By Loss and Sorrow, and Convinced Of Fearful Separation.

Anger Is Also The Principal Motivating Mood Of the "Vital" character. The "Vital" character Is Characteristically self-Indulgent, vitally, or physically. The Mood Of This Pattern Is Always Rather Rebellious. Indeed, Even the Most Apparently Carefree, self-pleasurizing "Vital" character Is Dramatizing Resistance and Refusal. The "Vital" character Is Founded On An Angry Reaction To Controls and Demands. The Characteristic Behavior Pattern Associated With the "Vital" character Is A Chronic Effort To Resist, Refuse, or Avoid The Controlling Influence Of others (or Even Of the mind) On The personal bodily Existence Of the conditional self. And That Angry

Mood Is Originally Developed In the years of infancy, childhood, and adolescence, Generally In An <u>Aggressive</u> and Rather adolescent Reaction Either To The Feeling Or To the Actual experience Of Being Too Much Controlled and Threatened By others, Especially adults.

The Dawn Horse Testament

* * *

Egoic self is strong, yes! Because you are angry. And anger is a technical fault. Those who are My devotees know where anger is. Anger arises in the solar plexus as a great heat, a fiery energy that runs up the front of the body. It runs up the <u>front</u> of the body, but the heat of Spiritual Force should run up the back of the body.

Anger is like vomiting, a reversal of the current of life-force in the frontal line of the body. Those who are angry throw up the life-force in front. But the front of the body is supposed to conduct the descending current, the cooling, relaxing current. Those who are chronically angry reverse this current from the solar plexus just below the ribcage, creating great heat in the head, in the face, all over the body. Anger is a disease, a reversal of the natural current of the body, which should descend in front and ascend in back.

You are so involved in anger because of your upbringing and because of all the previous lifetimes you do not remember. You are habituated to angry reaction toward embodied existence. Taken by itself as a matter of fact, embodied existence is totally worthy of anger. <u>Totally</u> worthy of it! You are therefore justified in your anger. But when you understand yourself, understand the mechanism of this reaction, this fire in the front of the body, and can relax that automaticity, then you can receive the cooling force of My Spiritual Heart-Transmission, which cools and relaxes the face, the chest, the heart, the solar plexus, the abdomen, cools you in front, relaxes you in life, enables you to re-order your life sanely, relieves you of all your un-Happiness. Then, via My Baptizing Power, the Fire of My Spirit-Current Awakens.

The Fire of My Spiritual Life-Current belongs in back, up the spine or in the central line of the body. It has nothing to do with negative or reactive emotions. First, you must understand yourself and overcome this revulsion, which is really like vomiting all the time. Anger is like throwing up all the time from this place just below the ribcage. You tighten up there, and then you throw it up through the heart, through the throat, through the face. You get flashes of heat in the face and you become aberrated. The heat boils your mind, boils your brain, interferes with the subtle mechanisms in the brain, in the hypothalamus and so forth, if you want to get technical about it. It increases the heat in the midbrain and it aberrates you.

The fundamental aspect of this angry orientation is the throwing up of life in the front of the body. Anger heats the brain in its central compartments and throws off hormonal chemistry that aggravates the rest of the body. You are not merely angry, you see. You are habituated to anger because of the difficulties of life and the models of the people you have grown up with and the training you have received and the aggravated education you have endured. All these influences have nothing to do with Spiritual life but only with ordinary suffering.

You must understand most fundamentally the mechanics of your self-contraction and what you do under various circumstances when you react and engage this mechanism, when you throw up the life, when you throw it back to the Divine angrily instead of receiving it from the Divine Person. You must be completely free of this orientation so that you can receive My Divine Blessing and breathe It down, conduct It down, inhale and receive It, open up your heart to It.

Feel Me. This is the first moment of Grace, not merely to taste My Blessing sometimes, but to be in a position to accept It and grow on Its basis, to use My Blessing as the Means of your Spiritual transformation.

*   *   *

Like children and adolescents, in your egoity you do not think you must be obliged by what you understand. You think you can be secretive, egoically "self-possessed", cloudy, dark, self-indulgent, dramatizing. You think you have a right to such dramatization. In fact, you think such dramatization is ordinary life, and you think it has no consequences.

When you were a child and a teenager, perhaps your immaturity did not have great consequences because you were surrounded by the shroud of adults' protection. But now that you are an adult and My devotee, you are responsible for the environment that makes life positive and whole. Therefore, you do not have the right to dramatization. You are now obliged by the passage to adulthood to manifest the sign of your best understanding, which has been Given to you by My Divine Revelation. You must show it fully, bodily, enthusiastically, happily, emotionally.

* * *

You no longer have the right to your bad days or your phases. Bad days and phases will occur in the process of the sadhana of the Way of the Heart, but I do not want to see a sign of them on your face or in your outward life. I do not want to see any drama. I have not come so that you can persist in stupidity and mediocrity, showing Me no life, no energy, no intelligence, no attention. Those tendencies are there in you, but so what? So you will have to do a little sadhana. The little difficulty required of one who lives the sadhana of Satsang with Me is nothing compared to the sadhana the seeker must perform. I expect you to accept this responsibility and to live in Satsang with Me and always to be Happy. If some circumstance within or without is temporarily giving you apparent trouble, I expect you to be Happy and to live this Satsang with Me with great energy, and never to turn away from Me. If you do all that is Required of you with great energy, you will see a transformation that will amaze you. And I expect your sadhana not to stop but to increase.

* * *

When do you ever get serious about yourself? You are in the same mud with everyone here, going to death [snaps His fingers] any moment now, all under the same sentence, stuck in the hell-house, waiting indefinitely for the execution. You all know it is going to happen, but you hope it will not hurt too much. And in the meantime you are hoping that life will be amusing and consoling and that you will not be so afraid. Thus, you keep piling in the consolations so that you can be immunized against your fear, which is the fundamental thing you are trying to avoid—not death but fear.

You are always trying to avoid fear. You will use almost any device in any moment to avoid fear, to avoid sensitivity to the situation you are really in. You hardly even participate in this existence, in this moment, because you are afraid of fear. You will not renounce sufficiently to encounter and go beyond your fear so that you are clearly here, clearly existing, bright, free to renounce this contraction here, like that [snaps His fingers]. As long as you are afraid of fear, you will not really renounce this contraction. You will toy with it, play with it, think about it, wonder about it, and keep introducing the delays.

In any moment of your conditional existence, you do have the power somehow to prolong your insensitivity to fear by consoling yourself, immunizing yourself, fooling yourself, occupying yourself, distracting yourself with this, that, or the other object—always selecting the objects that are the most consoling, that enable you to relax the most, to feel immune the most. You are basically seeking immunity, not self-transcendence. You are not motivated to self-transcendence. You are seeking immunity. You are seeking to be dull, unaware of fear, or the fundamental sensitivity to your circumstance here, in which your very existence could be hacked off, like your head by a sword, in any moment.

Nonetheless, in every moment you suffer limitation, search, agony, the pain of the contraction of your own body-mind, and still you will not relinquish the contraction. Rather than do that great act of devotion to Me, you prefer to console yourself, think yourself into insensitivity, react yourself into insensitivity, create a dullness physically so that you can be insensitive to the thing you know is always there: Fear. Ending. Unconsciousness. Blackness. Utter separation.

* * *

All doubt, despair, and fear become insignificant once the intention of life becomes love, rather than dependence on love.

* * *

Fear, egoity, self-Contraction, or Un-Love Is Chronically Expressed Through The Complex Ritual Of Rejection, or The Communication Of The Dominant Idea "You Do Not Love me". Once This Is (In The Way Of The Heart) Truly, and Completely, and Most Fundamentally Understood, The Ritual Of Rejection, Fear, egoity, self-Contraction, or Un-Love Can Be Directly Transcended, If Only It Is Summarily Replaced By The Ordeal (or Discipline and Practice) Of self-Transcending Love, and (Then, By Grace) Heart-Communion With and (Ultimately) Heart-Communication Of The Divine Self-Condition, In The Form "I Love You".

The Dawn Horse Testament

* * *

Rather Than Struggling, Turn to Me

SRI DA AVABHASA: In the instant when reactive states of mind, emotion, and body arise, then desires, motivations, and obsessive fascinations also arise, high and low, as methods of relief from the problems and tensions of the body-mind. Such is the origin of egoic "self-possession", temptation, and "sin", which means to "miss the mark". The reactive and independent body-mind is turned upon itself, and so it avoids or "misses the mark" of all relations—with all others and with Me, the Incarnate Divine Person.

In the Way of the Heart, the mature and truly human individual is able to inspect and understand this cycle of reaction, egoic "self-possession", and tension-release, in his or her own case as well as in the case of others. Because he or she is My devotee, such an individual does not indulge the egoically "self-possessed" sense of dilemma, nor does he or she indulge the tendencies that automatically arise to relieve him or her of the self-contraction. My devotee only observes the whole pattern in every moment, and so resorts to none of it. My devotee yields the egoic self instead to feeling-Contemplation of Me, in every instant of self-contraction, or dilemma. My devotee always bypasses the ordinary destiny of problems and solutions. My devotee abandons the problems and solutions of the reactive and independent body-mind in moment to moment feeling-Contemplation of Me.

This is the practice of My devotee—always to meet the Mark. Therefore, My devotee remains creatively effective, whole, essentially simple, and utterly free of the illusion of separation from Me, or from What is Real, Divine, Love-Blissful, and Great.

*   *   *

If you are making an effort to overcome one or another aspect of your egoic self in any moment, you are not practicing the Way of the Heart. Whatever characteristics you notice in yourself at any moment—your anger, your lustfulness—cannot be transcended by noticing them and then making a great effort to overcome them.

You may experience a basic sense of anger, for instance, every day of your life. The Way of the Heart is not to observe yourself to the point that you notice you are angry all the time and then you make every effort and use every aspect of My Wisdom-Teaching, interpreted from your egoic point of view, to somehow rid yourself of anger, or to be happy rather than angry, or even to be just pleasant rather than angry. Such effort is not the Way of the Heart. Such effort is the convention of the un-Enlightened paths. It is the natural sign of the ego, or the conditional individual without Divine Self-Realization. The sign of the Way of the Heart is feeling–Contemplation of Me, and, thus and thereby, of That Which already Transcends whatever limitation you are observing.

Rather than struggling with anger, Contemplate Me. Rather than trying to rid yourself of anger, give <u>Me</u> your attention. If you do, you will naturally observe that anger passes in that moment, and then in the next moment. Ultimately, it will be washed from you altogether.

The Hymn Of The True Heart-Master,
"I Am Grace Itself" section

* * *

The psychiatric point of view attempts to locate events that occurred early in life and that have had an effect on one's psychological disposition thereafter. In most cases, a perception rather than an actual event caused the reaction. In any case, freedom from reactivity is not a matter of remembering an incident from the past but of relocating one's emotional capability in present time, so that you can be responsibly emotional, or feeling, in your association with the Divine, with the universe, with all the relational factors of existence.

Recontacting the emotional force of the body-mind is essential to the development of the Spiritual process, and likewise it is essential to the regimen of emotional healing. Therefore, if shocks occur in the life of your child, or in the life of anyone, you must introduce the nurturing, intimate quality. Help the person to feel beyond the shock by re-attracting his or her emotional force when you notice it is becoming depressed or reactive.

One is a growing personality one's entire life, and therefore one should live in a culture of elders, a culture of wisdom, in which everybody is treated as a growing personality, one's reactions are observed, and one is drawn out of them. When you notice that an individual has been startled and made reactive by something that may have intruded upon him or her, you must learn how to re-attract the person—adult or child—physically, mentally, and emotionally into the relational environment, the universal pattern of existence.

That someone has become involved in a reactive mode is not an absolutely negative event. Simply notice it and re-attract the person to relationship. Every individual is in a moment of growth. As beginners in the Way of the Heart, you people are not finished. Whatever your chronological age, you are not yet truly human adults. As a matter of fact, you are frozen in levels of reactivity that belong to the first, second, and third stages of life.

The community of My devotees must know how to introduce cultural circumstances that will draw an individual's fundamental energy and attention, body and mind, from the field of reactivity and that will reintroduce the reactive personality into the continuing pattern of growth. Growth does not end. There is a summation of growth in the seventh stage of life, which is Revealed and Given by Me, but until that time one is involved in a process of growing as an individual, of adapting to further stages of association with the phenomena of existence.

The process of dramatization must be noticed by the elders of the culture of the Way of the Heart and by the force of the general community of My devotees. The factors of reaction, contraction, and egoic "self-possession" that have been introduced into an individual's life and that have inhibited the person's growth and adaptation at particular stages of life must be observed. On that basis, there must be the artful introduction of cultural influences that attract the individual out of the states of reactivity.

* * *

Reactive emotions and inappropriate behavior in general are secondary symptoms of a primary frustration. What is being frustrated is intimacy, or life-positive, associative energy. Thus, you cannot deal with the secondary, reactive emotions directly, as if they were the point. What the person is actually suffering is the point, and it is what must be addressed in him or her. A circumstance must be provided wherein the primary emotion of love can be chosen and expressed in any moment.

*   *   *

It is not just that mind or thought must cease to bother you, but the whole affair of your life must change. However, your life does not change, as you begin to realize, through the hard knocks of trial and error, by your trying with all your strength to manipulate it into something different, manipulating mind, emotion, body, energy. Manipulations do not do it, not even mystical Yogic manipulations, or religious and Spiritual manipulations. None of it works.

What does transform a reactive life is the heart-felt, devotional response to Me, the Incarnate Divine Person, Who Is your Real Condition, the Divine Self-Condition of the heart and of the whole body-mind.

*   *   *

The secret of living with children, as with all human beings, is that everybody stays happy, ecstatic, full of pleasure. If you can find the pleasure or the free attention in a child, then you can redirect him or her. But if you confront the aberration that is present in the moment, the child will not come out of it, because he or she has a ritual to perform. And it is the same with adults.

Therefore, the secret of truly human life is to live in the Happiness of Satsang with Me. Such Happiness is the responsibility of My devotee. The secret of living with others in the culture of the Way of the Heart is to locate the free attention and essential Happiness in them and in yourself and to redirect them to their sanity by that means.

*   *   *

In the Way of the Heart, anger is not transcended through suppression, nor is anger transcended through release. Anger is transcended through feeling in relationship, first in relationship to Me and then in relationship to others and the world. Therefore, when someone is angry in the community of the Way of the Heart, you must constantly deal with the person's primary emotion of related-ness, or love, and enhance that emotional sensitivity in the person, rather than dealing problematically with secondary reactive emotions.

* * *

The Oriental defense simply and thoroughly "considers" and understands the energy represented by an opponent, and deals with the energy that is in the opponent in such a way that one does not necessarily win but the conflict is transformed. The Western way is to see the angry other and to become angry and to become involved in an immediate confrontation. The Eastern way is to transcend anger altogether and simply study the opponent and constantly step aside from the blows. It is to dance with the other by not becoming the opponent of the other. When you enter into dance with the other, the energy is transformed.

The dance that is suggested is essentially a moral gesture, in which self-transcendence is the mood of one's relationships altogether. There are very few incidents in which any confrontation is appropriate.

* * *

Change your way of action, and the subjective dimension of your existence will change naturally. The born condition precedes all subjectivity. When you are un-Happy, you want to manipulate your subjectivity first—your feelings, your thinking, your conceptions, and your feeling-conceptions. You want to change them before you will change your way of life. You want to be free "inside" before you will love, before you will act differently.

You must act differently first, and not be concerned that the feeling and thinking aspect of the body-mind remains full of tendencies. Do not be concerned about them. They are just the signs of the old way of living. You must Contemplate Me with feeling-devotion and then act in love, with energy, with life, in all your relations, in your disposition moment to moment, under all conditions. You will observe in the midst of such action that the subjective dimension is also gradually penetrated and transformed. Its negativity, its reactivity, becomes unnecessary and ultimately obsolete by virtue of your different action.

As My devotee, you either change your action through feeling-Contemplation of Me or you do not. You must begin to do it. There is nothing more that can be said, nothing more convincing than that. You simply must begin to do it. As you begin to do it, the vulgar disposition of your internal life and your subjective tendencies will continue. You must not be concerned about them. Tendencies are only the signs of your old way of living. Let them pass. Live differently now. Love. Serve with feeling. Put your attention on My Argument. Be transformed by the hearing of it. And act differently. The new subjectivity will follow. Subjective changes, internal changes, emotional and mental, will follow.

Be My devotee and feelingly Contemplate Me. And on that basis, start to act differently. Stop presuming the separative position. Stop being angry and sorrowful and fearful in your relations, and bring energy into them. Be happy in them. Be enthusiastic in them. Bring life to all beings. Bring life to the tree. Bring life to the door-knob and to Me! And you will see your subjective life changing, over time. It may remain completely wretched for 25,000 births. Do not be concerned about it.

* * *

The father-force makes the demand, frustrates you, evokes the capability in you to overcome an obstacle, to deal with yourself, deal with what is difficult, and move into new areas of experience and growth.

* * *

Practice of the Way of the Heart is all that is sufficient and necessary. If My devotee dramatizes the ego-game, he or she should simply receive the discipline of intensified practice. Absolutely! That is it! Without fail!

If someone is having difficulty, "consider" what the person should combine with his or her regularly expected practice over the next three days or so. Interrupt the flow of the person's expectations for three days.

* * *

In the community of My devotees, every one knows what every one else has the tendency to become (when irresponsible) and the possibility to become (when responsible). And all serve one another at the level of that understanding. They all also know the functional character and capability of each other, and they amuse and enjoy and serve and employ one another at every appropriate level. But responsibility for functional life must always be assumed and demanded in the truly human community. When it is not, that failure of responsibility will weaken the community.

* * *

Spiritual life is a crisis. Therefore, spiritual life does involve discomfort at times. When discomforts of the crises occur, this does not mean that spiritual life is failing, or that you are not good enough for it. Crisis and discomfort <u>must</u> occur. The crisis, or turnabout, is what it is all about. It is supposed to occur. You are supposed to suffer the purifying events. You are supposed to encounter resistance in yourself. You are supposed to discover all kinds of garbage in yourself. So why should there be any special resistance to it when it occurs? There may be discomfort, and you may wish you did not have to go through it. But apart from that, there is no reason why you should be overwhelmed or completely disenchanted by the fact that you are witnessing a period of intense conflict, crisis, suffering, and disturbance. The more time you waste identifying with all of that, the less sensitive you become to the event. Therefore, Satsang, devotion to Guru, and a loving and intelligent approach to all of life should naturally increase or intensify in the periods of apparent discomfort.

All of these apparently disturbed or crisis episodes in this real process of spiritual life are themselves very intelligent, very meaningful. They have a great deal to show you. The more capability you have for passing through these times, the more useful they become. The man or woman who is really using this process can be passing through this crisis almost continually, with great frequency and intensity, and yet, like a soldier on the march, such a person never misses a step, never reveals it in any peculiar, outward manner. He or she continues to function, and apparently only enjoys life. He or she doesn't get involved in a whole drama of upset. But in the beginning, when a man or woman is just beginning to pass through this kind of crisis in consciousness, there tend to be reactions and breakdowns whenever this crisis process begins. In the beginning there is very often an emotional collapse, even a physical collapse. There are these episodes that have an almost psychotic quality to them. And it is during those times that the person is wondering whether to come here or not and all of that. But as one passes through these purifying episodes, one begins to realize how one must function in terms of the real spiritual process.

When this event begins to arise in the mature disciple, there is always already something familiar about it. One knows the signs, one knows what is about to occur, and one knows the kinds of reactions that will build up. One knows that, instead of clenching one's teeth and resisting it, one should find some more work to do during that time. Instead of planning a vacation or a binge when one sees a crisis coming, one cancels all forms of entertainment or ordinary distraction, every thing that one would normally use to distract oneself from one's usual state. One plans a lot of work for the coming days. One plans on an ordinary, functional life. One makes good use, really good use, of these episodes. The more intelligent one is, the better the use one makes of them. The less intelligent one is, the more capable one is of binding distraction at that time, the more one will look for means to dramatize one's state, and to distract oneself from the lesson that turns purification into transformation.

You must know that everything I am doing is a means to bring about this crisis. I desire this crisis in you. I don't want it not to happen. I don't want to console you. I don't want you to be happy in your unconsciousness. I want you to become sensitive to your actual state. I want you to know very well what you are always up to. I want you to become capable of seeing yourself under all kinds of conditions. I want you to see the machine of your ordinary activity. And I want it all to collapse. I want it to come to an end. I want the death of all of that.

The Method of the Siddhas

* * *

70

If you dramatize reactivity, you must discipline yourself, go to the meditation hall more, study, change the mind, submit it, and work out whatever is frustrating you. In any moment of difficulty you may not be able to change your state absolutely, but do not, therefore, dramatize it. Do not abuse Me, your True Heart-Master. Do not abuse your spouse, do not abuse your friends, do not indulge in your reactivity.

Suffer your reactivity yourself and bring it to more study. Surrender it in feeling-Contemplation of Me. Exercise yourself in devotion to Me. Deny yourself casual time for a day or two or three. Redress the wrong, and clarify your practice.

* * *

SRI DA AVABHASA: In the Way of the Heart, whenever you notice you are at your worst, go on retreat, or fast. Religious practitioners have always practiced retreat and fasting in difficult times, thus demonstrating that they knew what they are doing. Instead of dramatizing, which is the common choice when things seem not to be working out for you, drop out of the sphere of objects, others, seeking, and the dramatization of reactivity and desire, and go on retreat. Go on retreat for a day, for an afternoon, for several days, for some weeks, for however long it takes.

Apart from such formal retreat, which you should resort to as often as such dilemmas arise, you can also add a discipline to your daily life that is a kind of retreat for My devotee in the Way of the Heart. That discipline is to fast, while going about your daily business, from the sphere in which the dilemma is appearing. Instead of (while in a fit of potential dramatization) trying to work out something with someone about this, that, or the other thing, fast from the conflict. Do not associate with the person for the moment or even for some while. Do not enter into intimate occasion, if the disturbance is occurring in your emotional-sexual intimacy. Drop out of the sphere of objects and others and the search associated with it. Collect yourself to Me, "consider" My Heart-Word, and straighten yourself out.

These are the religious means. However, you tend to do what worldly people generally do. When you fall into these difficulties, you do not make use of the means to which you have already committed yourself as My devotee. Instead, you tend to abandon those means, you dramatize, and you create a struggle. If you should find yourself in such a difficult moment, fast, go on retreat—before you dramatize. If you do not fast or go on retreat, you will inevitably dramatize. And if you dramatize, you create difficulties, you make errors, you say things you should not say, everybody tries to address you, and people must use up their energy to deal with you as some adolescent character who is totally unavailable to any wisdom at all.

In fact, you all are wasting much of your time in cultural discussions with one another by addressing people who are already involved in a dramatization, whereas you should have noticed what they are doing and sent them to take a retreat or to fast. Therefore, establish the fundamental principle of this practice as the basis for your dealing with anything. Obviously, when things are more difficult and you are rather overwhelmed, you must apply the most fundamental principles of the Way of the Heart and resort to them. The Way of the Heart is about self-understanding and self-transcendence, not about perfecting the circumstance of your relations for their own sake.

DEVOTEE: I notice that in those moments of reactivity or seeking, the same objects always come up.

SRI DA AVABHASA: As an egoic character, you are patterned toward particular forms of seeking. It is likely that the patterns will continue to show themselves in a similar form over and over again. These repetitive patterns are exactly what you should fast from, because your purpose, since you are committed to the Way of the Heart, is to deal with yourself, not to make a utopia out of the conditional world, whether in the larger sense or up close.

DEVOTEE: So to deal with those objects of desire is to fast from those objects of desire?

SRI DA AVABHASA: If necessary. When you are capable, when the real arms of practice are in place in you, then you can deal more directly with your reactivity, your desire, your seeking for relations, objects, and others. When you have sufficient clarity, then you can be more outspoken and functional in your relationships. But if you do not have such clarity, it is time to fast.

*   *   *

In the Way of the Heart, the dietary discipline is senior to the emotional-sexual discipline. Without an understanding of oneself as a food body—which is what the flesh body is, a food body, made of food and about the process of food—without such understanding and without being responsible for the body as such a mechanism, you cannot be direct and clear about the emotional-sexual dimension of your life.

* * *

The gross body is, very simply, the food body. The gross body itself depends on (and is made of) food. The quality and quantity of food largely (or very basically) determines the state and desire and action of the physical body and the sense-mind. If food-taking is intelligently minimized, and if the food selected is both pure and purifying, then the physical body (and even the total mind and the emotional dimension of the being) passes through a spontaneous natural cycle that first shows signs of purification, then rebalancing, and, finally, rejuvenation. Therefore, if food-taking is controlled, the physical body itself, including its desires and activities, becomes rather easily (or simply) controllable.

The Da Avabhasa Upanishad

* * *

Only a benign, pure, vital, and complete diet can serve the body's Communion with the Divine Reality.

* * *

If the process of breathing is consciously exercised, and you become aware of breathing as a constant process of energy and feeling rather than mere huffing and puffing, then economization and control of emotional reactivity will become more and more natural to you in daily life.

* * *

When you are breathing, feel it, bodily and with emotion. Whatever you are <u>doing</u>, feel it altogether. Feel into all relations constantly. But whatever you are thinking or feeling <u>about</u> what you are doing or have done, feel what you <u>are</u> doing instead, and feel the breath of living.

If you are angry and too full of self-expression, inhale and receive and be vulnerable through all relations. And make sure the inhalations on the left side are full and clear. Then breathe evenly in the Happiness of My "Bright" Company.

If you are sorrowful and full of self-pity, exhale, blow out the lungs, and bring energy, love, and strength into all your relations. And make sure the exhalations on the right are full and clear. Then breathe evenly in the Happiness of My "Bright" Company.

If you are afraid and full of doubt, breathe deeply and fully, with feeling. Breathe equally in and out, fully and clearly. Then breathe evenly in the Happiness of My "Bright" Company.

And when fear, and sorrow, and anger are restored to the balance of life, My Divine Love-Bliss, Which Exceeds and Contains and is Ever Free of your illusion of separate life, may come forth to Claim your attention.

* * *

The devotee must continue to live and enjoy the Condition of Satsang, even though he or she may feel the rising tendencies, the negativity, the symptoms—physical, psychic, internal, in the external conditions of life, everywhere. Even so, live this Satsang, enjoy this Satsang. It is the only principle that is free of all of that, and if you live the transformative conditions of Satsang, Its intelligence replaces the unconscious activity of suffering. To live Satsang makes the search and its motivating dilemma obsolete.

The Method of the Siddhas

* * *

CHAPTER 11

Do Not Be Concerned

SRI DA AVABHASA: Part of the discipline of the Way of the Heart is not to be concerned that the physical, emotional, and mental signs of your old way of living continue. Allow them to come and go, rise and fall, without concern, without dramatization. Persist in feeling-Contemplation of Me and live the discipline of love, physically, vitally, emotionally, mentally, and (in due course) Spiritually. By living that commitment as a discipline, you will see the old adaptations fall away and become unnecessary and obsolete.

New adaptations of existence naturally come into being when you change your act—it is as simple as that. But you must persist in this discipline. Do not be concerned when subjective stuff arises. It eventually disappears, if only you persist in feeling-Contemplation of Me.

* * *

Turn Your Heart-attention To Me, and Do Not Measure That Turning Relative To Whether Or Not Your mind Stops and You Feel Better. Love Me, and Do Not Measure That Loving Against Whether Or Not You Still Feel Negative emotions and Confusion. Give Your life To Me. Turn bodily To My Bodily (Human) Form. Feel (and Thereby Contemplate) My Bodily (Human) Form, My Spiritual (and Always Blessing) Presence, and My Very (and Inherently Perfect) State At all times. And Do Not Measure That Giving, and That Turning, and That Feeling-Contemplation Against The Measure Of Whether Or Not You Feel pains in Your body.

Therefore, Always Maintain The Discipline Of That Giving, and That Turning, and That Feeling-Contemplation. It Can Be Done, If You Do Not limit or Deny That Giving, That Turning, and That Feeling-Contemplation By The Reading Of Problems In Your body-mind. That Giving, That Turning, and That Feeling-Contemplation Can Always Be Done. Truly, You Can Never Be Disabled In Terms Of That Giving, That Turning, and That Feeling-Contemplation.

The Dawn Horse Testament

* * *

Everything in you that is other than the Awakened heart makes your practice a dynamic process. This means that there will be times when you feel overwhelmed by your negativity and your symptoms. You must have more humor about all of that. You must observe its arising enough so that it has no more significance to you than a headache—expressed in psychological terms. When you can view it in that way, then the negativity is just something you live with. It does not animate you particularly. The tendency simply persists. And that is all it is: a tendency, a setup in the nervous system and in the endocrine system at the moment. It is a setup in the bloodstream and in the wave patterns in the brain at that moment.

The heart is not bound by any of that. It observes all of that. It sees what a cranky animal the psycho-physical person is and has some humor about it.

* * *

You can go through the crisis of reactivity the way the usual person goes through it, without any consciousness, just dramatizing it. Or you can see the tendencies arising in you from hour to hour and remain in Satsang with Me, going about your practical business without becoming concerned for it.

See the appearance of these things as what they are. They are the signs of an eternally ongoing purifying event, like creeps crawling up out of a well into the sunshine. These things want to creep out into the landscape. But if you dramatize them as soon as they get into your eyes or your mind, you fail to let them get out of the well. When you just step out of the sunlight, which is Satsang with Me, the creatures stay trapped in darkness.

Only if you live without concern while these things are arising do you allow them to pass into the landscape, to become unmodified again, not binding. They will be released if you will do the sadhana of always abiding in Satsang with Me.

* * *

Truly human life, or the life of devotion to Me, begins when you are adapted in the moment to a Principle of love that is undeniable. Even though subjective tendencies arise, as My devotee you do not read your life into them. You do not animate them. Instead, you Contemplate Me with feeling-devotion, and, thus turned at heart to Me, you go about your business, with fundamental indifference, letting the tendencies rise and fall. If you persist in this responsibility over time, in Satsang with Me, then these archaisms of the conditional personality become obsolete.

*   *   *

Patterns and experiences always come and go. That cycle never stops—never. A Realized being still experiences that cycle, manifesting within and without. It is just that his or her presence in the midst of it is of another order.

Practice of the Way of the Heart is not a matter of being concerned about precisely what to do about these qualities that arise in you. It is a matter of remaining in your true Condition, which is Satsang with Me. There will be periods of dullness, of the tamasic quality, when you are just stupid, without any clarity whatsoever, when you do not remember anything about what you have understood, when you have no capability whatsoever to be intelligent, to speak clearly, to be direct with anyone, to feel that you have surrendered your separate and separative self. But that tamasic quality will always come and go. No one ever eliminates it entirely. It is always there, as one of the qualities of existence.

Just so, at other times you become intensely active to the point where you have no peace. You have all kinds of energy, and you are full of creativity, endless thinking, motivation, and obsessive concern, some of which is even apparently "positive". This is the rajasic quality.

There are also times when you become very clear, very straight, very simple and full. Everything becomes obvious, and no effort is necessary. This is also a quality, the sattvic quality, the quality of harmony.

These three qualities come and go all the time. They never stop alternating. Their rising and falling is the law. All these qualities have their place, but, because of your improper relationship to them, they become binding. They repeat themselves, and you

77

become fixed in certain states or moods that are negative, rigid, immobile.

When Consciousness Identifies with any quality, Satsang has ceased to be the obvious principle. Consciousness does not realize that It is Witnessing the event, that the event is purely a modification of Itself, of Consciousness. All tendencies in relationship to the qualities of Consciousness, whether of identifying with them or of resisting them, have the same limiting effect. That is why the Guru appears. The Guru comes to establish another principle. Living this binding reaction to qualities is what is meant by "karma". Karma reinforces the limiting qualities.

If you feelingly Contemplate Me, your True Heart-Master, instead of being consistently concerned and reacting to the circumstances of life, positive or negative, that relationship itself, Satsang with Me, purifies the karmas and allows the various qualities to assume their appropriate force in body and mind. The conscious being ceases to identify with the qualities that arise.

* * *

The Secret of How to Change

True change and higher human adaptation are not made on the basis of any self-conscious resistance to old, degenerative, and sub-human habits. Change is not a matter of not doing something. It is a matter of doing something else—something that is inherently right, free, and pleasurable. Therefore, the key is insight and the freedom to feel and participate in ways of functioning that are right and new.

The tendencies and patterns of your earlier adaptations are not wrong. They were appropriate enough in their own moment of creation, and there is no need to feel guilt or despair about them. Likewise, efforts to oppose and change them are basically fruitless. Such efforts are forms of conflict, and they only reinforce the modes of egoic "self-possession".

What is not used becomes obsolete, whereas what is opposed is kept before you. Therefore, the creative principle of change is the one of relaxed inspection and awareness of existing tendencies and persistent, full-feeling orientation to right, new, regenerative functional patterns. If this is done consistently and in ecstatic resort to Me, your True Heart-Master, free growth is assured.

Have no regrets. Resort to Me in Truth and in the present. All that has been done by anyone had its logic in its time. Only Satsang with Me avails. Whatever is your habit in this moment is not wrong. It is simply a beginning. No habit is necessary, but it is only tending to persist, because it has not yet been replaced by further growth. Hear My Wisdom-Teaching of Truth, and understand what is the right, ultimate, and regenerative pattern of each function of the body-mind. Feel free of all negative judgments about what you have done and what you tend to do. Turn with full feeling-attention to the creative affair of new adaptation in most positive Communion with Me, the Incarnate Divine Person, Who Is Alive as all beings.

*   *   *

CHAPTER 12

Your Relationship to Me Is Sufficient to Overcome All Reactive Patterning

SRI DA AVABHASA: The emotional force of the individual being is like an infant. It has no ability to change merely because your mind has other plans or because you change your physical habits. This very primitive emotional reaction was created before your sophisticated mental and physical development. You have accumulated years of physical and mental development, but the emotional development, the disposition or range of your emotional existence, was determined much earlier, in infancy when you were in a totally unsophisticated state of perception, and at a time when you perceived things in an exaggerated fashion.

The primitive, infantile emotional reaction is a reaction to the perception of how things are, not simply to what might actually have occurred. From the infantile, unsophisticated mental and physical point of view, very simple little intrusions, which, from the point of view of adults, are part of the ordinary social involvement of human beings with one another, can be perceived to be profoundly threatening and suppressive. And such intrusions do affect the individual emotionally in a very profound and suppressive fashion.

The emotion of the human being is the primary controller of the very condition of mind and body, the very condition of the chemistry of the body-mind, the blood stream, the nervous system, the endocrine system. All the systems of the body-mind are controlled by emotion and, therefore, all of those systems are controlled by a very primitive, infantile, emotional reactivity. Thus, if you would develop the Spiritual process, you must be drawn into a fundamental responsibility while your emotional life is still in a very primitive condition.

The other aspects of the body-mind that are appealed to in the process that is the Way of the Heart—the mind and the body—are in a more highly developed state than the emotions, but they are dissociated from the fundamental emotional force of the body-mind. Therefore, although you may change mentally and physically, nothing fundamental changes in you because it is the emotional force that must be brought into the sphere of your practice of the Way of the Heart.

That emotional force is held in place by very primitive kinds of reactions that are not informed by sophisticated thinking and high levels of physical development.

* * *

SRI DA AVABHASA: The heart of every individual Stands Free. This is what must be Realized. The apparent impurities of the feeling being are impurities in the functional Circle of the body-mind. They do not belong to the heart. Even so, the heart of the individual may seem to be confused by them.

Reactive and ordinary emotions are not the expressions of the heart, or the feeling being, but of the complex personality, the extended personality, the functional personality. The feeling heart does not exist in space. It is the free, feeling dimension. The bodily locations are the extended personality, and they are peripheral to the heart, just as everything that seems to be objective is.

DEVOTEE: A way to say this is that the Heart Itself is Consciousness, Which is Prior to all conditionality.

SRI DA AVABHASA: And all conditionality is only an apparent modification of It. This all becomes clear in the seventh stage of life, which I Reveal and Give to you. Even so, from the beginning of his or her practice of the Way of the Heart, My devotee must function from the heart, which is simply the free, feeling characteristic of devotion to Me and commitment to the ordeal of sadhana in My Company. Everything observable is peripheral to that devotional commitment.

* * *

The Way of the Heart establishes the foundation of human sanity, which is the re-orientation to the relational condition itself, rather than to the reactive condition of subjectivity, contraction, the avoidance of relationship.

*　*　*

It has come to My attention that one of My devotees has sought counseling to alleviate life-problems she feels are a result of abuse of her as a child. I must emphasize that the Way of the Heart in itself is sufficient practice. Counseling and other therapies need not be added to it.

This woman is completely capable of going beyond her limitation this very day, if she will simply resort to Me with her whole heart and allow her life to be conformed to Me through the practice I have Given her. If she simply will enter fully into feeling-Contemplation of Me and allow her devotion to Me to purify and change her life, then her past experience will have no power over her whatsoever.

The devotional relationship to Me is not based on the presumption of any problem at all. The devotional relationship to Me is the Circumstance that inherently transcends all problems, and, therefore, all limitations and all obstructions. Whatever the experiences of the past, the heart is not even in the slightest touched by them. Therefore, the devotion My every devotee feels for Me in his or her heart has no limits, no problems, whatsoever.

The disadvantage of clinical therapy of any kind is that it presumes a problem, and even meditates on it. This woman reports that she values being involved with others who had an early-life experience similar to her own. In other words, because she is involved in her "case", she looks for the company of others with similar difficulties. People who presume problems pursue the "bad company" of those with like problems.

Instead of meditating on her problem, she should live in My Liberating Company constantly, pursue the "Good Company" of My devotees, and relinquish the orientation of problem and "case" through the clarity of her real heart-devotion to Me. If she will go to the meditation hall and spend an hour or an hour and a half with Me, magnifying her devotion to Me for real, she will immediately be set free of any need to continue to be involved with this problem.

Whatever her experience of being abused as a child, it amounts to absolutely nothing in comparison to all the ways one may suffer in this world. In some sense, it seems she is even clinging to this problem, so that having been abused is part of her self-image. The events themselves are long past. Only the ego is left behind.

To presume that these past experiences can limit her practice of the Way of the Heart is to presume that other life-experiences can limit her practice in the future. This is not the presumption of My true devotee. My true devotee does not struggle with "case" or the past in any form. Therefore, My true devotee does not require therapy to heal the heart and the mind. All My true devotee requires is Me.

Satsang with Me, devotion to Me, moment to moment, is sufficient to relieve My devotee of the limiting effects of all the sufferings of the past, and the limiting effects of all the sufferings that are possible in the future.

Truly, then, it is not therapy that this woman is lacking. Truly, she is not lacking anything. The most that can be said is that she should magnify her devotion to Me and allow herself to relinquish her past, her "case", and her reactivity.

She is no longer suffering from being abused in her childhood. She is suffering from her own activity. She is suffering from her own avoidance of relationship, and that is what she is dramatizing in relationship to Me. She can utterly relinquish this dramatization and easily practice beyond it if she will give Me her <u>heart</u> for real.

This is My Recommendation, not only to this woman but to everyone who would embrace the devotional relationship to Me and practice the Way of the Heart in My Company. I do not Recommend therapy, or conversations with others of a similar past, or any other kind of involvement in "case". This woman may choose counseling, if that is her intention, but it is not My Recommendation.

She should "consider" My Instruction to her and decide what she will do. It is time for strength of heart and not indulgence in reactivity and weakness. The heart was not abused. She should stop pretending that it was. It is time she stopped abusing men with her reactivity and the activity of avoidance.

* * *

Through feeling-Contemplation of Me, cease to live an invisible script and become capable of a free and passionate life that is utterly one with the Inherently Spiritual, Transcendental, and Divine Reality. When the unconscious is thought to be a "something" that is literally hidden, then you must find some way for it to reveal itself and you start looking for inward signs. "Unconscious" is perhaps an unfortunate word, because the patterning is not unconscious. It is fully conscious. It is simply not mental, and it does not have the form of mind. It is pre-mental, not unconscious, and it is effective in every moment of conditional existence.

Each moment of conditional existence, then, is the place where you must observe the pattern of your tendencies. Observe it also when you remember your childhood and when you have dreams. But such are relatively rare experiences. In contrast, many other experiences are arising continuously—you need not even look for them! You must simply observe them as they arise, and you will see the pattern there. The interpretation of life, then, is senior to the interpretation of dreams.

The "Narcissistic", "Oedipal", or egoic bond is broken not by treating it as something deep inside you that must be rooted out and destroyed but by being completely available to observe the pattern that is arising in every moment, until you Stand in the Position that is Prior to the hidden author of the hidden script. I Call you to Stand in the Position of Self-Existing and Self-Radiant Consciousness Itself, in Most Perfect Heart-Identification with Me, noticing the Love-Blissful Spiritual Current of Life in the midst of whatever form of conditional existence is arising in this moment, and noticing also the Consciousness that is aware of It.

That Stand in Consciousness Itself loosens every knot. Ultimately, in the by Me Revealed seventh stage of life, It Divinely Transfigures and Divinely Transforms everything. No amount of mere analysis does it. No number of extraordinary incidents of remembering your childhood or dreaming dreams and interpreting them in Freudian, Jungian, or anybody else's style is such Liberation or can produce It.

* * *

You must renounce sorrow. It is not that you must figure it out or analyze yourself or go into reveries and try to discover when it first appeared and what is holding it in place. No. You must sacrifice it, relinquish it, Stand Prior to it, be in a senior position relative to it. You must surrender it, just that, period. No mind about it. It is just a mechanism, a level of vibration, if you will, a thought. It is just something to be let go of. If you want higher thoughts, greater thoughts, you must sacrifice the ones you are tending to have right now. But you must do it intentionally, and, therefore, consistently. You must make it into a way of life. Your way of life must become one of intentionally and consistently relinquishing your association with lesser tendencies.

The Da Love-Ananda Gita,
"I <u>Am</u> (My Self) What you Require" section

* * *

As you develop your practice in My Company and contact Me through all the opportunities of Satsang with Me, all the contents of your "Narcissistic" ego, or your karmic personality, come into awareness, or into the view of attention. As these contents arise, practice the exercises of "conductivity" and the "conscious process" in daily life and meditation, but always in direct Communion with the Divine Power and Being Transmitted in and through and As Me, your True Heart-Master. As these contents arise in My Company, they are purified by My Spiritual Heart-Transmission. They are stimulated by My Transmission and they are lifted off, or changed— either instantly, or through a process of trial or a sequence of changes. The contents of the ego, or the body-mind, or self-contraction, are reduced, broken up, and in one or another way eliminated by My Divine Work. This is literally, and not merely figuratively, so. When I spend time with you, or sit with you to Grant you My Darshan, I Magnify My Spiritual Heart-Transmission to you, and It Combines with the various contents of your conditional being. My Transmission is Self-Radiant Energy and Self-Existing Consciousness. In Satsang with Me, this is what you confront in your life and meditation. This is the character of My Divine Siddhi. And It spontaneously Works to stimulate the contents of your conditional self, in life, in meditation, and in moments of repose. That Siddhi also breaks them up and eliminates them in a process that is not possible by any other means. Ultimately these contents are eliminated by My Transmission Work, and they are returned to the Primal Energy-Condition, or the Ultimate Condition of Divine Being.

The Hymn Of The True Heart-Master,
"I Am Grace Itself" section

* * *

In time, the force of negative emotions is undermined in the process of yielding all the content and consciousness of your life to Me. The more perfectly and intuitively you are turned to Me and the more abandoned life is in you, the less there is of negative emotion as a chronic, fixed tendency. All emotion is useful. However, you are locked into patterns that stimulate inappropriate episodes, just as in general everyone lives in a chronic emotional state of always manifesting characteristic emotions that are perpetually called into being by the circumstances of life. But if you establish your life in right relationship to Me, through the sacrificial, or devotional, process of the Way of the Heart, then you will also see, secondarily, the emotional pattern of your life begin to break up.

* * *

All tendencies are simply fixed reflections of old activities or adaptations. Therefore, all tendencies are dissolved or made obsolete by present sacrificial devotion to Me, or unobstructed feeling-Contemplation of Me. Such unobstructed feeling-Contemplation of Me is love. If it is lived in the moment of any tendency, the tendency itself is dissolved, or made unnecessary and ineffective in that moment.

* * *

Transcend Reactivity, but Do Not Lose the Virtue of Your Emotion

SRI DA AVABHASA: There is an exoteric religiosity in the world that falsely requires people to have no emotions—never to feel guilt, never to feel sorrow, never to be afraid. It is true that through submission to the Divine Being human beings must transcend chronic and reactive fear, anger, guilt, sorrow, irony, and the rest. But there are moments when any of these responses is completely appropriate, just as the physical body has reactions that contribute to its survival, such as pain. If you could not feel pain when touching something hot, you would not be able to protect yourself. Just so, you are emotionally equipped with survival mechanisms in the form of responsive emotions.

* * *

Perhaps in an instant a reaction cannot be avoided. If a tiger jumps out of a bush, fear occurs—fine. But to make life out of such reaction, even when the tiger disappears, that is the dramatization of reactivity.

* * *

Fear is perhaps the appropriate response to the attacking lion, and even then one's response should not be prolonged and debilitating fear but sudden and great strength. Fear is not intended to be your chronic state.

* * *

Love is a wound, a sorrow, a gesture beyond the separate and separative self. To love is to be wedded to the other, not just in the man-woman relationship but in all relationships. It is to be beyond oneself, even to be beyond the other, to go beyond the other's limitations, to exceed even sorrow but without excluding it.

The best thing that could possibly happen to you is that you become a raw nerve-end, a broken heart, unconsolable, with sorrow on your face—and ecstasy as well.

* * *

To be fiercely angry sometimes is good and necessary and right. It is part of your creative capability to deal with things in this world that must be changed. On the other hand, chronic and petty anger, anger that is not rising on love and that manifests in a life that is not otherwise Divinely Enlightened, must be transcended. But anger cannot be transcended through mere suppression. Anger is transcended only through love of Me, through understanding yourself in feeling-Contemplation of Me, through hearing My Wisdom-Teaching of Truth, and through practical responsibility. When you become truly responsible at the heart and whole bodily, then all of your potential emotions attain their natural form and occasion, as do all of the functions of the body-mind.

* * *

Yes, overcome your petty reactivity, but do not lose the virtue of your emotion. Communion with Me is enacted through feeling-intuition. To be manly, whether man or woman, you must remain sensitive to how things are in the world. The parental message of the world is always that you stop being difficult, that you suppress the emotions that create an unpleasant atmosphere. If human beings become overwhelmed at some point by the great Parental State, it will be because human beings will have renounced emotion, ceased to be angry, ceased to be even capable of anger.

You must be able to transcend your anger in Communion with Me. You must also be capable of anger, of sensitivity, in the face of the utter stupidity of the subhuman society at large in which you live. If you fail to maintain your understanding, your right appreciation, your right emotional response to the world as it is—and to yourself as you tend to be—then you will not grow. You will become benighted through the loss of emotion. You will look at the world, and it will all seem fine.

Things in the world need not be wonderful before you can be Happy. You must Realize the Happiness That I am always Transmitting, Which is Transcendental in nature, Which is Love-Blissful, and Which is your fundamental capability, and the fundamental capability of all human beings, if they will respond to Me, no matter what the circumstances.

I refuse to be angerless. One who is angerless is exploitable. One who is angerless gives himself or herself up to the Parent-State, to the influences that control and exploit individuals arbitrarily. Part of the right disposition of My devotee is to remain appropriately angry, to remain fiery. All the conventional nonsense about angerlessness, lustlessness, emotionlessness, and lifelessness has been borrowed from exoteric oriental religion. In the Way of the Heart, you must be capable of emotion, and you must likewise transcend all self-destructive and other-destructive aspects of emotion through the creative life of devotion to Me.

* * *

The Spiritual practitioner does not cooperate with what kills human beings. But not to cooperate with destructive forces does not lead one to become an ascetic or a killer in one's own right or a revolutionary righteously snuffing people out. Spiritual practice has nothing to do with any of that, either. To practice the Way of the Heart is to find a place for real religious and Spiritual practice at the human level, in the miniature scale of intimate existence, but it is also to not cooperate with the negative features of human society.

As My devotee, you are not called to support negativity, and you should not do so. Do not be like the snake who heard a little bit of wisdom and would not even hiss.‡ Do not submit to being destroyed, but love others, cooperate with others, live with others, communicate with others. This is what I advise you to do.

* * *

‡ Here Sri Da Avabhasa refers to the traditional story of a venomous snake that hissed at people and bit them until a sage tamed it, admonished it for its evil ways, and then taught it to repeat a sacred mantra and not to harm anyone. The snake practiced these disciplines diligently—so much so that some boys, emboldened, beat it nearly to death. Later, when the sage found it in ill health and heard the story, he said, "You are such a fool! I asked you not to bite, but I didn't forbid you to hiss."

You notice that, habitually, whatever arises, you feel in relation to it either appropriately or inappropriately. If you see a gorilla chasing you, the appropriate emotional response is to be afraid—and also to run, hopefully. And the inappropriate response is to laugh and start telling the gorilla stories about your childhood. If a person goes to a funeral, the appropriate response is to weep or feel sorrowful and be somber, and an inappropriate response, at least from the conventional point of view, is to laugh and do a tap dance, in effect to deny the fact of death. What I am suggesting is that appropriate response, or what one might call "appropriate affect", at best is only a logical style of limited emotion relative to some apparent fact. It is not Feeling without limit. It is the limitation of Feeling, even though it is appropriate. And, likewise, inappropriate emotional responses are limitations on Feeling, clearly. In other words, no matter what arises, whether you tend to react appropriately or inappropriately from a conventional point of view, you always present yourself as a limit on Feeling. And this, as you might gather, from My "Point of View" is inappropriate!

In other words, you must do more than feel afraid when it is appropriate to be afraid, and sorrowful when it is appropriate to be sorrowful, and gleeful when it is appropriate to be gleeful. You must Feel completely, without obstruction, in which case you will not merely be afraid, or angry, or sorrowful. You will feel anger, sorrow, fear, and that which is causing or suggesting to you to be angry, sorrowful, fearful. And by being completely free to feel these feelings, you will not merely dramatize these feelings, although you might tend also to continue to dramatize them to some degree, but you will simply feel. The feeling of the appropriate emotion will become Feeling Itself. Eventually, it will become Feeling simply, or Feeling without obstruction.

Remarkably enough, the reason you are so disturbed about the facts of life that might make you fearful, sorrowful, and angry is that whenever something arises that you might appropriately be angry, fearful, or sorrowful about, you do not feel it completely. You limit your feeling of even these reactions. And you certainly limit your feeling of the circumstance, or the condition, that is arising. You are always exhibiting the evidence of limited feeling, obstructed feeling. If feeling becomes limitless, if you do not contract, then feeling becomes Being Itself—no reaction, no contraction, Feeling without limit. That Feeling goes beyond fear, sorrow, anger, and conventional happiness and loving attitudes.

What is It? It is Love-Bliss. It is the Self-Existing and Self-Radiant Force of Being, Who I Am, without the slightest obstruction. It is Divine Enlightenment. It Divinely Transfigures the body-mind and becomes a Power, a Great Power, and—because now you are looking at manifestation through this color, this "one flavor", this Free Force or Free Energy—It even allows you to interpret everything differently. Now you will not be saying that manifested existence is evil or suffering or sinful, or that others are unloving, that you are mortal, that you are going to die, that it is a terrible life, and so forth. Instead, you will regard all of manifested existence to be pervaded by My Love-Bliss. Not merely Bliss coming at you from every direction, but Love-Bliss, Self-Existing and Self-Radiant, Radiating from every direction in the Place where you Stand, as you, and everywhere, altogether. I have no center, no bounds, no limits. My Love-Bliss is Happiness Itself. And, when you Realize Me Most Perfectly, you Realize My Love-Bliss Itself, Happiness Itself, and you are Free to feel without limit, not obstructed in your attention.

When, by Grace of My Spiritual Heart-Transmission, your attention is without limit, it is Divine Consciousness Itself, just Consciousness. When, by Grace, energy is without limit, it is Love-Bliss Itself, or Happiness Itself. When there is no limit on energy and attention, there is only Self-Existing and Self-Radiant Divine Being, without limit—and even the whole world becomes obviously That. And you, in the form of the manifested personality, become someone who is active as the Divinely Transfiguring Power that is Inherent in the realm of conditional Nature and that Transcends it also.

* * *

Love is more than fear, sorrow, and anger. It is not less than these. Thus, the love by which My true devotees move in relationship to Me and thereby to all beings, processes, and things is not the weak, desiring, and inward feeling-conception of the usual man or woman. It is full, it is free action, it is strong. The love which is the active principle of real Spiritual life in all realms, high or low, is alive only where fear, sorrow, and anger are presently and fully encountered and transformed in the individual. Love is alive only in one who is completely in touch with his or her own fear, sorrow, and anger. One who cannot permit, encounter, and face these tendencies in the contracted body-mind cannot transform them at the heart.

* * *

When, in the Way of the Heart, self-transcending responsibility characterizes the individual, the self-defining, contracting, tensing effects of experience will become less and less profound. And, in that case, daily existence will cease to be a constant effort to overcome obstacles and purify or save the egoic self, but it will instead become ecstatic self-sacrifice through practice of the Way of the Heart in My "Bright" Company.

Such an individual is profoundly responsive and alive. And he or she transcends the frustrating and reaction-forming power of experience by intensity of participation rather than unresponsive coolness. Such a person is not weak, but strong. Such a person's freedom is shown in his or her aggressive, self-yielding resort to feeling-Contemplation of Me under all circumstances. Such a person is not passionless. Rather, that one's passion is pressed to Me.

* * *

PART III

The Humor of Loving When It Is Most Difficult

You Are Not
the Guilty Party

A CONVERSATION WITH SRI DA AVABHASA

SRI DA AVABHASA: [to a devotee who is about to leave Sri Love-Anandashram in Fiji to return to his service in the United States] You had better lay it down before you leave, Brian. When you work for the Free Daist Communion, you must do all beings some good—this is no time to be trying to relieve yourself of your karmas. You cannot get rid of those karmas unless you surrender them to Me. So do you have anything at all to tell Me?

BRIAN O'MAHONY: Sri Gurudev, underneath my efforts to serve You I am fundamentally a destructive, angry person.

SRI DA AVABHASA: Mmmm. The same old stuff. [Laughter.] A fundamentally angry and destructive person. You presume that you should feel guilty about being the asshole that you are.

"Consider" this, Brian, "consider" this: No matter what arises, in body or mind, you are always observing it. These faults, these sins, these impediments, these inadequacies, these obsessions, these darknesses—you simply Watch all of these things. You simply observe them, do you not? You observe them. You are not the guilty party. From the "Point of View" of Consciousness Itself, you are the "Watcher", the Witness of these things.

Even in this moment, do you have a thought? Ah, you see? You are watching it, are you not? Are you aware of this body? Are you aware of all these beings here?

You have only observed everything that has ever occurred, is it not true? Therefore, you are not guilty of these limitations—you are merely observing them. Even this guilt, even this sense that you are angry, disturbed, not adequate, not perfect, even that mood is something you merely observe, ultimately. Is this true or not?

BRIAN: It is true.

SRI DA AVABHASA: Thus if, by real practice in My Company, you will Realize Identification with Consciousness Itself, with the Witness-Position of Consciousness Itself, you will know that you are not in the position of being guilty. If there is any guilt, ultimately you are only observing it. Am I right or wrong? Even now, you are always in the Position of observing what arises. If you will grow beyond the beginning and the advanced stages of life in the Way of the Heart in My Company, ultimately you Realize that you are not other than That Which merely Witnesses what arises. Everything that arises is a relation of yours, then, is it not?

BRIAN: Yes.

SRI DA AVABHASA: Therefore, the practice in the ultimate stages of life in the Way of the Heart is to take up that Position in which you merely Witness what arises. It is to be Identified with Consciousness Itself.

All these impressions you receive at the level of mind from popular communication, popular society, popular religion, popular psychology, all of this guilt and sense of being "me" that you inherit socially, is part of the effort people make to somehow keep from murdering one another. It has absolutely nothing to do with the Truth. There is no reason whatsoever that you should be possessed by an image of your own existence that is somehow guilty, inadequate, limited, unimportant, angry, or however else you might characterize your sense of yourself.

If you simply inspect your experience in My Company, you will ultimately discover that you are always That Which Witnesses this arising. In fact, it is only when you identify with what is arising that you identify with the persona that feels guilty or not guilty or adequate or inadequate. Through this identification with the born personality, That Which Witnesses all of this feels Itself to be the mind, feels Itself to be the body. But you are never actually in that born position. You are always in the Position that is aware of these conditions. Thus, practice in the ultimate stages of life in the Way of the Heart is first of all to be able to acknowledge that this Witness-Position is your Position.

You are the one who is observing the process of arising conditions. You have not created a fraction of it. You have not made a hair on your head. You have not made a hair in your armpit. There is not a piece of your body that you have made. Am I right? Not a piece of it! There is not one piece of your mind, therefore, that you have made. You have made none of it. You are observing it.

Your tendency to identify with parts of the process of arising conditions and to differentiate yourself from other parts is the very process by which you get into trouble. It is by that process that you develop a negative self-image, feel a problem, feel that there is something to work out, something to release, that there is some goal, some search, that is appropriate for you. This occurs only after you relinquish your presumption of your Real Position and begin to believe that you are in a position in which, in fact, you have never been and in which you do not exist in this moment. You have never been in any position other than the one that is simply observing what is arising.

And that is the cure, you see. To notice this fact via feeling-Contemplation of Me and to accept it, to presume that Observing Position, to be established in Me as Consciousness Itself, rather than in the position of the mind, the body, and all the complications of the relations of these, is the cure.

To understand your True Position washes you. This understanding is forgiveness, penance. To understand your Real Condition most profoundly is to be forgiven. It is to bypass the whole affair of guilt and all the other results of identifying with the body-mind.

Why should this fact be so difficult to accept? You are in that position at this very moment. Ultimately, it is completely obvious to you that no matter what arises, you are simply observing it, watching it. Am I right or wrong? Right now, as you are listening to My voice, in your intuition of the ultimate stages of practice in the Way of the Heart, you can appreciate that you are observing this event, can you not? You can appreciate My Argument that, ultimately, you are observing this body, these sensations, these thoughts that are arising.

Therefore, what you refer to as your "self" is ultimately just that which is observing this, is it not? Has it ever been any different? Throughout your life you have been indulging in beliefs that you are the body, that you are the mind, that you are this limit, that you are that limit, that you are in this circumstance, that you are in that circumstance. But look at the power of that which is observed and see if it can determine the attitude, the mood, the presumption of that which observes it.

There is a great Liberation in simply and directly noticing your actual Condition. There is more to Most Perfect God-Realization than that noticing, but that noticing is the beginning of practice in the ultimate stages of life in the Way of the Heart. When you mature to that degree in My Company, you begin to really accept your actual Condition, Which is That of the Observer of all of this arising. But, in order to truly Stand in that Position, you must go through a profound ordeal of preparation and purification. You must observe your tendencies, understand all of your complications, and relieve yourself of the motions of attention, relieve yourself of the various forms of identification with the process of arising conditions, relieve yourself of all the efforts of conditional energy through your feeling-Contemplation of My bodily (human) Form and, in due course, My Spiritual (and Always Blessing) Presence.

To participate in that process via feeling-Contemplation of My bodily (human) Form is the beginner's practice. As you mature into the more advanced stages of life in My Company, you participate in that process through feeling-Contemplation of My bodily (human) Form and My Spiritual (and Always Blessing) Presence. From the initial moment of listening to Me, through the first stage of the "Perfect Practice", which is the stage at which feeling-Contemplation of My Very (and Inherently Perfect) State becomes your capability and your responsibility, your practice is simply a matter of relieving this Witness of the motions of attention.

The forms of identification, differentiation, and desire, the things that one does in reaction to what is Witnessed, are all motions of attention. The beginning of Wisdom, then, is to observe yourself as you are. Forget philosophy, religion, and all the garbage of life. What precisely is your situation in this moment? Even now, you are That Which is Witnessing these arising conditions, whatever That Which is Witnessing this is altogether. Ultimately, you Realize that you are just That, and there is no doubt about it.

There is no way to deny this Truth, is there? It cannot be denied, except by the ego. Only the ego denies That Which is totally, absolutely obvious. Practice in the ultimate stages of life in the Way of the Heart is the practice of immersing yourself in That Which is the Witness and then discovering Its Status, Its Condition.

Before you can submit yourself to that Witness Perfectly, you must relieve yourself of all of the habits that you have developed in relation to what you observe—all your tendencies to identify with the body, with the mind, with reactive emotions, with a history, with a past, with a present, with relations. The beginner's practice that I have Given to you in the Way of the Heart is a way of relieving you of this burden, of releasing energy and attention from the habit of identifying with certain aspects of what arises and differentiating yourself from other aspects of what arises. You want to be, or think you are, some things, you desire some other things, and you absolutely do not want to be or to associate with some other things. That complex of identification, differentiation, and desire creates the complicated existence of egoity that I call karma. Such karma is simply what results when this Witness becomes implicated in what It observes and thus forgets Its own Position.

Great Wisdom in the ultimate stages of life in the Way of the Heart begins when you simply and very directly notice and Realize that you are always in this Position of simply Witnessing what arises. On that basis you take up the profound discipline of the first stage of the "Perfect Practice". What you call "I" is just the body-mind. "I" is not the Witness. "I" is not even independent. "I" should be submitted to the Divine, to the Condition of non-separateness, and stop differentiating itself, sizing itself up, being just "this" and not "that" and playing off all its objects and relations.

The first task of practice of the Way of the Heart in My Company is to uncomplicate the "I", to understand the "I", to release the "I", to submit the "I" to Me, the Very Divine Being in which it arises. But this is just the beginning of your practice of the Way of the Heart. It only prepares you to receive My Spirit-Baptism and to practice in the Spiritually activated stages of life in the Way of the Heart. And that reception of My Spiritual Heart-Transmission purifies you further, so that energy and attention are freed and you can begin to practice in the ultimate stages of life in the Way of the Heart.

When you are thus prepared, you take up the "Perfect Practice" wherein you immerse yourself in Me and submit yourself to the Condition in Which you always Stand, Which is the Condition of simply Witnessing what arises.

Thus, you say, for example, that underneath your interest in service there is this angry character. But that angry character is just something that is observed. It is not even unique. There is no reason to feel guilty about it. It is simply something to understand and, ultimately, to merely Witness. Why should you identify with it? All it is, is a system of tendencies. You did not make it to begin with anyway, so why should you feel guilty about it? You did not make the universe, you did not make your body, you did not make your intimate partner, you did not make anybody, you did not make anything whatsoever.

What business do you have being guilty? All that you are, or all with which you seem to identify, is just a pattern in conditional Nature. It is My business. Let it be My business. Resort to Me and, by that devotional resort, ultimately your responsibility becomes a matter of Being As you Are, As you always have Been, As you Are from the beginning, As you Are in Truth.

Ultimately, you are just That Which Witnesses this arising. Even now, you do not have to be concerned about the existence of it, the fact of its arising. Your responsibility is simply to understand yourself and submit to the discipline of being My devotee. I Am the Inherent Being in Whom these complications are released. To live that discipline of devotion to Me is your business, not to be guilty about what arises, not to be self-conscious about it, not to say, "I am this terrible person, look at poor me, forgive me, change me," and so forth. You do not have to do anything of the kind.

Your position is like that of a snail at the bottom of the ocean, which sticks its slimy body out onto the sandy bottom and looks back and sees this fantastic, spotted cowry shape. That shape is the body-mind, the egoic personality. It is angry, it is sexy, it is fat, it is skinny, it has innumerable qualities. You are only looking at and describing what you see. You do not have to identify with it. Just like the snail, you never made that body-mind to begin with. It happened spontaneously, innocently, by virtue of laws that appear in cosmic Nature. There is no reason to feel guilty about it whatsoever, and, therefore, there is no need for a savior to relieve you of this guilt.

You have never been in a position that requires a savior, a God who will relieve you of guilt. You already Stand in the Transcendental

Place, the Free Place, the Divine Place. What you need to do is be submitted to Me.

The first stage of that submission is to understand this body-mind most fundamentally, submit it to a real discipline in My Company. That most fundamental self-understanding allows you, to a much greater degree than you now enjoy, to be free in relationship to experience, to realize that you are already Happy, to accept My Grace, to feel My Spiritual Heart-Transmission and be Happy in Me, not striving to become Happy. Give up your need for forgiveness. Give up your guilt. Give up your self-identity, your ideas of yourself acquired from your past, your experience. Give it all up. Bring it to Me in one flower, one leaf, one cup of water. Do it in one act and give it up to Me completely, and be most fundamentally free of it, forever. That is what it means to hear My Argument.

Such hearing, or most fundamental self-understanding, is forgiveness, because it totally relieves you of your need for forgiveness. Understanding does not smack you on the head as if you were a poor, independent being and say, "You are forgiven." Understanding undercuts the whole affair of guilt, that search. Ultimately, you are Awakened to the Realization that you have never been in a position in which you needed to be forgiven.

Now, occasionally you do need to be forgiven in some ordinary, conventional social sense. If you do some rotten thing to somebody, then you must set things right with them and say, "I am sorry I did that." And they say, "Okay, good." That is ordinary, human forgiveness. But you do not need Ultimate forgiveness. What you need from the Ultimate Being is that understanding that relieves you of this obnoxious burden of identification with cosmic limitation. What you need is My Divinely Enlightened Argument, which draws you into the "consideration" wherein you ultimately Realize that you are already Free and that everything with which you have ever been associated is a pattern with which you have been involved naively, a pattern that you have not even created and that is not a real burden. It is just stuff. All you need to do is submit yourself to Me and this whole matter of your situation will begin to clarity itself.

The first thing you must do is not to find forgiveness, but to understand yourself most fundamentally and stand free of the self-contraction to that degree. In order to continue to grow beyond that stage of your practice, you must, based on most fundamental self-understanding, see Me and live in continuous Communion with Me, with That Which is Inherently Perfect, with That Which is Absolute, with That Which is Grace.

That Inherently Perfect State, that Absolute Grace, is the Force that I bring to you. I do not bring conventional forgiveness, because I do not regard you as a being who needs to be forgiven in any ultimate sense. What you imagine you need to be forgiven for has no ultimate significance. What you need to become involved with is not petty fear and wondering and un-Happiness relative to your apparent patterns. What you need to become involved with is My Very (and Inherently Perfect) State. That is what I bring to you. That is the significance of your relationship to Me, and it comes to you gratis, directly. You do not have to be forgiven to live in My Divine Company, to Commune with Me.

I do not put any obstacles between us. I do not make you be a lesser being, a karmic personality, or a demonic, sinful character who must be forgiven in order to enjoy Communion with Me. I call you to understand yourself and, on the basis of that understanding, to live in your natural Continuousness with Me. Do you understand what I am talking about?

Submit yourself to Communion with Me and give up all this petty nonsense of your inner character and your hidden faults. Everybody in conditional Nature is full of faults. What is perfect, anyway? Have you seen something perfect in conditional Nature today? Where does it sit, where it is floating, where is it swimming? There is nothing perfect in conditional Nature. When some being, some appearance in conditional Nature, achieves Identification with the Inherently Spiritual and Transcendental Divine Being, then a kind of Perfection is displayed, but it is the Inherent Perfection of That Which Transcends Nature. You find that Inherent Perfection in My Company. That is good. That is why I am here.

I am not fooling you. My Inherent Perfection is a unique and monumental occasion, and It relieves you of your sorrow, your foolishness, your un-Happiness—relieves you of it instantly, generates an understanding in you that relieves you entirely of your life of seeking and ultimately installs you in the Position of the Witness of all that arises.

All the disciplines of the Way of the Heart, which are part of your daily practice, are simply part of this whole affair of releasing

THE INCARNATION OF LOVE

energy and attention from what you are ultimately only observing and restoring you to balance, to equanimity, releasing self-imagery and inner life, so that you may mature to the point of Realizing That Which you already Are. Then the ultimate discipline to which I Call you can be fruitful.

That discipline is so direct, so simple, that it could be Realized in this very moment, if your energy and attention were free. In fact, you already Stand There. You are already simply observing what is arising. It is already true that that which observes what is arising now is not identical to what is arising. It is just observing what arises. It is just Consciousness Itself, Being Itself, Eternally Full. Through hearing My Argument and receiving My Spiritual Baptism, you can Realize that you are in that Position.

Accept the reasonable discipline that will release your energy and attention from the complications of all that is arising. That practice includes everything that prepares you to practice the "Perfect Practice".

You must embrace the discipline of your current stage of practice in the Way of the Heart and have it fulfill its purpose in a finite period of time. When you have fulfilled this preparatory course of practice, when you have heard Me and seen Me, you will, by Grace, Stand as the Witness of all that arises, in the first stage of the "Perfect Practice". Then, by your continued real and right resort to Me, you will be immersed in That Which is the Source of the Witness, in Consciousness Itself, or the Feeling of Being, in the second stage of the "Perfect Practice".

Therefore, you must allow your practice to be fruitful, real, and direct.

Do you have the slightest idea of what I am talking about, Brian?

BRIAN: Absolutely.

SRI DA AVABHASA: When you take up the "Perfect Practice" in My Company, you begin to acknowledge Me as That Which Is, Where you Stand, That Which is in the Existence Place, That Which is the Force, the Power, the Depth, of the Position in Which you Witness everything. You begin to acknowledge My Grace in a totally different sense, no longer as something outside you. My Grace is not you in this independent sense, but It is you as this Witness, as Consciousness Itself.

When and if, by Grace and in due course, you take up the "Perfect Practice" in My Company, you will submit to Me in the Place Where you Stand. I Am That Well, the Depth of It, the Fullness of It, the Absoluteness of It. Thus, you Find Me as the Divine Self and you begin to practice entering into the Feeling of Being in the second stage of the "Perfect Practice".

In the second stage of the "Perfect Practice", when you can enter Perfectly into the Feeling of Being, there is Great Wisdom, Absolute Sublimity—and My Absolute Gift is Given. When conditions reappear to that Sublimity, this is the State that I call "Open Eyes". Conditions reappear, but they have no power to qualify that Happiness, that Divine Sublimity. All conditions are utterly and instantly, tacitly, Divinely Recognizable as just a play upon That.

This is the "Natural" State of Divine Self-Realization, seventh stage Sahaj Samadhi. It is the Realization that one is that Divine Self-Condition, Being Itself, without qualification, Consciousness without limit, Love-Bliss, Original, Uncaused, Simple Being Itself. All of this arising is obviously That and has no power over It.

It is to this Realization of the by Me Revealed and Given seventh stage of life in the Way of the Heart that I Call you, not to the life of sinners, forgiven or unforgiven. All of this complex, psychiatric garbage that you have inside and outside yourself, all of your seeking, all of your failure to understand, all of your complicated thinking have nothing to do with the Way of the Heart. I Call you presently, always, to receive My Gift of this Freedom.

Accept My Revelation through understanding, through Communion with Me. Accept the discipline that I Offer to you. Simply do that discipline until you are prepared. Go through this process of learning, of self-observation. Be submitted to Me. Do not be a fool. Do not be a worldly person. Be a renunciate. Hear Me and see Me. Be completely submitted to Me. Free energy and attention to fulfill My Admonition to enter into the Feeling of Being, to be submitted to Me as the Condition in Which you Stand. You will submit to Me more and more fully, more and more Perfectly, without agitation, without distraction, and then My Great Mystery will suddenly be Obvious, by Grace.

DEVOTEES: We are so grateful for this Truth. We are so grateful for the Way of the Heart in Your Company. We are so grateful to You, Lord.

CHAPTER 15

Assume Relationship

SRI DA AVABHASA: As My devotee, your function is not to analyze and convince others but to be communicative with others and to assume relationship as the principle of all your communications. Do not react to the present attempts by you and others to withdraw from one another. Do not try to argue another out of withdrawing from you or dramatizing un-love in relationship to you. As soon as you stop assuming that relationship, you have lost your humor and you must try to deal with your intimate from the point of view of the drama of humorlessness. If you assume your relationship with the other person as the principle on which you communicate and live with one another, there is no possibility of losing your humor.

*   *   *

If you assume relationship with someone, then anything you talk about with that person has the quality of humor. You can laugh about it, you can be free with it, you can play games with it.

*   *   *

You can fail to assume relationship only if you <u>decide</u> to be unconscious. Then you have nothing but ways to assume that the relationship does not exist. But there is only relationship. Even in purely human terms, there is only relationship. Everything relates to everything else. Everything is interdependent. There is one great process, and all beings are involved in it, so there are only relationships.

Now, there are special kinds of relationships. One has a different relationship to one's grocer than to one's intimate partner. There are agreements, contracts, special forms of relationships. But even though you may not be a close intimate of another person, the relationship with that person exists. Whenever you communicate with any person, relationship is the condition that already exists, and relationship is the source of humor and intelligence. On that basis communications occur.

Ordinarily, people do not communicate while making the assumption of relationship. They communicate while making the assumption of alienation, separation. Therefore, they approach one another in fear and mystery, in doubt, as if they did not have anything to do with one another, as if they had to prove something to one another. They do not assume that the relationship already exists, and so allow the force of relationship, which is life and love, to undo limitations.

Such people are always trying to create relationship from a point of view of disadvantage, of alienation, of separation. But you cannot <u>create</u> relationship. You cannot discover relationship as the end phenomenon of a long series of talks. Relationship is not established as a result of something that somebody does. An act by someone else may remind you of relationship, but it does not create it. Relationship fundamentally already and always exists. It always has existed, and it is your Condition in Truth, Realizable in Satsang with Me.

* * *

Relationship is always already the case. If you are sitting in the house, weeping, screaming, feeling upset and negative about somebody you live with, then this is your suffering. This activity is your suffering. Remember that person. Remember the relationship. Live the relationship. Let the force of life move again, and there is no suffering at all. You've obviated that whole "tour", including the making up and everything else.

The Method of the Siddhas

* * *

CHAPTER 16

Do Not Blame

SRI DA AVABHASA: As long as you do not get the Lesson of life, as long as you think that life is about becoming Happy, you can blame anybody and everybody. But when you understand the Lesson of life, you understand that your Realization of Happiness is a matter of what you do. It is your responsibility only. There is nobody to blame. In fact, there is everyone to praise, no matter what anyone does. All others are serving your Happiness because they serve your responsibility. No matter what occurs or what anyone does, you have the choice to transcend your own contraction—or not.

*   *   *

"Consider" this: Every time you dramatize reactivity, you are thinking you are the victim of someone or something or some event—every time. Reactivity is the sure sign that you have this point of view. If you react and dramatize reactivity, you are always blaming the event, blaming the other, instead of introducing the self-responsible discipline into the occasion of difficulty or stress. Always. It is always so.

Of course, there are all kinds of events in life, and there are reactions to them. Therefore, perhaps you cannot altogether stop reacting to the events of life. But to dramatize the reaction, to extend it into a whole period of drama, irresponsibility, egoic "self-possession", weakness, non-practice, is to act like the victim. It is to blame the event, as if the event or the other is the reason that you are weak, the reason that you are not responsible, the reason that you cannot deal with yourself, the reason you get crazy. It is your own reactivity, and you must become responsible for it. Every time you dramatize reactivity you are blaming something or someone and not being responsible for yourself.

Before your reaction becomes dramatization, you must deal with the reaction itself. And to truly deal with the reaction itself, you must come to the point of most fundamental self-understanding, before the reactivity, before the action that precedes all reactivity, all desiring, all seeking. You must become responsible for that action in every instant—moment by moment. Especially from that point of view, then, you can retard the dramatization of reactivity.

* * *

Westerners—and Westernized people everywhere—are always looking for somebody or something to blame. There is nobody and nothing to blame. Even the latest psychiatric wisdom is all about blaming something or other—you know, your parents, your past traumas. There is always something to blame, always somebody to abuse, as if somebody or some experience is the reason that you are so messed up. You are the only reason.

Whatever you may have experienced in your life, it is your reaction to it that is binding you, and you must deal with your reactivity. There is nobody whatsoever to blame. In order to stop blaming everyone and everything and the universe itself and whatever you think God is, you ought to get down to dealing with yourself.

* * *

All martyrs feel very self-important. To view yourself as a victim is to be very self-important. It is strong egoity, manifested in a particular fashion. A strong egoic tendency is also what you got out of your childhood, a great sense of self-importance and difference, even superiority.

Everybody has difficulties. Life is difficult, and it requires something of you. Another way of characterizing the so-to-speak "victim" consciousness is that it is always looking for something or someone to blame even for the most petty of life's difficulties and demands. If you feel you are the victim, you always look for somebody or something to blame, some past incident, whatever it may be, to justify your lack of responsibility, your lack of clarity, your lack of effectiveness.

It is not just in reaction to the most traumatic of life's incidents that this mechanism is generated. It is an ordinary mechanism, and it is also culturally enforced, and socially reinforced, politically reinforced, reinforced by social and political institutions even. It is not associated with traumatic life, really. It is just the strategy of living life in such a fashion that you are always relieved of responsibility, because there is always something or someone to blame and you, therefore, need not be responsible. You just presume that the seat of responsibility is not in yourself but in all the causes in your life. And they are just what they are, so there is nothing you can do about it.

You are always running through the time-streak of memory to find where you were victimized, to find what there is to blame, what incident you can blame for your trouble, what people—mommy, daddy, whoever else—what incidents, what experiences, what diseases. You are always going down the time track to find what to blame and then dramatizing being victimized there and receiving sympathy from everybody else about your bad experience.

Responsibility is in the person, the "own" state, the ego place. That is where responsibility must arise. You must understand that it does not make a bit of difference who has done what to you, or what experience you had in the past recently, long ago, before this lifetime, in this lifetime—it does not make any difference. You may discover how in the past you established patterns that are effective now, but there is no true healing in such discovery unless you get down to the "consideration" of your responsibility for your own reaction, ultimately for your own self-contraction.

In the "own" position, the egoic self-position, you must realize responsibility for your own reactivity, your own dissociation, your own separativeness, your own generation of a victim ritual. There will be difficult events in the future just as there have been difficult events in the past. How are they to be dealt with? By responsibility for your own reactivity, your own egoic "self-possession", your own self-enclosure, your own dissociation, your own separativeness.

This is the key to healing people of their various disorders and life-problems—the development of responsibility, not the constant finding of things to blame and, in effect, practicing shamanistic rituals to just relax your mind so that now you feel cured. No—responsibility is the key, responsibility for the ego-act, the self-contraction itself, and all the reactivity, dramatization, seeking, desiring, pursuit of objects and others and so forth that arise by your own act.

Realize that responsibility, and love, forgiveness, flows from you toward all events, all past, all future, all present, and you can live freely and transcend life-difficulties. That is religious life manifested in action.

Of course, the religious life most fundamentally is about self-transcendence to the point of Most Perfect self-transcendence and Realization of the Divine Self-Condition. But as a manifestation in life, it shows itself through responsibility for the self-contraction, not through rehearsing the victim rituals.

* * *

There is absolutely no one to blame. Blame is the game of evading responsibility. All your indulgence in reactivity, as if you have reasons not to grow! You have none.

* * *

Do not blame anybody ever again. Embrace the discipline of blamelessness. Never blame anything or anyone ever again. You have no right to blame anybody. It is all your personal business. Therefore, as My devotees, embrace one another personally, cooperatively, as such responsible people.

* * *

In your fitful association with others, objects, relations, experiences, you become less and less aware of your fundamental Happiness, the Self-Existing and Self-Radiant Love-Bliss of Divine Being. And becoming thus dis-eased, analyzing your "problem", and diagnosing it, you tend to do the opposite, which is to separate yourself from relations. You start blaming the world or blaming the body-mind, blaming others, blaming birth. And then you try to get rid of all that, as if when you finally and exhaustively cut everything away, you will suddenly find out that you are Happy.

* * *

You alone, you entirely, you as a manifested personality, are the only structure that limits feeling. Nothing else does. Nothing else has the power to do it. When everything suggests that you are not responsible for the limitation on feeling, it is because you have already relinquished your responsibility. You project your un-Happy state on everything, and you feel that everything that arises is just cause for the limitation that you place on feeling. In that disposition you are blaming everyone, you are blaming the universe, you are blaming God for your un-Happiness. Therefore, you look to every-one, to the universe, and to God to relieve you of your un-Happiness, whereas you and only you are the cause of it, and therefore you and only you through your devotional surrender to Me can do anything about it.

*   *   *

Be free of betrayal, or the presumption that you are not loved and that you are weak, separate, starving, and never full or inher-ently blissful. Be free of your infantile philosophy. Bring an end to the perpetual adolescence of seeking in dilemma for the absent bliss. By existing as love in love with Me, be free of the search for love.

*   *   *

You are not certain of being loved and, thus, you do not love. But to love is the Law. You must love, regardless of the circumstance. The essential principle of Spiritual life is unobstructed feeling-Contemplation of Me, enforced via all functions, in all relations, under all conditions. The principle of Satsang with Me is to be real-ized as love in all the complicated mechanics of your relationships and at every developmental stage of your practice in the Way of the Heart.

*   *   *

CHAPTER 17

Be Wounded, Not Insulted

SRI DA AVABHASA: For those who Are Committed To Love (and who Always Commune With The One Who Is Love), Even Rejection By others Is Received and Accepted As A Wound, Not An Insult. Even The Heart-Necessity To Love and To Be Loved Is A Wound. Even The Fullest Realization Of Love Is A Wound That Never Heals.

The Dawn Horse Testament

*   *   *

The egoic Ritual Calls every individual To Defend himself or herself Against The Wounds Of Love and The Wounding Signs Of Un-Love (or egoic self-Contraction) In the daily world. Therefore, Even In The Context Of True Intimacy, The Tendency (Apart From Spiritual Responsibility) Is To Act As If Every Wound (Which Is Simply A Hurt) Is An Insult (or A Reason To Punish).

The Reactive Rituals Of egoity Must Be Released By The self-Transcending (and Then Spiritual) Practice Of Love. This Requires Each and Every Practitioner Of The Way Of The Heart To Observe, Understand, and Relinquish The emotionally Reactive Cycle Of Rejection and Punishment. And The Necessary Prerequisites For Such Relinquishment Are Vulnerability (or The Ability To Feel The Wounds Of Love Without Retaliation), Sensitivity To the other In Love (or The Ability To Sympathetically Observe, Understand, Forgive, Love, and Not Punish or Dissociate From the other In Love), and Love Itself (or The Ability To Love, To Know You Are Loved, To Receive Love, and To Know That Both You and the other, Regardless Of Any Appearance To The Contrary, Are Vulnerable To Love and Heart-Requiring Of Love).

It Is Not Necessary (or Even Possible) To Become Immune To The Feeling Of Being Rejected. To Become Thus Immune, You Would Have To Become Immune To Love Itself. What Is Necessary (and Also Possible) Is To Enter Fully Into The Spiritual Life-Sphere Of Love. In The Way Of The Heart, This Is Done By First Entering (By Heart) Into My Company (and, Thus and Thereby, Into The Company Of The Divine Person), and (Therein) To Submit To The Divine Embrace Of Love, Wherein Not Only Are You Loved, but You Are Love Itself. Then You Must Magnify That Love-Radiance In the world of human relationships.

If You Will Do This, Then You Must Do The Sadhana (or Concentrated Practice) Of Love. As A Practical Matter, You Must Stop Dramatizing The egoic Ritual Of Betrayal In Reaction To The Feeling Of Being Rejected. You Must Understand, Transcend, and Release The Tendency To Respond (or React) To Signs Of Rejection (or Signs That You Are Not Loved) As If You Are Insulted, Rather Than Wounded. That Is To Say, You Must Stop Punishing and Rejecting others When You Feel Rejected. If You Punish another When You Feel This, You Will Act As If You Are Immune To Love's Wound. Thus, You Will Pretend To Be Angrily Insulted, Rather Than Suffer To Be Wounded. In The Process, You Will Withdraw and Withhold Love. You Will Stand Off, Independent and Dissociated. You Will Only Reinforce The Feeling Of Being Rejected, and You Will Compound It By Actually Rejecting the other. In This Manner, You Will Become Un-Love. You Will Fail To Love. You Will Fail To Live In The Sphere Of Love. Your Own Acts Of Un-Love Will Degrade You, Delude You, and Separate You From Your Love-partner (or Your partners In Love) and From Love Itself. Therefore, those who Fail To Practice The Sadhana Of Love In their intimate emotional-sexual relationships, and In human relationships Generally, Will, By That Failure, Turn Away (or Contract) From God (or The Great Condition That Is Reality Itself).

The Dawn Horse Testament

* * *

Love Does Not Fail For You When You Are Rejected or Betrayed or Apparently Not Loved. Love Fails For You When You Reject, Betray, and Do Not Love. Therefore, If You Listen To Me, and Also If You Hear Me, and Also If You See Me, Do Not Stand Off From Relationship. Be Vulnerable. Be Wounded When Necessary, and Endure That Wound or Hurt. Do Not Punish the other In Love. Communicate To one another, Even Discipline one another, but Do Not Dissociate From one another or Fail To Grant one another The Knowledge Of Love. Realize That each one Wants To Love and To Be Loved By the other In Love. Therefore, Love. Do This Rather Than Make Any Effort To Get Rid Of The Feeling Of Being Rejected. To Feel Rejected Is To Feel The Hurt Of Not Being Loved. Allow That Hurt, but Do Not Let It Become The Feeling Of Lovelessness. Be Vulnerable and Thus Not Insulted. If You Are Merely Hurt, You Will Still Know The Necessity (or The Heart's Requirement) Of Love, and You Will Still Know The Necessity (or The Heart's Requirement) To Love.

The Dawn Horse Testament

*   *   *

CHAPTER 18

Serve the Person
Who Makes You Angry

SRI DA AVABHASA: You may have particularly strong resistance to certain people in whose company you feel anger, righteousness, or other strong and negative feelings. Serve those you have conflict with, rather than engaging in gossip, complaint, and righteousness in their company, all of which are forms of withdrawal or contraction-reaction. Really serve. That is, direct your attention and energy to their good and well-being.

When you have conflict with someone, it will not help you to try to identify and analyze the reasons for your difficulties. There are no reasons. There are only justifications for withdrawing your life-energy. And it is not simply a matter of not loving the person. Observe yourself in that relationship, and you will see that you are actively manufacturing non-love toward the other person.

Your appropriate activity, then, is not to try to create love for the person. You will only create self-consciousness and not love. You need not love the person at all. Simply direct your energy to that person, serve that person, sacrifice your refusal to share life-energy with that person. The more you understand under the conditions of such service, the more such service will itself be revealed to be love.

*   *   *

There is no true Awakening without a change of heart, a literal purification, a redress of wrongs, and a change of habits.

*   *   *

You will notice that in the face of any difficulty you resort to a sequence of devices and strategies. You must discover the root of all of that and see what you simply need to do. Understand that there is no resolution until there is the release of the self-contraction.

In the face of the difficulty, you might try various psychological devices, various ways of thinking about it and knowing about it to make you feel better—including, perhaps, wishing you could punch somebody in the teeth. But you will realize eventually that the only way you will feel full and Happy under such circumstances is to no longer contract from the difficulty.

This is why I have told you, for example, that you should never become involved in a destructive intention when dealing with people who oppose what you are doing. Obviously you must deal with the situation, but your dealing with the situation should not be unlike your blessing of others. In other words, it is not by contracting from difficulty and doing evil deeds but by transcending the self-contraction that you become effective in adversity.

All the negative feelings that arise because of self-contraction must be transcended. You will notice that the reason you feel bad about a difficult situation is that you are contracting from it. When you stop contracting from it, you will feel Happy in Divine Communion. Nevertheless, the situation will still exist to be dealt with effectively.

*　*　*

You Must Not Withdraw From Grace-Given Divine Communion (or Become Degraded By Un-Love) Even When Circumstances Within Your Intimate Sphere, or Within The Sphere Of Your Appropriate social Responsibility, Require You To Make Difficult Gestures To Counter and Control The Effects or Undermine and Discipline The Negative and Destructive Effectiveness Of The Rituals Of Un-Love That Are Performed By others.

The Dawn Horse Testament

*　*　*

CHAPTER 19

Forgive

SRI DA AVABHASA: To be human is to love, to forgive, to concretely handle all business, to purify, to set oneself and all others free, to generate a circumstance for continued existence that is not time-bound so that you have time to invest yourself in timeless activities—meditative feeling-Contemplation of Me, Ishta-Guru-Bhakti Yoga in the Way of the Heart.

* * *

Never submit to hatred. This discipline is difficult, yes, it is always difficult. But it is your obligation. See what a wound life is. I Call you to forgiveness, love, acceptance of limitations. This is what love requires. This is what love does.

* * *

Every individual is only seeking not to be destroyed.

The Liberator (Eleutherios)

* * *

There are two forms of forgiveness, or two options, that you may choose in relation to anyone.

The greater option is to grant forgiveness in the form of great energy, love, regard, help, friendship, and upliftment. That is one option, and in certain relations and in certain moments it is an option you call upon yourself to exercise.

The other option, which is really the fundamental motive or force of forgiveness, is to ignore the offense, to forget about it, to not give attention to it. Perhaps the fundamental definition of forgiveness is to just forget or ignore the offense. Such forgetting has the force of forgiveness because it gives no negative energy.

You may be troubling yourself because you cannot forgive those who have negative feelings about you, in that you cannot love them and cannot just be happy about them. Perhaps in some moments every now and then you achieve such love, but you are struggling as if forgiveness and right relationship to these individuals means you must magnify radiant love toward them. You need not feel guilty because you cannot do that. If you can do it, fine—to do so is healing and the ultimate form of forgiveness. However, the form of forgiveness for which you are also responsible is forgetting, or ignoring, or non-attention.

Therefore, give no attention to those who want to harm you. Do not give them any attention, and you will therefore not give them any negative energy, you will not curse them. Forget about them. Put your attention somewhere else.

Just so with your own difficulties or the difficulties of others with whom you are intimate—if you cannot give radiant, loving, blessing energy, that is all right. It is simply not your moment for such energy. You can ignore them, however. You can forget about the offense, you can refrain from talking about it, you can be reticent, you can be silent, you can occupy yourself with your practice. You can do all those things, can you not? Then forget. That is forgiveness.

Forgiveness is to forget, to not make curses, to not hold others to account. You can always do that. Therefore, always do it. Then, in unique moments, grant great energy and attention, full of blessing and support and helpfulness. Do not feel guilty if you cannot. Do it when you are given the Grace to do it. But in all your moments forgive by ignoring and forgetting. Have nothing to do with the offense, and go about your own business.

To do this is not a curse, you see. In fact, it is the denial of curses. Therefore, at least forget. That you can do by meditating and by occupying yourself with service.

Do this practice in general and in relation to the most difficult moments of life. Do it with one another. Do not spend time in talking about your "case" or anyone else's. You need not agitate yourself constantly with the difficulties of others. You have your own difficulties, anyway! You know the moments that are your charismatic moments of blessing and help and touching and laying on of hands. Those moments occur only at certain times, however. Most of the time the difficulties of others are their own business. Fail to curse them by forgetting them. Occupy yourself with Divine Communion and your own real practice. Do not pass on bad thoughts, which are effective curses. Just forget about it. That is forgiveness. To forget is to forget to curse. To ignore is forgiveness. It is the principal form of forgiveness, and you <u>can</u> be responsible for it.

You need not feel guilt because you cannot bless and love and radiate to everyone who lives or who curses you. Ignore their curses, ignore their faults, ignore their person, and occupy yourself with feeling-Contemplation of Me. Curse no one. Love them or forget them. Do not curse. You need not feel guilt, because you can <u>always</u> forget to curse. Simply put your attention somewhere else, and do not imagine that you are guilty because you have not magnified great blessing. Such blessing is virtue, but it is a special Grace for special moments. Do not curse.

All you need do to not curse is to forget about it and put your attention somewhere else: Contemplate Me. Go to the Communion Hall. Serve. Study. Overcome the thought. You can do that. You already know that you can do that, but do it rigorously, constantly, and be sensitive to those moments in which you can magnify great energy, great enthusiasm, great feeling. When the capability for giving special attention to someone arises, give it. Do not fail to do so. You will not be able to help yourself in any case, so magnify your feelings in those moments. To do that is not forgiveness—it is blessing. Forgiveness is to forget about it and to go about your business.

*   *   *

Particularly as Westerners, you are habituated to a kind of conventional ritual of forgiveness, a kind of institutionalized forgiveness, not only as it may appear in certain religious societies, but in the context of ordinary living, where you play a similar forgiveness game—the only real effort you have to generate is to get up the nerve, the courage, the energy, to ask for forgiveness. And, having done that, then, forgiveness is supposed to be automatic so that you will be able to presume it. There may be somebody there, functioning as a priest or whatever, who says, "Now that you have asked for forgiveness, you are totally forgiven." And then you need not be concerned about it anymore. Or, perhaps, five or ten minutes of a religious ritual is sufficient for forgiveness.

But that is not how it works in general and for real. Of course, sometimes forgiveness is believed, accepted, and becomes effective suddenly, easily. But basically forgiveness is a process. It is an aspect of sadhana. You must know in yourself what you will have to do before you will even accept forgiveness from someone, from anyone at all, from Me.

Forgiveness requires not merely that you exhibit the courage or the good manners to ask for it, but that you discipline yourself, endure the tapas of purification, and repair the wrong and the one or ones you have wronged. It is not that you can merely do some physical thing or other and feel forgiven now because you have given somebody something and he or she should be satisfied. You cannot get away with that, either. You must endure the process of purification and reparation, or restoration. You will not even really accept forgiveness if you do not do this. Not really. Not deeply. Not in a fashion that changes your life and your disposition. To do wrong is to live wrong. To undo wrong, to be forgiven, you must change your way of life.

In principle, forgiveness is constant. My Forgiveness is already Given. But if it is to be effective, if you are to receive it, if the process is to be complete, you must do the sadhana. You must integrate yourself with forgiveness. You must commit your life, your body-mind, to the process. And that is where the fault is—in the body-mind.

Sometimes, in some kinds of moments, forgiveness can be received quite suddenly. Such forgiveness is a Grace of a sudden kind. Relative to all else, relative to that life for which you need to be forgiven, you must do the sadhana.

Your history of betrayal, of abuse, of exploitation of Me or of others is not going to be vanished because you say you are sorry, or ask for forgiveness. You cannot presume that you are forgiven at the other end without reparation.

Such asking for forgiveness is just a formality. It is not real. There is no change of life, no reparation, no restoration, no right relationship to Me or to others you may have wronged, no real dependence for the forgiveness of the one you have wronged. It is just something you feel you can presume on your own. You think you do not have to change anything. You think you can do anything whatsoever, simply say you are sorry, and that means it is all

119

right not to deal with it anymore.

Such is the popular ritual of forgiveness. It is not real, whether done in the religious manner or in an ordinary social manner. That is not how forgiveness really works.

Something like this also appears in the context of intimate relationship where, apart from the casual "I love you" statements people may make, they rarely say "I love you" to one another with any kind of seriousness. People even feel in themselves reluctance to say it to someone with whom they would be intimate. Very often intimates chide one another about this, "Why don't you say the words?" You probably have said it yourself in some ridiculous moment or other.

Of course, there are perhaps some superficial aspects of intimate relationships that may prevent this kind of communication, either through words or through some sort of feeling, but a level of it is also very much the same as this matter of forgiveness. People think they can say "I love you" to someone, and it covers everything, and it is totally believable, totally real. Whereas you must <u>live</u> love. It is not romantic.

Part of the reluctance to say "I love you", aside from the negative reasons for not saying so, has to do with the fact that love is much more profound than this kind of saying. To say it reduces it to something banal, to reduce it to romance, to reduce it to some superficial communication.

Well, then—know something about forgiveness. Forgiveness is like love. It <u>is</u> love. To expect it to come about and be real simply because you say some words, or make almost any kind of gesture in the moment, is to ritualize it. You must live out the process wherein things are purified. You must live out the process wherein love is really experienced, believed, accepted, lived in relationship. You must do this in intimacies and friendships. Above all you must do this with Me.

And what have you done in your relationship to Me, that qualifies it as real love? You have been willing to go to your ritual occasions and say it in one way or another. You tell one another that you love Me and that you are My devotee. Yet look at what you do, at what you have done. Look at your reluctance. Such refusal is not purified by a statement, by a letter, by a report, by an apology.

An "I love you" does not do it. An "I love you", or a "forgive me", can be felt as a kind of mockery, because it does not touch it. The matter is very profound.

Something must be done. You must change your way of life. You must become real. You must really be My devotee.

* * *

CHAPTER 20

Be Served

SRI DA AVABHASA: The ego is capable of knowing an infinite number of offenses. And these offenses serve until the ego is undone. If, as My devotee, you are smart, you will allow such offenses to serve you. You will be happy to let the world become totally offensive. You will allow the world's offenses to show you the dimension of your own lack of wisdom, and you will learn from it.

* * *

Negative circumstances in your life, including encounters with negative people and negative forces, provide a circumstance of creative struggle whereby you must come to understand that you cannot be snuffed out or destroyed, that a greater Power is available to you than any negative circumstance represents, however strong the negativity may seem.

Your encounters with negative forces and negative individuals may be difficult, but such encounters serve you. The reactions they awaken in you are expressions of your present psycho-physical technique that you must overcome. Merely to encounter difficulties does not justify egoically "self-possessed" frustration and the abandonment of your practice of the Way of the Heart. Rather, you should accept the lessons provided by difficulties and, in feeling-Contemplation of Me, surrender the negativity in yourself that is stimulated by an encounter with what frustrates you. That is one dimension of your dealing with difficulties.

The next dimension of your dealing with difficulties is positively to meet negative conditions with the disposition of surrender and, through feeling-Contemplation of Me, to create an opening for the Divine Force so that It may Accomplish changes.

* * *

CHAPTER 21

Release Guilt

SRI DA AVABHASA: Guilt has no place in the Way of the Heart. Discipline, however, has a great place in the Way of the Heart. You have not originally sinned. You are not priorly guilty. In the circumstance of this life, suffering this life, you not even knowing what it is and not having created it, how can guilt be suggested? Responsibility is suggested! Discipline of Submission to Delight, to Happiness, to Bliss—that is suggested. I am to be noticed! Forget guilt and blame and self-consciousness! These are man-made, I Say. My Heart-Blessing does not merely Answer you. It Relieves you even of your questions. Through feeling-Contemplation of Me, you move into a different place, luxuriate in another Process.

* * *

This practical discipline should be fulfilled by you to whatever degree you find the capability in yourself. To whatever degree you fail or find yourself unable to fulfill this discipline at any time, simply observe yourself, be easy, be full of enjoyment, make your actions at least an indulgence that does not harm others, and continue to turn to Me and with feeling-devotion, from the heart. The more you mature in My Company, the more you will fulfill this discipline. The more you fulfill it, the more you will see of your turning from the Divine Self-Condition That Is Incarnate before you. And the more you see of this turning away, the more responsible you will become for your turning to Me.

* * *

As My devotee, you must constantly surrender all concerns for what you have done in the past, or what negative tendencies, accumulated from past actions or experiences, you feel to be lingering within yourself in the present. All conditions must be observed, but they must be simultaneously released via devotional and responsive feeling-Contemplation of Me.

The Divine Being, Truth, and Reality is Love, Wherein everything that is merely true is Outshined by What <u>Is</u> Truth. Therefore, all beings are tacitly, or in every moment, forgiven, or Liberated from the past—if only they will turn (or "repent") from the tendencies of the past and enter whole bodily into present and Ecstatic Communion with Me.

* * *

Whoever loves in the present is not bound. This is the Divine Law. Where there is love, there is release of karma, or the effects of the past. To love is to be "forgiven", or released from past un-love and the destiny past un-love creates through accumulated reactions and the tendencies established by past experience.

* * *

PART IV

Basic Practical
Instructions

CHAPTER 22

Do Your Relations Some Good

A CONVERSATION WITH DA AVABHASA

SRI DA AVABHASA: Did you have a problem with your father?

DONOVAN TRAIN: I think it is fair to say that my father represents all the tendencies in myself that I am most disturbed by and . . .

SRI DA AVABHASA: [Laughing.] You hated your father—is that what you are trying to say?

Apart from your father's personal qualities, which presumably were ego-bound and difficult to endure, you must understand that he is also your inheritance. He was the stream of influence in your early life that would have made you a man, that would have helped you to invest yourself in masculine responsibility. And all you feel about it is complication, hatred, dis-ease, dislike. Whatever there may be in his character or signs or actions to justify it, you are denying yourself your initiation into manhood. You are refusing to invest yourself in manly responsibility. You are denying yourself your maleness, your male humanity, your own masculine responsibility, your own husbanding obligations.

You cannot hate your father forever. You must understand him. You must understand yourself. You must forgive him. You must accept the male inheritance and allow it to be balanced, if you will, in relationship to a woman. But if all you are going to do is dramatize your entire life about a disinclination relative to your father, you are not only expressing a reaction to him but you are denying yourself your own male humanity, because he is the stream of your inheritance of that obligation.

Fathers are how men get to be men. And if, somehow or other, there is a complication in that—you become too attached to women, you become effeminate, you may become homosexual (there are many reasons to be homosexual, of course, including biological ones, but this is psychologically part of how it may arise). You may develop along with all kinds of male weakness, fear, anxious life—then you cannot imagine yourself being a man or husbanding another. If you think your father was such a jerk, you are denying yourself your own inheritance and obligation.

This is why love and forgiveness must come about in all children. Eventually, sooner or later, you must accept the most positive inheritance of the male and the female and overcome your psychological problem about it. Your parents are the only ones you have. They are your seeds of humanity. And you must straighten out your relationship to them, if only for your own sake and for the sake of everyone else you are relating to as an adult. You must deal with your reaction to your parental inheritance, whatever may have occurred in your life with your parents. What occurred there are the acts of nature, the reactivity of egos, the natural and ordinary human signs. And you cannot hate all that forever without destroying yourself.

DONOVAN: The way I have done this, my Lord, is just by maintaining a very superficial relationship with my father, in which I do not express . . .

SRI DA AVABHASA: The main way you have done it is by your own reactivity and by the design of life in which you have invested yourself because of it. There is a psychological truth in the traditional admonition that you must overcome the reaction to your mother and your father, so that you may live a life free to invest yourself in the Divine Source of existence. If you do not overcome this psychological complex, you invest yourself in impediment and in a destiny with which you will curse your life. It is important for the sake of your parents—and it is also important for your sake and for the sake of all those to whom you are related—that you overcome these reactions, these difficulties, of your early life.

What you have principally inherited through your parents are the male and female signs. If your parents were limited, you must still overcome your reaction and forgive them and—"meet some other people", you know? Get out of the house, meet some other men and women, become a man, become a woman. And, as My devotee, yes, find Me out.

To deal with this emotional-sexual complication or problem, you must deal with your mother and father. Your emotional-sexual complication is not just a matter of what you do in intimacy or in sexual intercourse. It is a matter of the mind, the emotional-sexual mind, the origin of which, in your present lifetime, is in your experience with your mother and father. You have been patterning your life, since birth, on the basis of your imitation of your mother or your father or both, and on the basis of your reaction to them. And you always thought you would never live like them! But you are living exactly like them, because of your imitation of them and your reaction to them.

Therefore, so that you can deal with your emotional-sexual problem, I Call you to investigate, observe, "consider", confess all the signs of your early life, your reaction to your mother and father, whatever happened. Work out the matter of forgiveness and love-expression with them. By this you purify yourself and all your future relations and all your present relations, and you purify your parents as well.

This is a necessary service, and a necessary part of growing in the religious life. Without it, there is no growth in religious life, and there is no growing up in emotional-sexual terms. As long as you harbor your problems with your mother and father, you will never straighten out your emotional-sexual life. Mark My Words! Never!

Do not just harbor these reactions. Your model of emotional-sexual intent, desire, seeking, interest, the way you relate to males, females, all that is based on your primitive origins in your childhood household, or whatever the circumstance of your infancy and childhood. It is entirely based on it. You must deal with it. You have no choice. You cannot be straight with anyone until you do.

Anyone, or almost anyone, can function sexually. Almost everyone can. That you are sexually active does not mean that you have straightened out your emotional-sexual life. You think that maybe that is so, because of the message of orgasm and the consolations associated with it. But why all the dramatizations in these relationships? And why all the things you do with male others, female others? Where does it all come from? Yes, there are all the inherited karmas of presumed previous existence, previous to this lifetime, whatever the form of your previous existence. But you can readily observe the origin of your dramatization in the sign of your childhood, your relationship to your parents, your reactions to them, and the whole psychology and all the visions, thoughts, patterns, and so forth, you have inherited from that reaction.

You are never going to make Yoga out of your intimacies, or straighten them out in the ways I have told you to straighten them out, until you deal with this, the fundamentals of your emotional-sexual character. You are not free to be a man, if you are male, until you have dealt with your problems with your father. You are not free to be a woman, if you are female, until you have dealt with your problems with your mother. You are also not free to be a man until you have dealt with your problems with your mother. And you are not free to be a woman until you have dealt with your problems with your father.

You must deal with this. Your entire life is patterned on it. You must become sensitive to it. Without such understanding and purification, all of your emotional-sexual life is a dramatization—all of it. That is why I Call you to the most serious investigation, "consideration", and confession of your origins in this lifetime in relation to your parents, the circumstance of your early life—everything thoroughly confessed, understood, in the context of devotion to Me, all forgiven, letters written, telephone calls made, visits—it is your business. And, by the way, giving short shrift to your mother and father on the telephone is not dealing with it.

There must be forgiveness, assumption of your own maleness, femaleness, responsibility for your relationship to male others, female others. This is the clarity necessary for a renunciate or for My devotee of any maturity. It is absolutely necessary.

DONOVAN: In fact, Sri Gurudev, I am intending to visit my father on my way home from this retreat.

SRI DA AVABHASA: Whatever he does or says, make sure that what you say and do is full of love, full of tears too.

DONOVAN: Ten years or so ago, I went to him with this intention, and I began expressing my love to him. We were riding along in a pickup truck, and he was obviously embarrassed by what I was saying to him.

SRI DA AVABHASA: So what? You do not know how much of a conversion he will go through when you get straight with him. You have an obligation to be straight. Endure his embarrassment. Whatever is necessary for you to say, feel, express, and weep about, you be sure you do it. You may never get another opportunity.

Do him some good. Do yourself some good. Do all your relations, including your intimate partner, some good. Make sure you handle this business.

*Know My Love
and Grant It to All Others*

S RI DA AVABHASA: Find out what true Happiness is in every
moment and communicate that Happiness.

*   *   *

The Happiness of Which I Speak is not just a matter of feeling
good and being able to smile. That is not Happiness Itself. At most
that represents a kind of ordinary personal equanimity. The
Happiness of Which I Speak is spelled with a capital "H", and It is
the Love-Blissfulness of Divine Being Itself, Prior to the body-mind
and its relations.

*   *   *

Happiness is simply the Self-Radiance of the Divine Self.

*   *   *

Nothing could be more mad than to be Happy in this place,
because there is really no justification for it. It is not reasonable to
be Happy. If you thoroughly examine this world, there is reason to
feel very un-Happy. Even a little pleasurableness thrown in is not
enough to overcome the conviction of darkness that you get when
you really see what is happening here. Therefore, not any philosophy you can base on your experience here makes you Happy.
Complete release from implications, from the force of this dreaming, from this appearance for which you cannot account makes you
Happy.

And it is already miraculous. Nothing fantastic has to happen.
You already cannot account for a single thing in this room here.

The mere existence of anything is beyond comprehension. It is sufficient to boggle you. You do not know what a single thing is. You cannot build any great programs for victory on the basis of such Divine Ignorance. On the basis of that Divine Ignorance, you are naturally disposed to all of this arising, and you may be led into the intuitive acknowledgement of the Divine Self-Condition of all of this arising.

* * *

Before you start imagining a program for your ultimate victory or defeat, by desiring and creating circumstances for yourself, just before all of that happens in this moment, just before you believe all of that, you are Happy. That Happiness is your true Condition. All the rest of it is an hallucination by which you program your life. Therefore, the matter of sadhana in the Way of the Heart is simple. It is not complicated, not a complicated involvement with all of the stuff that obsesses you. Wherever all that is seen and yielded, your conscious awareness assumes its native, intuitive Condition. That Condition is Satsang with Me. That is Divine Communion. That is what all of this is about.

* * *

The Price Of Happiness In every moment Is Release Of self-Contraction (and Release Of The Search To Acquire, Hold On To, or Strategically Escape the conditions Of conditional Existence). This Release Is Possible Only If There Is Most Fundamental self-Understanding. And That Most Fundamental self-Understanding May Be Fulfilled, Most Ultimately and Most Perfectly, Only By Distracted Love Of The By Grace Revealed Person Of Reality, Truth, and Happiness.

The Dawn Horse Testament

* * *

This is the demand which always obliges My devotee and with which My devotee is always at odds by tendency: You should look and feel and be and act completely Happy under all conditions.

* * *

Love is the energy of My Transmitted Happiness. If you are My devotee, then you know that Love, that Blessing, and It Falls on you every day, It Fills you up, It makes you Ecstatic, and you grant It to all other beings. Your entire life is the work of that granting of Love. Your life is finding every way possible to grant Love to everyone, because by granting It you magnify your participation in It—remarkably, paradoxically.

* * *

An appropriate order of life must be established, in which there is room for absolute blissfulness. . . . When the life is only open, when this incredible Force is flowing through, it churns you, it purifies the life. Then there is nothing at last to be unhappy about, nothing to think about. The flood of enjoyment rushes through the body, dissolves the mind, overwhelms the life. The real intelligence of conscious life begins to intensify and function in place of ignorance. And that intelligence has no answers. It has no questions. That state without answers and without questions is the true state. From that state, the "creation" of marvels begins.

The Method of the Siddhas

* * *

Ishta-Guru-Bhakti is ecstasy. Now, as such an ecstatic heart, free to bring the love-principle into life, do it! And do it in your intimacies. Do it in everything.

* * *

In the Way of the Heart, ecstasy requires the entire body. Sexual activity is a means of ecstatic living, but you must not reduce your ecstatic life to sexing. Yes, use sexuality in that ecstatic manner, but you must also have the ability to drop out of the social persona and live an ecstatic life every day. This is the primary function of true religion.

Conventional, or exoteric, religion, however, is not about that. It is about the social persona, which commands people toward moral and socially productive activity. Social productivity tends to be the whole of conventional religion. That is it. The social structure commands you to be the social persona only and not to be ecstatic. However, people collapse under the stress of that demand, and they adapt to a merely self-indulgent life, exploiting drugs and alcohol, even sexuality, because they are under stress.

It is neither right nor natural to divorce yourself from ecstasy.

Ecstasy is the primal function of the human being. The social function is certainly useful and necessary. But it must not be enforced to the degree of excluding ecstasy and the actual practice of ecstasy. If you have such freedom, then your fundamental exercise is in the religious life, and not merely in the exoteric religious life, which reinforces the social personality. So-called moral and socially useful activity is really the only purpose of exoteric religion. True religion is esoteric. True religion may combine itself with things that are otherwise considered exoteric, but it is about ecstasy. It is about ego-transcendence.

If you are free to live a truly religious life, then you practice ecstasy under all kinds of circumstances, all the time in fact. In the Way of the Heart, such ecstasy is feeling-Contemplation of Me to the degree that you manifest love, incarnate love and its signs, in daily life. Therefore, as My devotee, Contemplate Me and do not just live a moral life. Live a life of love in My Awakening Company. Then practice all the meditative and other exercises that are occasions of ecstasy—Puja, chanting, song, praise.

The whole process of truly religious or Spiritual life is about ecstasy, or transcending egoity, to the point of Realizing Me, or the One Who Is when there is no contraction, the One Who Is the Divine Self-Condition.

True religion transforms life and touches all aspects of your living. True religion, then, is a primary requirement of human beings. It is not merely something that comes down through time that should be used to command moral or socially useful behavior. It is a culture and a key mechanism for the fulfillment of what a human life is about. It is a heart matter. And it is about ecstasy, or the transcendence of egoity.

* * *

CHAPTER 24

Say the Words of Love

SRI DA AVABHASA: I Call you to investigate, observe, "consider", and confess all the signs of your early life, your reaction to your mother and father and all the rest. Clear all that up and, if your parents are still alive, work out forgiveness and the expression of love with them. By this you will purify yourself and all your future relations, and you will purify your parents as well.

* * *

DEVOTEE, a man: On one occasion, I brought up the subject of my son to Sri Gurudev. I said that our relationship was okay, but somehow it seemed lopsided and unresolved. He asked me about my son, who is grown now.

We talked a little about it, and then He asked me, "Were you a good father?"

"I think so, yes."

"Do you love him?"

"Oh, yes."

"Do you ever tell him you love him?"

"Yes."

"Does he ever tell you he loves you?"

"Yes."

"Well, then, you have no problem. You tell each other that you love each other, you embrace, and you say goodbye. No problem. But you usually have to say it three times—"I love you, I love you, I love you, my son."

* * *

Do not just wait until you are on your deathbed to tell your friend that you love him or her. Invest yourself in the business of love, now, presently. Purify yourself with Truth, and thereby purify others. Relieve all beings of the imposition of the insult of cosmic Nature and un-Happiness and bad deeds. Be relieved, and relieve all, by the force of Truth.

That is it. That is what I call "assuming the relational discipline in the Way of the Heart".

* * *

Part of the reluctance to say to anyone that you love the person is that you do not want to trivialize your love. There is a great deal of this reluctance between intimates, between emotional-sexual intimates, for instance. Women tend to be more emotionally expressive and more emotionally expectant than men. Therefore, women tend to complain that their male intimate does not say the words "I love you" often enough.

You know that trivia. The drama appears in movies, so you all know about it. You have probably played it out yourself. The woman wants the man to say "I love you", and he does not say it enough. Part of the male reluctance is an unwillingness to trivialize love, to say words without sufficient expression that the feeling will be noticed or felt to be enough, therefore always being required to be blapping out the greeting-card message. Part of the reluctance is the unwillingness to trivialize love, or the feeling of embarrassment because you do not want to trivialize it.

Another element of it, however, is just the refusal to love—not merely the refusal to say love but the refusal to do it. Again in man-woman relations, if the man actually did love more, the woman would be more satisfied.

* * *

DEVOTEE, a man: In June 1992, while on retreat at Sri Love-Anandashram, I had the rare and auspicious opportunity to embrace Da Avabhasa. During our long and very emotional embrace, He whispered in my ear.

"And do you love your intimate partner?" He said.

"Yes," I replied.

"Do you tell her this?"

Again, I replied, "Yes, Beloved Lord."

"Tcha," He said. "You must tell her that you love her many times every day. This is part of the man's Yoga in an intimate relationship. Will you do this?"

"Yes," I responded from my heart. "I will."

"Tcha," He said again. "And tell her that I Love her and want to see her very soon," He said.

"I will, Beloved Lord. She will be very pleased. Thank you."

"Tcha," He responded again as He continued to Embrace me in His massive, gentle arms.

*　*　*

The cure for the great emotional neurosis—the program of "Narcissus" that I have "Considered" at length with you—is praise. Not praise of you but praise communicated by you. In order to praise another, you must transcend your envy and your self-defense by which you strive to appear superior. In order to praise anything, you must transcend your own position. Thus, praise is one of the ordinary disciplines of a naturally serving life wherein you grant life to others. Your communication of praise enlivens your friends.

*　*　*

CHILD: Heart-Master Da, I have a personal discipline not to be righteous. But I'm still righteous a lot, and I cannot really find a way to stop it.

SRI DA AVABHASA: What do you mean by "righteous"?

CHILD: Well, I try to be smart, you know. I do things like telling somebody something, just walking by somebody and saying something to him, not really meaning it, just being rude.

SRI DA AVABHASA: Are you angry about something?

CHILD: I am angry when I say it.

SRI DA AVABHASA: What are you angry about?

CHILD: Well, I am just inside myself.

SRI DA AVABHASA: Why do you think you are angry? Do you feel angry a lot?

CHILD: Not too much, but sometimes I feel real angry.

SRI DA AVABHASA: Is being righteous a way of being angry?

CHILD: Yes.

SRI DA AVABHASA: So?

CHILD: Do You have a way that You can tell me that I can stop being righteous?

SRI DA AVABHASA: Yes. If you love. If you will love people and persist in that feeling, allow yourself to love people all the time, then you will not be righteous in the way that you are talking about. It is fine every now and then to tell somebody where he or she is at—you have to be able to know the difference between behavior in people that is all right and behavior that is not all right, or that is negative. But if you love them, then you will know the difference between the things they do that are good and the things they do that are not. And you will be able to talk to them about the things that are not good without being righteous, without being angry. You will be able to be Happy with them, because you will know at that moment that you also love them. Whereas when you are being righteous, you are not aware of the fact that you love them. You forget about that for a minute.

You must learn about this loving feeling. Whenever you do not love, whenever you do not feel, you start getting angry. And after you have been angry for a long time, you start getting afraid. You start to feel bad. So you must learn how to be able to love all the time, how to feel all the time. You must be able to feel the world.

A lady who was just talking to Me said she gets up in the morning unhappy about the fact that the world exists. The mood she is in at that moment is not the mood of someone who is My devotee. My devotee wakes up and, even though things may not be going too well, he or she feels Me. My devotee knows that the Divine Being, Truth, and Reality is all over this world, all inside the world, inside everyone and outside everyone. My devotee feels that the world is about the Divine, that the world is about Love.

But the people one sees on television and people who are not being Happy do not know that the world is about the Divine. They do not know that the world is about Love. That is why they do not love very much. That is why they are always talking about themselves and about negative things.

Therefore, if you are angry and righteous, it is just that you have forgotten for a moment that the world is about the Divine, and that the world is about Love, and that you are about Love. There is nothing you can do about being righteous if you forget to love, if you forget that the world is about God. You cannot stop being righteous by trying not to be righteous. You will stop being righteous when you forget about being righteous, which means you must remember to love.

You are all the time remembering what you must remember to be angry and righteous. Instead, you must remember what you must Remember to be Happy, and that means you must Remember Me. You must Remember the Mystery in Which you live. You must remember to love, and you must love, and you must practice loving people. Do not wait for love to just happen. You must <u>practice</u> loving people. And you must communicate love to them. You must <u>say</u> you love them. You must do things for them that are full of the feeling of love for them. You see? So, find out what you must Remember to be Happy, and do that. If you do that, then you will forget to be angry and righteous.

Sometimes you may have something to say to somebody about something that he or she is doing that is not very good, but what you say to that person will not be the same as righteousness. You will tell this to the person because you love the person. And when you tell the person, you will even <u>sound</u> like you love that person. There are even bad people here and there. You probably have not met any really bad people lately, not any <u>really</u> bad ones. But even the really bad ones are alive in the same world. They are with the Divine just like you. They have some things to learn, but you cannot teach them without loving them. You cannot teach anybody anything without being Happy with the person. And you cannot be Happy with anybody else unless <u>you</u> are Happy. You cannot always wait for others to do something to make you Happy. <u>You</u> have to be Happy, and then you make other people Happy, too.

* * *

CHAPTER 25

The Wound of Love

SRI DA AVABHASA: The ego, "Narcissus", the self-knot, is always defending itself, always seeking isolation and immunity from relations.

*   *   *

Love one another and there is nothing cool about it. What I mean by this love for one another is to become wounded by love, to submit yourself to love, to live in the world of love, and to make your relationships about love. Be vulnerable enough to love and be loved. If you do this, you will be wounded by this love but you will not be diseased. The wound of love is the "hole" in the universe, and ultimately it is Realized as such.

In this hole in the universe, this Domain of Feeling without armoring, without self-contraction, the great Physics, the great Science, the great Possibility, is evident. Hardly anyone in human history has known of It. Human beings in general do not want anything to do with It. They do not want to come close enough to It to be wounded in their intimacies with one another. It is the doorway to Divine Transfiguration, Divine Transformation, and, ultimately, Divine Translation, or Outshining of phenomenal existence. It is the way into the Divine Self-Domain.

You must be wounded in order to Realize Me. You must be wounded to hear Me and see Me. Such Realization is felt even physically as a kind of wound. It is felt as intense, armorless vulnerability.

If you can begin to awaken to this principle, then you will love others, your sexuality will cease to be problematic, your friendships and your community life will become possible. You will make a different kind of community, a true Spiritual community of My true devotees, which is a process available to only uniquely free people. This wound enlivens you. It releases great force, great energy. It releases all of the armoring of the usual personality. It enables you to love, to be in love.

If you become thus wounded and enter into such intimacy with one another, then in your emotional-sexual relationships you will not have any troubles with your promiscuity and your lack of interest in one another and all the petty problems you make for one another in your unconverted emotional state. All of that completely disappears.

Such is the kind of process you must be involved in as a result of our "consideration" together. Therefore, you must make a community of love with one another, a truly Spiritual community.

* * *

If you enter into this process of self-knowledge and knowledge of another, it will break your heart. It did Mine! Yet as dreadful as it is, it is the best thing I ever did. The best thing that could possibly happen to you is for you to become a raw nerve-end, a broken heart, unconsolable, with sorrow on your face and ecstasy as well, no longer a conventional man or woman, no longer able to put on the social false face—incapable of it, with no argument, no anger, no feeling rejected, you responsible and you dying, and no absolutes coming to you through the bodies of others.

Everything you console yourself with is a lie. When you get down to the bottom of it, broken-hearted in your distress, maybe you will discover what "in love" is. It is not about what you must do. It is about transcending yourself, about not fulfilling yourself. And it is not amusing. It is passionate and it is terrible.

* * *

You must submit to Me emotionally. To submit to Me emotionally means you cannot let emotion assume a contracted form, become a reactive state, in relationship to Me. You must simply feel whatever is the case. You must put yourself in a position to be wholly vulnerable to whatever is the case, through feeling. Feeling is a kind of touch.

* * *

Divine Self-Realization is not the avoidance of the pain of life but it is to suffer it to the nth degree, to the point of Awakening, to the point of Freedom, to the point of being utterly transformed, in effect, by love, to murder the murderer, to be Free of limitations— but not by evading them.

Mediocrity is the universal solution of humankind. Mediocrity, superficiality, convention—this is how people desensitize themselves to reality, to death, and to the great requirement that is the Heart Itself, Which is the Depth of existence. You are always ready to make an arrangement that is sort of smiling and superficial, that desensitizes you and makes you get pleasant. You are always ready to do that, but that is not it.

If you were sensitive to the situation you are always in, you would be serious all the time. You would not settle for mediocrity or superficiality. Superficiality would not occur to you. You would never lose the Heart-Wound, ever. You could be in a circumstance that, to all appearances, is the most pleasant, amusing, and happy, in the ordinary sense, and have tears in your eyes because you feel where you are, you feel your situation, you feel your limitations, and you will not endure being limited. You press yourself beyond it. You do not submit to superficiality or casualness. That is what it takes.

*   *   *

The Reactive Rituals Of egoity Must Be Released By The self-Transcending (and Then Spiritual) Practice Of Love. This Requires Each and Every Practitioner Of The Way Of The Heart To Observe, Understand, and Relinquish The Emotionally Reactive Cycle Of Rejection and Punishment. And the Necessary Prerequisites For Such Relinquishment Are Vulnerability (or The Ability To Feel The Wounds Of Love Without Retaliation), Sensitivity To the other In Love (or The Ability To Sympathetically Observe, Understand, Forgive, Love, and Not Punish or Dissociate From the other In Love), and Love Itself (or the Ability To Love, To Know You Are Loved, To Receive Love, and To Know That Both You and the other, Regardless Of Any Appearance To The Contrary, Are Vulnerable To Love and Heart-Requiring Of Love).

The Dawn Horse Testament

*   *   *

To be in love is embarrassing and awkward. Your face changes, and you become foolish, not so ready-made, buttoned-down, cool, and strategic. You consent to be in love only on very rare occasions, usually when you have realized some romantic sexual association. Yet to be in love, to be submitted into the Divine Self-Radiance, is the native state of human beings. God is love. That is true enough.

* * *

The great fear, and what no one wants to do, is to live the life of love. Nobody wants to do that. It is embarrassing. It is not consoling. It involves a profound responsibility. You cannot be a child and do it.

Therefore, you prefer the magic acts of self-destruction, the magic acts of dissolution, whereby you are not liberated from anything but, perhaps, relieved. You prefer orgasm to God-Realization and to love.

All of that is a reflection of your childishness, your recoil, your inability to go to school, to submit and be changed, to be responsible. You are self-destructive. Instead of celebrating, you poison yourself because you are refusing the moral obligation inherent in your True Condition, which is to love, to penetrate the whole force of your self-contraction, to be morally heroic.

* * *

The endless cycle of your own moods is not the Condition of Satsang. Satsang with Me is a "radical" Condition, and It requires everything of you. It requires you to absolutely lose face. You must lose face in relation to the Truth. It is quite a different thing from being caught nude in the subway. You lose face by exposing yourself absolutely to Me, the Divine Adept Who is your Real and Inherently Perfect Self, by becoming known.

* * *

Why be reluctant to love? It is your obligation to do so. Be aware of your reluctance, but surrender, forget yourself, animate yourself, be expressive, override your reluctance, do the counter-egoic act. If at first you are embarrassed about loving, love and be embarrassed. Then do it some more. Animate the throat, the voice of praise, the expression of love. Say love. Do love. Live love.

Oblige yourself. Do not just sit around meditating on your reluctance to do so. "Consider" the matter and do it. And then do it some more. And do it more and more.

Make agreements with others about how you will magnify your expression of love, and then oblige yourself to do so. It does not make any difference how reluctant you are. Love is a matter of your practice of the Way of the Heart, that is all. Confess all the reluctance, all the embarrassment, if it is there—fine. But this is the practice: Do it. Override your reluctance. The more you override it, the more you are purified of it. You are purified of your reluctance not by analyzing it and dwelling on it and meditating on it forever but by accepting the discipline and engaging yourself in this counter-egoic effort, this responsible practice, whereby you override the very thing you know is your impediment.

If to do so embarrasses you, so what? After a while you will notice that it is not embarrassing you anymore, because you are doing something else. Doing something else is what the religious life is about. Doing the other thing, the "else", the very thing you are reluctant to do—that is the cure. Instead of living like an addict, the ego, do the cure, do the other thing, do the discipline.

It is difficult. It requires a confrontation with your limitations. It requires you to go beyond them. But that is how it is. That is it.

*   *   *

CHAPTER 26

Undermine the Tendency to Create Emotional Dissociation

SRI DA AVABHASA: As My devotee, you should not indulge any separative activity in yourself at all. You can all see what separative activity is. It is when you withdraw from somebody. Is there anybody here who does not know what that is like? Everybody here knows that? Then you have received the initiation!

That is the avoidance of relationship. Before you do that, before you withdraw from somebody, notice that the person is already right there. Your relationship to the person already exists. Therefore, all withdrawing from that person is felt by you as pain. You suffer because you withdraw your life-force from them, and you likewise feel confused and upset.

Do you see how all of that is the life of suffering? Then do not do that anymore! Instead, live in relationship to others. Do not tolerate any withdrawal in yourself. Maintain your contact with that other person and deal with all the forms—even the subtlest forms—of that withdrawal in yourself, from this same point of view. And do not dramatize it anymore.

* * *

You must not forget. Never allow your "consideration" to degenerate into "let's pretend" and mere positive affirmation. There must be a real and direct feeling association among My devotees and a constant feeling practice of love-surrender to Me. You must literally practice this heart-felt surrender at all times, and you must literally oblige one another to do this practice.

* * *

The commitment to subjectivity is the withdrawing of life-energy, the withholding of feeling-attention, the failure to love. It is just as much a failure to love as all the outward, wild, gross activities people tend to do. Generally, however, people do not regard the failure to love to be a "sin". They think that "sin" is the indulgence of the senses, and they think that otherwise their subjective orientation is in the God-ward direction. But that is absolutely untrue. Subjectivity is just the other side of the body.

*　*　*

Love is unobstructed feeling-attention. It is human relational intensity—free of the recoil of egoic "self-possession", reactive or negative emotions, and absorption in the subjective stream of thoughts and images.

*　*　*

In general you tend not to engage the emotional dimension at all. You avoid it. You play the game of emotional dissociation from the world, from one another, and from Me, the Incarnate Divine Person. When you dramatize this problem of emotional dissociation, this quality of the collapse of feeling, energy, and attention, then you become a self-server, totally without clarity in relationship—not only in human relationships but in all relationships, and in relationship to Me most fundamentally.

This constant and unconscious effort to create emotional dissociation must be undermined. Serve one another by helping to break this habit and by re-establishing one another in authentic emotional association, in love-surrender through feeling-Contemplation of Me, and in a loving, radiant life altogether, in all relations. As My devotees, you must bring down this emotional barrier that exists between you and never again play the game of "let's pretend".

*　*　*

If you cannot feel, if the core of the being, the heart, is not active, then at the physical level you must indulge yourself in all the ways of gaining pleasure, from orgasm to drugs. If you cannot feel at the level of emotion, then you cannot live a life of love, you cannot be intimate. If you cannot feel with the head, at the level of mind, you cannot enjoy clarity of mind or "consider" things as they truly are.

Thus, feeling must be awakened from head to toe and from toe to crown, through Contemplating Me with feeling-devotion. Feeling must become natural to you. It must become your discipline.

*   *   *

The Realization of Truth is an emotional matter. The discovery is an emotional one, the change is an emotional one, the true practice of the Way of the Heart is emotional.

*   *   *

The "consideration" of the activity of emotional dissociation, or "Narcissus", must not be dropped. It is not something that as My devotee you take seriously only every now and then. It must be constant. You must constantly observe what you are doing at the heart and transcend it. That is what it is to practice the heart in every moment.

Therefore, you must be able to inspect the limit on your heart-response to Me, and, therefore, to all others, in every moment. You must be able to inspect the process of emotional dissociation, whereby you are always entering into the separative, subjective mood of the separate person, instead of the radiant, loving mood of My devotee, or the true person.

*   *   *

This is Wisdom: Always relax into the pains and circumstances of experience, and so remain in Communion with Me, rather than in confrontation with the modifications of life. Surrender to Me rather than react to experience. Do this consistently, under all circumstances, and thus remain always with Me and disposed toward loving self-release in all relationships. This is the human foundation of morality.

*   *   *

To found yourself in feeling-response to Me is the essence of all practice in the Way of the Heart.

The Da Love-Ananda Gita,
"I Am (My Self) What you Require" section

*   *   *

You can place only <u>one</u> limit on your practice of the Way of the Heart, and that is the limitation on feeling Me.

The Da Love-Ananda Gita,
"I <u>Am</u> (My Self) What you Require" section

*   *   *

What else can be called God, Truth, or Reality but That Which Is Self-Evident when all of dissociation is transcended? That Is the Divine Self-Condition, Which Is the Realization in the Way of the Heart. That Is the Person I Reveal to you. That Is My Realization, My Very (and Inherently Perfect) State, My Very Condition, My Work. That Is the One I <u>Am</u>.

*   *   *

CHAPTER 27

Giving and Receiving

SRI DA AVABHASA: To be Happy, you must receive life-energy from others. But to continue in that Happiness, you must also give life-energy to others. Thus, if you receive and also grant life-energy, then infinite delight and love and beauty can be enjoyed in your person. This will occur, however, only if you receive and transmit at the same time. Only! Only!

* * *

As My devotee, live in feeling-Contemplation of Me, submit yourself to Divine Communion in feeling-Contemplation of Me, and submit yourself to receive and to live with all others in the disposition of giving. This is the Great Law. That is it. That is the Law. Receive absolutely, and transmit absolutely. Do this, and you will be Happy. If there is a blank in your transmission, overcome it. If there is a blank in your reception, overcome it. The Law is to receive absolutely and transmit absolutely. That is love. That is it.

If there is no reception, there is no love. If there is no transmission, there is no love. Submit yourself absolutely. Receive the Grace, the Beauty, the Love-Bliss and Reality of the Divine and submit yourself to That. If you do, if you are in the position of receiving My Grace, My Love-Bliss, My Happiness, then what else will you do but love and give to everyone, in such a way that each can receive your transmission?

What else is there to do in this humble place between birth and death?

* * *

As My devotee, receive My Spiritual Heart-Transmission absolutely and love your neighbor, just as if that one were you, the same One, the same Love-Bliss, needing to be a terminal of such reception. Live in Me, submit yourself to Me, submit yourself to receive My Divine Blessing, and live with all others in the disposition of giving.

* * *

You need not put on a smile to change how you feel—<u>you</u> cannot even see it. Manifest a smile for the sake of others.

The Hymn Of The True Heart-Master,
"I Am Grace Itself" section

* * *

You must fulfill the sadhana of giving with a full heart, with no doubt of love, with no expectation. Grant the gift of the Divine Beloved. Love every being as the Divine Being. This is the sadhana. Do not expect congratulations. Look to the face of your friend, your lover, your beloved. Rejoice in that. Expect no personal word. Look for the joy of friends. There is no other compensation in this place.

* * *

CHAPTER 28

The Mother-Force
and
the Father-Force

SRI DA AVABHASA: One's psychological disposition toward the mother and father in the first three stages of life tends to be reflected in one's response to the Spiritual process. Although most people who are practicing the Way of the Heart are adults and no longer living with their parents, something about the psychology of the child-parent/male-female dynamic is still in place in their character, in emotional-sexual and other intimate relationships, and in every aspect of life, including (therefore) how they relate to the Spiritual process.

In My Description of the practice of the Way of the Heart, I have used the metaphors of the "Mother-Force" and the "Father-Force". The Father-Force (or male influence) is the controlling force, and the Mother-Force (or female influence) is the nurturing force. The Father-Force is associated with Divine Consciousness, and with the "conscious process" and concentration. The Mother-Force is associated with the Divine Spirit-Current, and with "conductivity" and the Yogic infusion of the body-mind by Divine Love-Bliss. In right practice of the Way of the Heart, both of these "Forces" (and dimensions of practice) are fully, rightly, cooperatively, and effectively embraced and managed.

The Hymn Of The True Heart-Master,
"I Am Grace Itself" section

*   *   *

151

After the individual's early stages of childhood, or at least after the second stage of life, the mother and father should not have to act in a parent-like fashion anymore. Even so, these two forces continue as the dynamic of the human situation that exists throughout your life, moving from mommy and daddy to the great forces of existence. You must grow, through your participation in that dynamic.

Eventually, you must mature sufficiently to be able to respond to My "Fatherly" side, My Demand, as well as to My Love. You must respond to both of these apparent Qualities. Your life must be participation in the dynamic of the One Reality, or That Which Is Great. You must respond not only to My Love but also to My Demand for your self-transcendence.

*　*　*

Some of you had stronger parents than others—you felt nurtured by the mother and not merely aggressively challenged by the father but drawn out by the father into creative participation in life. Some people have had better experience than others in the universe of meanings in childhood, and they tend to be more effective adults—not Enlightened, but more effective and happy in the ordinary sense.

*　*　*

The mother-force is nurturing, supportive, and it connects you to everything, makes you feel loved, makes you feel familiar, and evokes the loving, radiant response in you.

*　*　*

The mother means nurturing. She is a supportive force. At any rate, such is the role that the mother is expected to perform, even by the infant and the child. The father is a different force, however. The father means challenge—something quite the opposite of the mother.

*　*　*

The mother is primary. One who is not nurtured inevitably feels too much challenged. Such a person's unhappiness is primary evidence of the lack of sustenance, the disconnection from the Divine Source. And it is also an expression of confrontation with challenge. Thus, the description of someone's failure to be nurtured also applies to the person's being too much challenged. Both circumstances produce the tendency to depression and to feeling overwhelmed.

The mother is primary, and the father is secondary. If you are well sustained, then you can deal with challenge, with the forces of life that demand self-transcendence and sacrifice. In other words, you are only oversensitive to the father-force if you are already feeling the absence of the mother-force.

Whether you are male or female, you are sustained by the mother and challenged by the father. If sustenance is lacking, you tend not to feel connected to That Which Sustains, and you tend not to feel positive about existence. Then the father-force, the challenge of life, is simply overwhelming, and you become a self-protective, anxious personality.

*   *   *

If only the mother-force existed, you would die. The challenge must also exist. You must break away from the mother—but only from the stifling, protective force, not from the sustaining power. Then you must also find the father.

*   *   *

Examine the tradition of the American Indians. What is the basis of the culture whereby they train one another? It is a culture of testing. It is also a culture of compassion and love, but it is not a culture that affirms the principle of weakness. It demands that people grow. It equips people to grow, to be strong, to endure the limitations of existence, and to transcend those limitations.

Such a traditional culture stands in profound contrast to much of the traditional upbringing of the rest of humanity, who tend to resent demands and want to live like children, just being given the things of life that are satisfying. What has tended to disappear from the world is the attitude of manliness (male or female), or the willingness and the capability to live life as an ordeal that requires you to understand and transcend yourself.

That requirement is basic to everything that I have "Considered" with you.

*   *   *

Equanimity and Feeling

SRI DA AVABHASA: When feeling-sensitivity is exercised in relationship, one learns that one is more than merely physical. One is also a field of energy that extends to others and communicates emotional, mental, psychic, and physical states to others as well as to the realm of conditional Nature. Therefore, one must learn to be responsible for one's emotional, mental, psychic, and physical state by participating in, or surrendering openly into, the domains of the natural energy of the body-mind and its relations. Through such participation, one's social development and one's involvement in the realm of conditional Nature will develop as a moral and feeling gesture, rather than as an amoral (or egoically "self-possessed" and other-manipulative) form of conventional socialization and worldliness.

*   *   *

Because the direct communication of your state, your condition, to others in any moment has moral and Spiritual implications, you must become responsible for your energy—responsible, therefore, for your emotional state. You must keep the energy field of the body-mind in balance by transcending reactive emotions, and you must maintain a state of physical well-being and mental openness, receptivity, and clarity.

You must maintain a free psychic state. In doing this, you not only change your outward behavior, but you also affect your energy field and therefore your energetic transmission to others.

*   *   *

It is not readily obvious to young people, or even to many adults who have never undergone the true learning of the second stage of life, that they are manifested as an energy field. My early-life devotees must learn this through self-observation that is awakened in feeling-Contemplation of Me.

* * *

In the second stage of life, human beings learn about the energy field that is the dimension of the body-mind next in subtlety after the gross physical dimension. In the Way of the Heart, the child learns how to be responsible for this field of energy, how to communicate through it, and how to be sensitive and helpful to others via energy. Thus, the child learns how to do massage and the laying on of hands, and how to have an altogether healing, enlivening, and quickening effect on others.

* * *

What happens when you think a negative thought, by the way? If a plant can react to a negative thought—and it has been proven that plants do have such reactions—then anyone can think a negative thought that could influence you. Think about it. What happens when you think a negative thought?

* * *

In the Way of the Heart, the condition of children (and of adults) must be one whereby they are obliged to live with sensitivity. They must be obliged to be relaxed, they must be obliged to practice service in all relations, and they must be sensitive to and mindful of one another. Children (and adults) need to learn to serve others consistently as a real responsibility.

* * *

Sila, or equanimity, is fundamental to truly human life. Even though many kinds of disciplines are associated with the Way of the Heart, one aspect is of continuous significance throughout the course of your practice. That is this process of releasing energy and attention from the self-bond and enjoying the state of equanimity, or natural control over the outgoing automaticities of energy and attention.

* * *

155

In your relations with everyone, you should notice the same limits I observe in your personal service to Me. You are constantly tending to act in service to Me without the discipline of sila. In other words, you are tending to live out of balance. Therefore, you are inattentive to what is precisely required or requested of you. As a result, you create disturbances constantly, and you disturb even the process of communication, as well as what is supposed to result from communication. I Call all My devotees to practice sila—which is the discipline of the body-mind and the discipline of attention—first in devotional service to Me and then in relation to all others.

* * *

Through your right practice of the Way of the Heart in My Company, you are available in relationship. You are attentive rather than resistive. Therefore, you can be sensitive to people's requirements and know how to function around them. Your attention will be sufficient to know what people are really saying when they speak to you directly, and you will be sensitive enough to the signs you see in them to be able to serve their needs.

Simply by virtue of your noticing a person's state you should anticipate his or her request through your service.

* * *

You already know what the result is when you do not do what you should do and when others do not do what they should do. It is the usual ego, the troubled person who causes unlimited problems for himself or herself and for others. As egos, you not only create problems for one another by what you are doing and by what you are communicating (both verbally and emotionally in outward physical terms), but you also transmit your state throughout the universe, like a super-powerful transmission station. You particularly direct your limited state to those individuals, groups, places, and processes on which your attention is fixed.

You are always broadcasting your state to others. You literally bring about changes in cosmic Nature through your individual and collective habits at the level of energy, in the subtler dimension of personality and in the psyche. Thus, if your individual life and your relationships are to change and if human life is going to change altogether, you must become responsible for these habits. If you do not, then you will continue to act in ways that trouble and aberrate others, and you will also directly broadcast your aberration to others through the medium of your energy and your psyche.

Everyone is continually receiving these aberrated messages, and if you are not responsible for yourself you are affected by them in various ways. You involuntarily move into states of contraction, reactivity, loss of well-being, mental obsession, and all the rest of it. Very often these actions have nothing whatever to do with anything that is going on directly in your life. They simply come over you because of the mechanical clicking of your reactive "Narcissism" and its automaticities, but also through the reception of tendencies in the field of energy.

You receive these tendencies from people to whom you are related, and from all kinds of gross and subtle entities, both incarnate and discarnate. These other persons or entities may not have a particular intention relative to you, but they are in a certain state, and for some reason or other you become subject to them, come into contact with them, experience their influence, and then you yourself start undergoing changes. But, no matter what changes you tend to go through by these means, you must become responsible for them. This means you must, through feeling-Contemplation of Me, be awakened to self-understanding and (in due course) to Spiritually activated practice of the Way of the Heart in My Company.

Transcend yourself via feeling-Contemplation of Me and engage life on that basis. Then you will always be repairing and balancing out your body-mind, no matter what effects are tending to impinge on you. You will not become the persona who is characterized by these reactions, by these signs. You should always be able to purify yourself via your devotion to Me and your active resort to Me.

Among the things you must learn is how to identify what has to do with you and what has to do with someone else. You need not work out every apparent problem. Much of the time you simply must realize that the "problem" is someone else's problem, someone else's state! You need not investigate it at all. All you need to do is take a few breaths and surrender to Me. Let it go.

There are also things that you need to deal with that are part of your own mechanics and your relationships. My Wisdom-Teaching and your real practice of the Way of the Heart in My Company Give you all the arms that a human being needs for dealing with this manifested condition of existence. I have Given you everything you need for growing in the midst of every circumstance, and I am the Means by Which, Most Ultimately, you transcend all of it.

It is up to you to practice the Way of the Heart or not. You will not tend to practice if you are weak and unlearned. Therefore, you must learn and become strong first. Then by real practice in devotional relationship to Me, you will grow in Wisdom and strength.

First transcend yourself, then become strong via your reception of My Spiritual (and always Blessing) Presence, My Living Baptism. Practice in My Company. If you practice that which you have learned, on the basis of what you have understood, and if you practice on the basis of My Gifts to you, on the basis of What you have received in My Company, My Grace will magnify Itself in your own person and in all your relationships.

*   *   *

Do Not Become Bound Up in the Search for Dominance and Power

SRI DA AVABHASA: Cease to struggle with others and yourself. Do not become bound up in the usual search for dominance, consolation, pleasure, and release. There is neither Final Release nor Ultimate Happiness in the objective or the subjective realms of merely conditional existence.

The Liberator (Eleutherios)

* * *

Do not manipulate others.

* * *

The essential motive of a human being is to be universally attractive to others, loved by all, served by all, consoled by all. It is the desperate motive of power, the urge to manipulate independent self and others. It is all a symptom of fear—the failure to love beyond all limits.

* * *

The self-based, or self-contracting and self-preserving, conception of existence is manifested via the psychology of fear and conflict relative to all that is not the egoic self. Therefore, the psychology of egocentric existence is inherently disposed to seek control and dominance over all that is not the egoic self. For this reason, individual lives are a constant expression of anxiety, mechanically involved in techniques of self-manipulation (in order to preserve the egoic self) and other-manipulation (in order to control or dominate whatever is not the egoic self).

* * *

I Have Observed That human individuals In The First Three Stages Of Life Tend (Generally Unknowingly) To Relate (or React) To all persons (and Especially intimates, and Presumed rivals) of the Same sex As they Did (or Do) To their own parent (or Otherwise Principal early-life relation) of the Same sex. . . . Relations With all persons (and Especially the parent, and Also intimates, and Presumed rivals) of the Same sex Generally Tend To Be Associated With The Basic Struggle To Acquire A Powerful self-Image, An egoic Center Of Strength, or The egoic Ability To Compete (and, Thereby, To Survive, and Even To Dominate).

The Dawn Horse Testament

* * *

The usual man or woman, weak in love, seeks to control. The usual man or woman seeks knowledge, solutions, and power—to control what is beyond knowledge and beyond the waking or verbal states of mind. Such a person is often mean, righteous, rational, blithe, and apparently fearless. Such a person is always weak in love, in sacrifice, in sensual sensitivity, and in understanding of the essentially selfless, or undefinable, nature of the body-mind itself.

* * *

The usual man or woman seeks control by all means, since such a person fears that he or she and even existence itself are out of control. That person makes sublime sighs whenever he or she sees something orderly. But such a one does not understand that all order is an arbitrary design, made of repetitions of like things.

Order is Truth to Narcissus. Narcissus dies for the sake of order. Narcissus dies because of order. He is egoically "self-possessed", possessed of the repetition of everything he wants to continue to be. He repeats himself, literally. He is fixed upon himself, the symbol of certainty. At last, unable to yield to what is more than independent self, below thought, above thought, outside the thinker, he contracts upon himself, imploded on the instant of thinking.

* * *

A common misunderstanding of teachers and parents is that children are supposed to feel they are the center of everyone's life, almost to the point that they begin to think they are the center of the universe. There is no reason why that tendency should be reinforced in anyone, adult or child. Even at a very young age there is no cause for children's thinking they are the center of everyone's world. They must be brought into relationship with others. They must be served to move out of their independent self-involvement into the condition of relationship.

* * *

In your egoity, you tend not to presume the open, non-egocentric Divine Self-Condition and to allow the energy of life to flow through you in mutual interdependence with all other living beings. Rather, you attempt in every moment to draw all attention to the false and presumed "self" at the apparent center of experience, in order to reinforce the illusion of its existence. Every practice in the Way of the Heart acts to break through this self-enclosure by restoring you in body, emotion, and mind to the condition of relationship.

* * *

There is no game in God, no awful demand for clever victory in the world or in the inward domain. The eyes may remain open, and the body may move about, but Divine Self-Realization is always a matter of simple, direct, Ecstatic Heart-Identification with Me, the Love-Blissful Divine Person, Who is Alive as the world, Active as the body, Conscious as the mind, and Existing as the Heart of every being.

* * *

Do not imagine that you must have absolute knowledge before you will become Happy, participate freely, submit yourself, be a receiver and a transmitter. Live in My Love-Bliss, in Inherent Happiness now.

* * *

As My devotee in the Way of the Heart, once you are Awakened to the Wisdom of a self-transcending, or ecstatic, practice in relationship to the process of experience, then you gradually cease to indulge the automaticities of stress, self-indulgence, and exaggerated

efforts to know and to accomplish and to be overwhelmingly powerful in the world. You do not, however, turn upon yourself and
away from the relational patterns of experience. Rather, you simply
feel through and beyond the stress of events—you acknowledge the
component of self-binding contraction in every moment of experience and transcend that compressive force in direct relaxation of the
patterns arising in the body-mind.

*   *   *

You are mortal. And the only victory you have on Earth is your
devotion to Me.

*   *   *

CHAPTER 31

The True Politics of Human Relationships

SRI DA AVABHASA: No individual should live as the superior, or the inferior, or even the equal, of all others. Rather, each should live as the intimate servant of others through love. The true politics of human relationships is the politics of servants everywhere—every one serving, and every one served.

* * *

Some individuals feel superior, and others feel inferior, and some alternate between the two. Whatever your characteristic strategy of reluctance, it is not Ishta-Guru-Bhakti Yoga.

The Hymn Of The True Heart-Master,
"I Am Grace Itself" section

* * *

I said to some among you recently that My true devotee is nobody—not a climber, not a self-seeker, not a person designed by tendency to be prominent—although My devotee could be any of those. No one is inherently disqualified, but such social signs are not the measure. The humblest are the greatest. Those who relinquish the ego are the greatest.

There are all kinds of strengths in human beings. Anyone can be strong. But remarkably enough, those who may seem weakest, according to the standards of ego-survival, may potentially be the greatest.

* * *

I Am Realization Itself. Thus, in truly self-surrendering and self-forgetting, and therefore self-transcending, Communion with Me, the Realization is Accomplished, Given to you gratis, for free, immediately. Not that you can get puffed up and feel, "I've already got it because I Contemplate Da Avabhasa". It is not about such self-referring. It is about self-surrender, about self-forgetting, in feeling-Contemplation of Me. This Gift is not an attribute of the ego.

As My devotee, you have the right and the cause and the circumstance to be Happy, but not proud. Realization has nothing to do with you.

* * *

In the Way of the Heart, there is no superior person by virtue of experience, because experience is not the process of Satsang with Me. Satsang with Me is a sacred Condition into Which all My devotees enter and in Which all enjoy the same privilege and responsibility. Therefore, it is your responsibility to love and to be free and to break down the cult of experience, whether you have been My devotee for years or for three and a half days.

When you gather with others of My devotees to study My Wisdom-Teaching, or just to talk with someone who is My devotee, this responsibility I Give you holds at all times. Whoever is leading a study group or some other group in the culture of My devotees is not the authority, although you may tend to make it so and thus reinforce the need in that person to act like an authority, to pretend to be the source.

* * *

In the Way of the Heart, you are always observing that you cannot fulfill the discipline. You are continually being shown the failure of your life, the conventional strategy of your life, the false commitment of your life. Such inspection is what practice of the Way of the Heart is all about. It is not about winning! It is about Truth, Freedom in the Divine Reality! There are no winners in the Divine, none.

You must yield your victory. For most people Spiritual life suggests a kind of effort at the end of which they are supposed to be the hero, the winner, the victor. Such a view is an illusion. The fulfillment of the disciplines in the Way of the Heart is coincident with fulfillment of the Divine Law, which is sacrifice, or love.

* * *

The Way of the Heart is the Way of life in which you lose face in each moment, in which you are My serving devotee, the servant of the Divine Person, dependent upon the Service of the Divine Person. Unless such a literal and conscious and Ecstatic and face-losing affair appears in every moment as your life, you are not doing sadhana in the Way of the Heart.

* * *

I Love all My devotees. I Love each one of My devotees Perfectly. All My devotees have equal access to Me. All My devotees receive My Grace. You cannot get closer to Me by standing in one group or another. All My devotees are intimate with Me.

* * *

Because you live in a so-called egalitarian culture—egalitarian by presumption, anyway—everybody thinks (snaps fingers) "I am ready, I am up to it, I am it, I can read a book, I have got some ideas in my head—that means I am ready for the Ultimate Realization." DIVINE SELF-REALIZATION IS A GREAT WORK! A great doing! And you must humble yourself to do it, surrender yourself, equip yourself with humility and surrender. It is not huffing and puffing, full of words and nonsense! IT IS A GREAT MATTER!

The Way of the Heart, which I have introduced here, will go on and on and on if you will take responsibility for its practice. The Way of the Heart does not come to an end with My physical Lifetime. Likewise, the simple fact that you are in My Company does not mean that you will fulfill the Way of the Heart Ultimately in your present lifetime. Most of you will not. Nevertheless, if you will establish yourself for real, authentically, in the Way of the Heart, you will go on with it during this life and after it. Be grateful that it is so.

Establish your link to Me and to the Way of the Heart for real in this lifetime, and your practice of the Way of the Heart will persist. Stop all your pretenses, in the midst of an unsurrendered life especially. Do you think that just because you can think and become enthusiastic and indulge in grandiose self-imagery it means that you are up to Most Perfectly self-transcending God-Realization? No, it does not! How many great Saints and great Yogis have there ever been? To Realize the seventh stage of life (which is Revealed and

Given only by Me) requires more than Sainthood and mystical Realization—extraordinarily more than that!

You trivialize the God-Realizing process in My Company with your self-imagery. You imagine that just because you are in My Company, Divine Self-Realization is going to happen to you. You can begin that Great Process now, but most of you are not even going to come close to fulfilling it in this lifetime. And lucky for you that it goes on and on, that death is not the end.

Link yourself to Me, and the process will continue, after death and after future embodiments anywhere. Immense time is the context in which you should be My devotee.

*　*　*

There is no righteousness. There is only My Divine Happiness Itself. Go and make morality out of That. Go and make society, community, life, and death out of That. That is My Wisdom-Teaching.

*　*　*

DEVOTEE: I feel so unlovable.

SRI DA AVABHASA: You are unlovable? Out of all these billions here you are selected out to be unlovable? What makes you so damned important? All beings are lovable by those who can love.

*　*　*

In some sense, self-doubt is very amusing. Everybody has experienced it. In the mood of self-doubt, you find yourself to be uniquely unacceptable, uniquely wrong, uniquely incapacitated, incapable, undesirable. Actually, you are merely one among all others. Everyone is in the same circumstance. Nobody is uniquely divorced or divorceable from anything. Such a belief is an illusion, a naive and false presumption.

The opposite belief—megalomania, exaggerated egoity, an exaggerated sense of your own worth—is equally false and ridiculous. Nobody is that good, and nobody is that bad.

*　*　*

What is to be praised about each of you has to do with the Divine Being. What others love in you is not something to doubt or speak negatively about, but neither should you egoically identify with the praiseworthy characteristics. Everyone is in a position to be loved and even praised. Therefore, what is the justification for this ridiculous modesty or this ridiculous self-doubt? Instead of being modest or full of self-doubt, become a lover, become a sacrifice, grant life to others, and let the Beauty that is Truth Shine in your own person.

* * *

DEVOTEE: Sri Gurudev, I am feeling that Your future Work is with those who are ready for the Spiritually activated practice of the Way of the Heart.

SRI DA AVABHASA: My Work is with all My devotees. They are all necessary participants, not just the most advanced or the most mature, the renunciates. All. I Love all My devotees, and I accept and embrace them all in the particularity of their practice of the Way of the Heart.

* * *

You must love one another, have compassion for your limitations and the limitations of others, and forget about the fact that you are not perfect, and neither is anyone else.

* * *

There need not be perfection on Earth for Happiness Itself to Exist. All that is necessary is your Communion with Me, with That Which Is Inherently Perfect.

* * *

Your practice is not a matter of perfecting the body-mind. It is a matter of transcending it. If you transcend the body-mind from moment to moment, it will be transformed and show you signs. It may show you good signs one day, and you may think you are into "wow-ee!" evolution-land. Don't buy it! It will also show you negative signs.

Some day the body-mind is going to die. The natural signs take their time, and the body-mind drops off sooner or later. Consciousness Itself is not fundamentally affected by that event. It is affected in reaction, because of Its feeling of apparent association with conditions, but Consciousness Itself has never changed. It will never be any different than It Is right now. You cannot perfect It. It is simply what It Is. The Divine Is Eternally and Inherently Perfect.

The Hymn Of The True Heart-Master,
"I Am Grace Itself" section

* * *

Most people are hypercritical of others and find it impossible to associate with others truly or even to truly enjoy being alive because life is not perfect yet. Life is not wholly congenial to most people, so they stand back and criticize or simply have nothing to do with it.

A typical fault associated with egoity is that people are not very capable of relationships at any level. As My devotee, you must overcome this fault. You will never find justification in life for loving even one other person or even for being happy. Therefore, you must become wise. You must understand yourself. You must hear Me and see Me and Find Me As I Am, and, if you do, then you will acquire tolerance for the ordeal of life. You will re-acquire the capability for relationships.

The essence of egoity is the avoidance of relationship. The ego inherently contains the hypercritical disposition that results in withdrawal, dissociation, the withholding of love. The withholding of participation in life makes any human individual into a leech on the system of the world, looking for advantage without commitment, feeding off the energy created by the participation of others. Such an individual never becomes a participant in life, never dares to love or tolerate or commit to others, and never dares to make changes.

Instead of dramatizing that fault, as My devotee you must hear Me and see Me. In My Divine Company, you must become a creative participant in the Totality of life, Which is the Divine Reality.

* * *

The Way Of The Heart Is Not the path Of self-Fulfillment (or Of Fulfillment Of the conditional self). Therefore, Neither Is It The Pursuit Of physical, emotional, mental, moral, psychic, or Cosmic self-Perfection (or Of Perfection Of the conditional self). All Ideas (or Ideals) Of self-Perfection (or Of Perfection of the conditional self) Are conventions of egoity, and The Pursuit Of self-Perfection (or Of Perfection Of the conditional self) Is The Epitome Of egoic

Seeking. The Ideal Of self-Perfection (or Of Perfection Of the conditional self) Is Utterly Misplaced. Perfection Is Not A Quality or Sign Of what is conditional (and, Therefore, Necessarily limited, or inherently imperfect). That Which Is (Inherently) Perfect Is That Which Inherently Transcends the imperfect, the limited, and the conditional.

The Way Of The Heart Is Not the path Of self-Negation (or Of Negation Of the conditional self). Therefore, Neither Is It The Pursuit Of Perfect physical, emotional, mental, moral, psychic, or Cosmic self-Purification (or Of Perfect Purification Of the conditional self). All Ideas (or Ideals) Of Perfect self-Purification (or Of Perfect Purification Of the conditional self) Are conventions of egoity, and The Pursuit Of Perfect self-Purification (or Of Perfect Purification Of the conditional self) Is, Like The Pursuit Of self-Perfection (or Of Perfection Of the conditional self) In General, The Epitome Of egoic Seeking, Based On a Misplaced or egoic conception Of What Is Perfect.

The Way Of The Heart Is (Most Simply) The Progressive (and Direct) Practice Of self-Transcendence.

The Dawn Horse Testament

*   *   *

CHAPTER 32

Honor Your Agreements and Obligations

S RI DA AVABHASA: Your word must have the force of a vow, which means you must have more than the mere intention to do something. You must take into account everything you have committed yourself to do and make sure that you have not only the intention to accomplish it but also the means to do so.

* * *

Of course you should be able to change your mind, but in the Way of the Heart there is a practice for doing so that is part of your learning in the first three stages of life. To make such changes you must be in communication with the people with whom you have made an earlier agreement, and then you must change your agreements together.

* * *

The traditional "yamas" (restraints) and "niyamas" (observances), which are the religious and moral foundation of Spiritual life, involve responsibilities relative to mind (or intellect), speech, and body. They include the yamas of internal and external non-violence, truthfulness, non-stealing, celibacy (or sexual self-mastery), and non-covetousness, and the niyamas of internal and external purity, contentment, austerity, study of scriptures (and of the strategies of the egoic self), and worship of, or meditation on, the Divine.

* * *

Duty was always very much specified in the traditional religious cultures of the East. Likewise in the West duty must be specified. Secular obligations must be rounded out, made specific, and not allowed to overwhelm your entire life. Social obligations are fine. They make order, they help everyone to survive. But social obligations are not all there is. It should be understood that social relations are about duty, and they are appropriate, but they are not the whole of life.

Instead of indulging in social relations as if they are the be-all and end-all, instead of acting as though they are all that life is, you should observe your duty. Manifest your right attention to the matters that you must, but do not be totally aberrated by doing so. Do not renounce Me, your True Heart-Master, do not renounce the Way of the Heart, do not become stupid in the face of your ordinary obligations. That is not your duty. That is not what life is about.

As My devotee, from East or West, you should know what the social obligations are for real and not tighten them up so much that you have no freedom to engage in the experiment of life, in real sadhana. Do not allow social obligations to be piled on social obligations so that you are so limited you cannot do sadhana anymore, so that you cannot do anything but be a slave to secular purposes anymore.

It is important that you understand your rights and your real obligations and that you fulfill them. When the time comes, you can even renounce those—if you become a true renunciate.

* * *

CHAPTER 33

Transform Your Speech

S RI DA AVABHASA: Talk less.

* * *

What is true is all that should be said, and only when it is appropriate. Therefore, conserve communication.

* * *

Your speech should sustain you. Your life of speech should be a form of your communication in Communion with Me. Your speech and your eating and your every action should dwell in your feeling-Contemplation of Me.

* * *

The self-indulgent and irresponsible person is not aware that all action, all manifestation, is itself sacrifice. Speech is sacrifice. Sexual activity, even emotional-sexual relationship itself, is sacrifice. All action tends to break the life-current, the sphere of descending and ascending force. Where action is performed, the internal circle of life, or energy, tends to be broken and released temporarily. Do that enough, do it in ignorance and absolutely, and there is only death as a result. Do it intelligently, and it gives life, it generates life through relationship, for relationship is a universal duplication of the internal circle of energy. To sacrifice oneself, or open oneself, into relationship is to realize the greater Form, the true and perfect Circle, the Completion that transcends limited, or separative, individuality. Therefore, true and conscious sacrifice is a form of completion, not of interruption or separation.

The Method of the Siddhas

* * *

I have told you that speech is a form of sacrifice. It is a sacrifice of the life-force. It is not entertainment. People generally talk in order to empty themselves. That is another form of throwing the force out of this contraction so they don't suffer it anymore. Whenever there is speech, whenever there is communication with the environment, whenever there is relationship, whenever there is use of the life-force, it is sacrifice. Sexuality is a form of sacrifice. It <u>does</u> tend to make you empty, unless you know fully how to make use of that process, how to conduct its generative energy into the cycle of regeneration. If I sat here and talked endlessly, occasionally going to sleep and taking food here, the talking alone would eventually kill me. I would die from speech! Any exploitation of the life-force will kill you, and people are in fact dying from this abuse. People are dying from a complex exploitation of the life-force. They don't conduct it. They only <u>use</u> it. They don't refresh themselves. They do not live this circuit of energy even a little bit.

The Method of the Siddhas

* * *

Therefore, the True Heart-Master is Unique in the world. The devotional relationship to the True Heart-Master is the Unique Method of Awakening, provided by the Grace of God to living beings. The practice is to transform the activities and functions of body, mind, and speech into real and constant feeling-surrender to the One Who <u>Is</u> Present in and as the Bodily (Human) Form, the Spiritual (and Always Blessing) Presence, and the Very (and Inherently Perfect) State of the Master of the Heart.

The Hymn Of The True Heart-Master

* * *

When people talk with one another, they often talk about their hard times. They talk about difficulties relative to "money, food, and sex". They meditate on their difficulties through the instrument of social communication. Such social magic is a way of meditating on the failure of life, on one's self-indulgent and irresponsible life of conflict and seeking.

* * *

Speech should be responsible to My constant Blessing-Transmission, rather than betraying My Divine Presence in the service of childish reactivity and degenerative society.

* * *

Honesty is to be highly valued in the Way of the Heart—highly valued.

* * *

Traditionally, one of the primary disciplines is to be truthful, to be true.

* * *

Do not participate in gossip, or casual, negatively suggestive communications about other people. You are not practicing the Way of the Heart if you are only meditating on others' limitations, reinforcing and magnifying them, doing harm to others, and playing "gotcha" games. In the "village life" of conventional society, some sort of ideal form of life is projected onto everyone, and everyone talks about everyone else's failure to live it—and such talk is gossip.

In the Way of the Heart, there is never an appropriate time to casually discuss the failure of someone else's practice or to pass on rumors that suggest such a failure.

* * *

The usual man or woman thrives on irony, on subtle negativity. Until you have been transformed, at least to some degree, by your practice of the Way of the Heart, all your usual humor, so-called, is irony. Most of your conversation is irony. You tend either to be ironic with another, or else to tell another ironic stories about how ironic life is. Or how ironic it all was: "How ironic it was that this and that happened when I was twelve."

Not yet converted at heart, you generally communicate irony, rather than love. The analytical hammering of another, the righteous correcting of another's practice of the Way of the Heart, is a form of irony. And really it is fundamentally unnecessary. You should feel free to correct another when it is appropriate. But if your habit of correcting people becomes a repetitive liturgy, you must observe that you yourself are bound to the principle of irony, or "Narcissus", which is the refusal and withholding of love.

* * *

Do not ever manifest intolerance in your speech and life. You must exhibit tolerance, compassion, love, freedom from egoic "self-possession" in your life, in your speech, in all your acts. This is not a moralistic matter. It is necessary even for survival.

*   *   *

CHAPTER 34

Compassion and Tolerance

SRI DA AVABHASA: You are mortal, and entirely subject to the Mercy of the Divine. You own nothing, and you know nothing. No technique of meditation leads to the Divine Being, and there is nothing to be believed that is the Truth. Rather, you must be touched in your feeling by the unspeakable suffering of this world and return everything to the Self-Existing and Self-Radiant Divine Person.

* * *

So do not be stupid and cruel people. Be a little more humorous and loving, and acknowledge your friends compassionately. All of them are fleshily presented, and dying. All of your women friends, all of your men friends—everyone who lives is dying and is confronted with the most incredible circumstance. All are deserving of your love and compassion, and also of your demand for the discipline of love beyond egoic "self-possession", so that they too can enjoy the intuition of this Happiness.

Everyone is dying. All of these shapes get snuffed out with trembling stupidity and insanity. When the body dies, the brain becomes active for a moment, it begins to show you lighted shapes and to dissolve you beyond the elements. First you get fleshy, and then you get watery, then you get fiery, then you get airy, then you start screaming and nobody can hear you, and the body shakes all over the place, and then you are dead. I certainly wish you could acknowledge it while you are alive. If you can, you will love somebody, and if you cannot, you will not.

Do not pretend that you live in a Disney world of beauty. This life is many-sided, and you do not know what it _is_. And your Happiness depends on the total inspection of this life. Understand the situation you are in and become manly (male or female) on the basis of this observation, so that you may be lovers and friends. Acknowledge this terrible circumstance and be Happy, and stop placing stupid obligations on one another. You exist in a place that is open-ended, an edge to the Eternal, and you are dying. The only way you can comprehend this complication is by sacrificing it and becoming a lover and a friend. Nothing else you may project in your lifetime can change that. You are still a fleshy, homely being that can be crushed by circumstance.

* * *

Weaponry, non-cooperation, delineating your block, your little neighborhood, your nation, in total opposition with everyone else—that is the circumstance on Earth today. It is egoity gone wild. You think you are being rather mild about it because all you propose is to make a little circle with your intimate friends, but such is the principle that is making the politics of the whole Earth. I Call you to self-transcendence, cooperation, benign, compassionate awareness of other human beings and their stresses and their anger. This is what you must manifest. Mark My Words! You have always seen Me do so. You must also do so.

* * *

To live with one another freely you must love, tolerate, and be compassionate toward one another. Therefore, you cannot live with one another dispassionately, abstracted, as in the mood of science or egoity. You must <u>participate</u> in one another.

* * *

Individuals and cultures all stand and change within a single but progressively developing range of characteristic possibilities (or potential stages of life and Realization). The ideas or persuasions of any individual or culture are no more than an illustrative expression of the stage of life (or Realization) that is, to that moment (or in that moment), Realized. Therefore, every one must responsibly examine the Great Tradition that all have inherited. And, by this widest view, every one must understand and transcend the provincialism (or the narrow look) of every merely local (or limited and non-universal) inheritance or view. Indeed, by all of this (and by signs of speech and action), every one (and all) must, for the sake of all, promote the culture of true (universal) tolerance, which understands and positively allows all temporary views, and which Calls every one (and every culture) to true (critical) self-study, and to constant Growth and Out-Growing, and would, at last, be Given the Gift of an even Perfect Understanding.

The Basket of Tolerance

* * *

In every relationship and every circumstance, you must overcome your hypercritical orientation to others and to yourself, not gleefully or naively but through real self-understanding and understanding of others, so that you become tolerant.

* * *

You think that you are not going to make a difference. What you do does make a difference. Only people such as you can make the difference, by rising up and refusing the impulse to non-cooperation, by manifesting the principles in your religion in relation to all other religions, by manifesting the principle of compassion, cooperation, love. Manifest that in your personal life every day, or you are only supporting the destructiveness that is going on all over the world. You are alive at a critical time in this Kali Yuga. Am I asking too much?

* * *

All My devotees in all the communities around the world must voice, manifest, and demonstrate this point of view, this devotion, this acceptance of the law, this tolerance.

My principal Communication about the Great Tradition is *The Basket of Tolerance*. There is not a word in it of separateness, of hatred, of non-allowance of people and their traditions. If people want to choose Me, fine. If they want to choose something different, fine. Everyone should really choose his or her tradition, because those traditions, if you understand their right principle, are about cooperation, about tolerance, about living with one another, not about drawing the lines around.

* * *

The only ultimate "purity" is egoless Awakening to the Divine Self-Condition, Which Is Beyond or Eternally Prior to birth, change, experience, knowledge, and death. As long as you are manifested as an apparent individual in conditional Nature, you are necessarily "impure", neither good nor evil but a dynamic character moved by the inevitable two-sidedness of every function, every motion, and every event.

Therefore, My Wisdom-Teaching is also a plea for tolerance— tolerance for the proper "impurity" of human beings in the realm of conditional Nature, tolerance for human functions, human differences, human impulses, and human complexity, personal and social.

The Way of the Heart is not a matter of any righteous effort toward self-purification. It is a matter of freedom from that effort. Neither is it an evil or immoral life. The Way of the Heart is simply a matter of understanding what the right principle of life is from the point of view of Truth, through feeling-Contemplation of Me. On the basis of that principle, you become tolerant of others and tolerant of your own humanity.

* * *

As My devotee, you must know the difference between the Way of the Heart, which you practice, and the practice of some other. Knowing that difference, you should love others, tolerate others, bless others.

* * *

Tolerance is a sign you must manifest in the circumstance of "difference". Yes, maintain the integrity of your point of view and do the necessary and happy things you must do to survive as the gathering of My devotees, but also be tolerant. Make gestures of friendship to all other beings and all traditions, all schools, all Teachers, all Masters, everyone.

* * *

Do not yourself participate in separative movements, whether they be apparently Free Daist movements or any other kinds of movements. Your obligation as My devotees collectively is to manifest the sign of tolerance, truthful communication, cooperative living.

* * *

Sexual preferences, not only your preferences for sexual partners of the same sex or for sexual partners of the opposite sex but your preferences for anyone you want to be sexual with, are governed by all kinds of experiences—genetic inheritance, shocks, suffering, all kinds of things. What difference do your sexual preferences make—as long as acting upon those preferences does not harm anyone? Why should there be any intolerance at all of people's sexual inclinations? Such intolerance is insanity.

If you know the Sacred History of the years of My Teaching Work with My devotees, I Demonstrated to you total acceptance, total tolerance. I included you absolutely. You all, however, engaged in gross intolerances, non-acceptance and abuse. I allowed you all of your inclinations so that you could observe yourself, to know yourself and manifest whatever you are about. I skillfully related to you in every kind of circumstance for twenty years.

Now I Call you simply to do the sadhana of the Way of the Heart in the midst of the mixture of arbitraries that determine your design of preferences, your form of mind. You must plow through the mechanical destiny that your mind shows in every moment's preference. Therefore, you must exhibit great tolerance for one another.

* * *

You must be canny, real, and practical, as well as full of tolerance and love and wisdom.

* * *

You must, as individuals and as the community of My devotees, magnify the impulse toward tolerance and the requirement that people be sane and not opposed to one another. Adhering to a particular religious or social tradition is no justification for killing people. As soon as killing people becomes justified, there is genocide on a grand scale, as has been seen everywhere in the world in the twentieth century.

* * *

There is nothing lesser about people of any color—white, black, yellow, red, anything. Never size up race against race, tradition against tradition. Devotees should never indulge in that ritual of common society. You should demand tolerance, love, cooperation—that is your business on Earth.

* * *

CHAPTER 35

Bless All Others

SRI DA AVABHASA: In the Way of the Heart each one is responsible to bless all others. Therefore, as My devotee, bless everyone and everything with every action, every thought, and every breath. It is not possible to bless another by presuming a position of superiority for yourself or inferiority on the part of another. To bless another one must worship and acknowledge that one in his or her True Form, inhering in the Divine Reality, present as an expressive manifestation of the Divine Being.

Therefore, whatever your stage of life in the Way of the Heart, bless all others in feeling-Contemplation of Me, serve every being as the modification of the Divine Reality that I Reveal to you, acknowledge every being and condition in the "Brightness" of My Divine Company, and address everyone and everything in the same spirit in which you acknowledge Me. Only in this manner are you free in Satsang with Me, invoking and finding Me in, as, and through every being and condition.

Be My devotee, in Communion with Me. See all in Communion with Me. Through feeling-Contemplation of Me, worship the Divine Being, Truth, and Reality in, as, and through everyone and everything. Never be too proud to do this worship. Only this expresses true Realization.

* * *

My True Devotees Become Prayerful Instruments For conditional Changes That Serve their own human Well-being, self-Transcending Practice, and Most Ultimate (or Truly Divine) Self-Realization (and Also The human Well-being, self-Transcending Practice, and Most Ultimate, or Truly Divine, Self-Realization Of Even all human beings, and Also The Well-being, self-Transcending Practice, and Most Ultimate, or Truly Divine, Self-Realization of Even all conditionally Manifested beings).

The Dawn Horse Testament

* * *

The Prayer of Changes, which is practiced by My devotees in the Way of the Heart, is a resort to Communion with Me and the relinquishment of any negative mind and emotion that identifies with the "problem". It is the release of identification with all negative conditions and the assumption of an entirely right disposition, through Divine Communion.

The Prayer of Changes is the entire relinquishment of identifying with dis-ease or any kind of presumed problem. It is assuming Divine Communion, affirming a wholly right condition, and allowing that wholly right condition to be fully assumed, felt, breathed, and lived.

Therefore, the Prayer of Changes is not merely an interior exercise of pleading with Me for Divine changes. It is Communion with Me, wherein the point of view of the right, or positive, condition is assumed and then felt, breathed, and lived.

Therefore, if, as My devotee, you are really doing the Prayer of Changes, you are <u>doing</u> the changes. You are entering into the condition of Divine Communion such that you are already established in the point of view of the right, or desired, condition and, therefore, you are effective in implementing that right condition.

The Prayer of Changes should be practiced regularly by all My devotees, and it may be practiced in conjunction with daily formal meditative feeling-Contemplation of Me. It should also be done whenever a healing treatment is given, or instead of a healing treatment, perhaps in conjunction with the laying on of hands.

The Prayer of Changes should also be performed regularly by groups of practitioners for the sake of any particular individual or group of individuals, and for the sake of individuals outside the group. When it is done for someone who is not physically present, it is good practice to view the person's photograph, passing it among those who are performing the Prayer, especially if they do not know the person.

* * *

The Apparent individual, or Separate psycho-physical person, Cannot, By ego-Efforts, or in and of himself or herself, Directly Affect and Change any or all conditions, Universally, but, By Consistently Surrendering the ego-"I", and By Rightly Changing the mind, and By Consistently Maintaining the Rightly Changed form, or forms, of mind, The Devotee Of The Spiritual Divine Can, By Grace, Serve The Spiritual Divine, and Cooperate With The Spiritual Divine, and Submit all beings, forms, processes, and things To The Potential Influence Of The Spiritual Divine. And, Thus, By Effectively "getting out of the way", or Removing The mental, and Otherwise egoic, Obstacles To The Divine Spiritual Infusion Of conditional events, and By Generating Entirely Positive and Intensely Auspicious and Profoundly Felt mind-forms, The Devotee Of The Spiritual Divine Can Cooperatively <u>Allow</u> The Spiritual Divine To Pour Into, and To Directly and Newly and Positively Affect and Change, any particular condition, or conditions, At All.

The Dawn Horse Testament

* * *

PART V

Cooperative Community

CHAPTER 36

You Are My Gift to You:
Cooperative Community
in the Way of the Heart

SRI DA AVABHASA: Formal cooperative community (to the maximum degree possible for the individual) is <u>necessary</u> and <u>fundamental</u> to the Way of the Heart.

The Da Love-Ananda Gita,
"I <u>Am</u> (My Self) What you Require" section

* * *

Cooperative, human-scale community is the political, social, and cultural root-source of civilization. Cooperative, human-scale community is also the primary political, social, and cultural condition that civilization tends to destroy. Therefore, the struggle to re-establish cooperative, human-scale community, and, in turn, to re-establish, within the larger political, social, and cultural order, the virtues characteristically associated with cooperative, human-scale community, is the constant necessity and the principal political, social, and cultural revolution whereby civilization can be purified of its negative effects, and whereby the integrity of civilization (and of civilized people) can be restored. . . .

The negative evidence of the present global civilization is obvious at every physical and human level of the world—so much so that mankind has now clearly entered into a dark and darkening phase, with great potential for every kind of disaster, and yet, if truly humanizing Wisdom and real Divine Grace are accepted, with an equally great, and even greater, potential for a lightening, and more and more Divine, transformation. It is not necessary that I describe all the negative signs and mixed signs of the present civilization. Let each one enumerate the signs for himself or herself, and feel the human wound at heart. . . .

Of course, some have, in the present context of civilization, already tried to revolutionize their "civilized" lives by engaging efforts toward human-scale community. Those efforts or experiments have met with varying degrees of practical and human success to date. However, far more is required to achieve cooperative, human-scale, and truly humanizing community than present and past experimenters generally suppose or have supposed. For example, in the present ego-bound context of global civilization, there is a general tendency for community experimenters to try to create community on the basis of the same egoic principles that otherwise characterize the present civilization itself. Thus, present-time community experimenters generally try to create community on the (supposedly egalitarian) basis of the motives of competitive individualism (or egoity itself), even though they also want to establish cooperative principles and cooperative structures. As a result, experimental community efforts often are degraded and defeated by competitiveness, the tendency to pander to egoic preferences and egoic dramatizations (often in the name of egalitarian idealism), and a characteristic fear of (or a rather adolescent rebellion against) authority, hierarchy, and the hierarchical culture of respect (which are necessary to any truly human and cooperative community order).

There is a profound difference between true (and necessarily sacred) community and mere practical (political, social, and cultural) communalism (whether such is viewed to be secular or religious or even sacred in its nature and intention). A cooperative, human-scale, and truly humanizing community is necessarily and truly sacred, rather than merely secular (or otherwise not truly sacred). That is to say, such a community is necessarily based on the motive of self-transcendence (rather than on the motive of self-fulfillment), and, therefore, it is not based on the search to satisfy the ego-"I" and the egoic motives of any of its members, but it is based on the devotion of each and all of its members to That Which inherently transcends each and all.

True community is necessarily <u>one</u>-pointed. That is to say, it is not focused in service to (and fulfillment of) egos (or whatever is

THE INCARNATION OF LOVE

many and separate), but in service to (and Realization of) That Singleness Which inherently transcends egoity and every limitation. The Real does not rotate around each and all, but each and all are Called and Obliged to surrender self and to forget self in participatory Communion with the all-transcending, all-pervading, all-embracing, and necessarily Divine Reality. And it is only the response to this Call and Obligation that can purify and restore mankind, one by one, each and all, by means of the benign and truly humanizing political, social, and cultural revolution that is the establishment of truly sacred and truly cooperative human-scale communities (and, by extension, the transformation of even the entire global civilization itself into a cooperative, rather than a merely competitive, world-order).

The Basket of Tolerance

* * *

Free men and women must create a refuge, or human sanctuary, for their growth, and this is not done in personal isolation, but only in intimate cultural cooperation.

* * *

There is no such thing as true religion without cooperative community. The sacred community is the necessary theatre wherein true religious responsibilities and activities can take place.

* * *

When I Speak to you about the discipline of cooperative community, I am Speaking to you very <u>realistically</u> about a condition of practice that, if rightly (and progressively) embraced, should increase the potential for Divine Self-Realization in the case of each and every practitioner of the Way of the Heart.

The Da Love-Ananda Gita,
"I <u>Am</u> (My Self) What you Require" section

* * *

True religion is not just the practice of community in itself. It is the practice of Divine Communion in community.

* * *

The internal business of the community of My devotees is the relationship to Me, the True Heart-Master. Wherever that is forgotten, offended, suppressed, minimized, made artificial, not served, the gathering of My devotees fails to be a true community. Therefore, Satsang with Me is the prize of the community of My devotees.

* * *

What I call "cooperative community" is the structure of discipline wherein (especially) the householder's way of life is structured in a specifically renunciate manner, and altogether made into a circumstance of life suitable for sadhana and real growth.

The Da Love-Ananda Gita,
"I Am (My Self) What you Require" section

* * *

You are called to live the practice of the Way of the Heart in cooperative community, but not because community itself is some sort of ideal or utopian circumstance or even possibility. The living community of My devotees is a form of sadhana. Its purpose, then, is self-transcendence and Divine Self-Realization Most Ultimately. Those who live this sadhana of cooperation in community with one another in the Way of the Heart are animating their commitment to Most Perfectly self-transcending God-Realization, and they are serving that possibility in one another.

* * *

If, as My devotee, you are truly practicing the discipline of cooperative community that I have Given you, then, as in your devotional groups you serve to increase one another's devotion to Me, so also in your daily life you give one another more and more opportunity, more and more time, more and more focus for truly God-Realizing practice. You accomplish things cooperatively, whereas if you left one another to your private householder games, you would basically be spending your life forever trying to organize and improve your ordinary social limitations and obligations. Nothing would be simplified, nothing resolved.

You must serve one another's true practice of Ishta-Guru-Bhakti in devotional relationship to Me, and you must understand the difference between truly God-Realizing sadhana and social religiosity.

189

Social religiosity is exoteric religion, socially based religion, more or less utopian seeking to fulfill the separate individual. That is not the Way of the Heart. That is not true sadhana in My Company. That is not esoteric Spiritual practice.

* * *

The community of My devotees should essentially be an environment where people live together who practice the Way of the Heart and serve one another.

* * *

The principal admonition of the Great Tradition has always been, "Spend time in 'Good Company'." Satsang, the Company of the Realizer and the company of those who love the Realizer, is the most auspicious association. As My devotee, absorb that Company in Satsang with Me. Imbibe it. Drink deep of it. Duplicate it.

* * *

The community of My devotees is in itself a form of meditation, a form of devotion to Me. Therefore, when My devotees come together, they tend to turn one another quite naturally to Me, to Satsang with Me. Individually, they tend to become associated with their dramas, their changes, their limitations. But as soon as they enter into one another's company, it is as if they were reminding one another of Satsang with Me, even though they might not outwardly be saying anything about it.

That reminder in itself is meditation. Therefore, you naturally feel it more strongly at those times of gathering. At those times you are entering into the company of many others in whom the devotional relationship with Me is active, perhaps in a different way than it is in your own case. Limitations that may be yours may not be active in some of the others, so you feel the Siddhi of My Blessing Company more purely represented to you at those times, because your own limitations are transcended by My Divine Grace as it freely appears in others. Just so, there may be areas in yourself that are not obstructed, but that are obstructed in others, and those others feel the Power of Satsang with Me more intensely because of your presence, or the presence of several like you.

* * *

True religion (in any and every stage of life) is always and necessarily and inherently a practice and a process that originates, develops, and continues to develop only in the context of a living and effectively functioning religious <u>community</u> (which, as a "culture of expectation and inspiration", must nurture, stimulate, support, guide, and direct, and thus both inform and test, the individual's religious practice and process).

The Basket of Tolerance

*　*　*

The community of My devotees is not supposed to be devoted to problems in people. The community of My devotees should at least be made up of real beginners, real practitioners of the preliminary disciplines in the Way of the Heart, who can help one another, who constantly support one another in their understanding, their real process of freeing energy and attention from self-bondage and from the presumed problems of existence.

*　*　*

You must find the ways to overcome the stresses of lower adaptation, to transform the chemistry of the body-mind literally, so that you can live your daily life without personal, social, cultural, and chemical stress. Such a life is not possible for a group of people until they manage to create sanctuary with one another—a mutually protected, stable, basically unthreatened way of life.

*　*　*

"We are threatened!" is the message of the news. It reminds you of your chronic situation. The theatre of the news is all about people who are threatening one another, either with terrible violence or with just plain social nastiness, exploiting one another to death. Human beings constantly reinforce loveless society in their associations with one another. You teach each other, and you pass on to your children all the techniques for living as a stressful personality. The usual person believes bodily, stressfully, that his or her life cannot, even should not, be long, that it is not good to be alive in the body, that human beings are only supposed to go elsewhere.

You harbor all these ideas that are life-negative in bodily terms, but Divine Enlightenment is to become <u>life-positive</u> in bodily terms, which is just the reverse of what you are tending to do. Human

191

beings are living way down at the bottom of their evolutionary potential. Nevertheless, if you, as My devotee, can personally, and with a few others, grasp the greater realities of the mechanisms in which you live, then you can practice a Way of life that stimulates and develops those greater factors.

You must have sanctuary, a relatively protected world, in which to do that, because, if you are going to rise above the civilization of the daily news, you must live in a manner that is superior to the way that people in general tend to live.

* * *

I used to point out that this gathering around Me, this community of a kind, even though it is not only imperfect but rather chaotic, is nevertheless useful. Although I criticized it more intensely than anyone, I also defended the community circumstance of My devotees when people became petulant or angry about it. Among its functions, and this is a great service, was to provide the opportunity for people to transcend themselves. After all, self-transcendence is the essence of what My devotees are involved in.

* * *

To live in the formal cooperative circumstance with others requires you to transcend your separate and separative ego-self, no doubt. Therefore, in the Way of the Heart, self-transcendence (in the case of each and all) is also the function and purpose of cooperative community.

The Da Love-Ananda Gita,
"I <u>Am</u> (My Self) What you Require" section

* * *

Community is the natural condition of all true spiritual activity. . . . I intend for this Teaching always to be displayed in relationship, because it is only in relationship that it begins to make any sense, that it begins to show itself. So there must be this functional confrontation with the Teaching by those who are using it. That confrontation is the <u>use</u> of it.

The Method of the Siddhas

* * *

An inevitable discipline is community, if one awakens beyond the principle of egoity. Therefore, as My devotee, you cure egoity, transcend it, work beyond it through the discipline of community or the opportunity to do that most creatively and effectively with those who are similarly inclined to the Way of the Heart. You must express that discipline in all relationships. You must overcome yourself, transcend yourself, in all relationships.

* * *

The sadhana of the religious life, and, in due course, of the Spiritual life, in the Way of the Heart is necessarily associated with cooperative community. In other words, it impinges on your life of relatedness and requires the discipline in relationship, requires you to discipline egoity in the context of relationship, egoity and separateness, self-isolation.

* * *

Suffering is felt, seen, experienced from day to day essentially in vital terms by human beings. The best "cave" is an ordinary life, a relational life, a functional life. That is where you find your discipline, that is where you become strong, that is where you become truly responsible for yourself. Relationships are the best circumstance of spiritual practice. Intimate relationships, functional conditions, these are the best "Bodhi Tree". These are the true "ascetic" practices.

The Method of the Siddhas

* * *

As renunciates in times past lived together in renunciate communities, ashrams, and hermitages, you, by your cooperation in community with one another, will relieve one another of many of the limitations imposed upon human beings by the demands of ordinary life, and, by sharing the burdens of even all the ordinary demands of life, you will give one another the gift of time for sacred cultural practice.

The Da Love-Ananda Gita,
"I Am (My Self) What you Require" section

* * *

It is good to live in community and develop cooperative systems, to get out of the ego mold, or the mold of the accumulator, the successful capitalist or communist, the successful ego that accumulates, stuffs himself or herself with everything from worldly goods to food to beliefs and phony ideals of all kinds.

*   *   *

My devotees must come to a point of understanding that to become My devotee, to become a member of this Communion, implicitly and explicitly involves them in an obligation to engage a total Way of life in relation to all My other devotees, and in relation to the world. Whatever their position or circumstance in the world, they must move into the society of this Communion and transcend the mind of "me and my castle, me and my ego alone, bodily fulfilling myself", and see how the law of cooperation, mutuality, and relationship, rather than independence, changes their relationship to the use of money, ownership, and land. My devotees must understand free cooperative association as the structure wherein all the goods of life exist.

*   *   *

The <u>fundamentals</u> of life must be pre-solved at the local level, at the regional level where the cooperative community exists. Within the community, every member should be guaranteed access to the basic necessities of life (provided each individual functions responsibly and cooperatively within the community). Basic solutions to human needs do not generally require resort to any of the resources of the State, but they should be managed locally in one's own community, and in natural cooperation with other communities. (In other words, first establish community and the planned solutions to fundamental needs, and, on that basis, see what kind of agreements are useful in cooperation with other communities and with large-scale cooperative agencies.)

*   *   *

People in cooperative community are yet "individuals", and, in general, they must each have their "families". Families and households also (naturally) have, to some degree, their own unique interests and purposes, or (sometimes) their own unique uses of time (and even of income)—that is all fine. Nevertheless, fundamentally (and relative to all matters), the principles of renunciation, simplification, and cooperation must be embraced and consistently demonstrated by every practitioner (and by every family or household) within every formally acknowledged cooperative community gathering of formally acknowledged practitioners of the Way of the Heart.

The Da Love-Ananda Gita,
"I <u>Am</u> (My Self) What you Require" section

* * *

To create a human sanctuary for greater adaptation and the ultimate transcendence of Man is a true urge, even the primal human urge. Human beings inherently desire a truly human and natural environment in which they can live without the chronic production of stress chemistry. Human beings want to be cured at the heart of their mind and thereby transformed bodily. And they know, deeply, psychically, that they cannot Realize that transformation until they can create a culture in which people can live without degenerative stress. Thus, sanctuary, or Spiritual community, is the motive in Man that contains the genetic secret of the next stage in human evolution.

* * *

On Sri Da Avabhasa's first trip to India in April 1968, He visited the small town of Mulund, just outside Bombay. His first impression was that the town was "a little dirt-road village with crowds of people—not a beautiful place". Taken to a small apartment building where He would spend the night, Heart-Master Da showered and then climbed the stairs to the roof of the building. In 1988, twenty years later, He described to His devotees what He saw from the roof:

SRI DA AVABHASA: As I came to the top of the stairs and onto the roof, the orientation was to the back of the building, whereas on the road I had approached the building from the front and the crowded, noisy town. Looking out in the opposite direction from the roof, then, I saw a completely different physical environment.

There was no way I could have presumed that anything like what I saw existed in this town. It was a large square with green at the perimeter. Everything was cleanly trimmed. There were decorative trees and plants and flowers everywhere, and walkways through a large park where a few people were calmly walking about, all of them very crisply and cleanly dressed in a style of clothing I suppose is characteristic of this group. They were all well washed and clean in their nice evening dress—families, women and children and men, walking together very calmly. There was no sound, no noise at all, in the park—whereas it was all noise beyond at the front side of the building.

The park was a picture of serenity and order, of people who lived effectively, people who could choose a way of life and by coopera- tion with one another command the quality of life that they chose.

It was quite different from what one sees elsewhere, in the little dirt-road towns that are called "cities" in the world, with all the noise and chaos of "put up with whatever your neighbor feels like doing" and "we all just do our thing". In such places, everybody puts up with what everybody else is doing. You hang a picture or set out a little vase of flowers, put in earplugs, and try, in your sheerest privacy and in the smallest space that you can call your own, to create something of the order of your own choosing.

Very few people have the chance to choose an order together, a way of life that is based on the Truth. Rather, everyone is wander- ing, doing their thing, ego-wise, and disturbing everyone else.

One of the virtues, then, of My devotees' choosing to practice the Way of the Heart together is that you can command the quality of space and time, at least on a much larger scale than you could otherwise, and more surely. If you do that, then your environments can become beautiful places where that order, that serenity, that quality of life that you live in My Company is shown, as well as places that are a sign of God-wardness and Divine Awakeness, or the Process that Awakens toward God and in God, and Most Ultimately As God.

* * *

A very powerful individual can make great changes, and so also can a gathering of people in a right disposition. The communi- ty of My devotees, therefore, will be very effective, more effective than a single individual of minimal Spiritual development. This is another reason why it is so important for the community of My devotees to grow in size and for the individuals within it to cooper- ate intentionally with one another relative to changes of all kinds, including the will to Divine Enlightenment for all.

* * *

You can assume a mutually dependent condition as soon as you see that there is something intelligent about doing that. You run into many difficulties, of course, because your entire life below the conscious mind is devoted to this private destiny, this affair of "Narcissus". It is filled with all kinds of equipment and strategies devoted to that end.

Therefore, as soon as you assume the discipline of relationship as your condition of life, you are going to see manifested in you all of these other urges and principles and strategies and demands.

*　*　*

Many of you have at one time or another expressed to me your feelings about organized spirituality, organized religion, whatever. People commonly have negative and resistive feelings toward all forms of community and human relationships. And the reason, the ultimate root of these feelings, is the tendency towards separation itself. In a certain sense you can see that it is completely justified. There is a great deal about organized spiritual and common life worthy to be resisted! On the other hand, Truth is manifested only in this relational condition, and It is perceived in relationship. It is a crisis that occurs in relationship. Therefore, the community of Truth, the community that lives this Teaching, is absolutely necessary. But what makes it a thing to resist is your lack of involvement in it, your separation from it, your dramatized resistance to relational and community life. The spiritual community must be alive. Every one must be alive within it. Every one must be active in relationship and must function within it. So if you do become active, responsible, alive, and intimate with others who are living this way, the whole sensation of resistance to so-called "organized" spiritual life will disappear, because you will be dealing with the problem of community only as that which it truly is: an expression of your own avoidance of relationship. But if you do not live this way, if you do not move into functional relationship to this way, you will only see it externally. Everywhere you will only see your reasons for separating from the Guru, the Teaching, and the community, because you will have made it into something without life, something worth resisting. Therefore, it is the responsibility of those in this Ashram to live this way, to become active in it, to use it, and to become responsible for it.

The Method of the Siddhas

*　*　*

Truly human politics is in the sphere of relationships, experienced on a daily basis, where the individual's voice and experience can be heard and dramatically felt.

* * *

I have described the practice of the Way of the Heart in the context of what I call a "cooperative democracy", in which men and women are, in principle, politically, economically, and socially free. Therefore, as a matter of your practice of the Way of the Heart, you must demonstrate this principle. I presume the liberated state of women. It is part of My fundamental address to women. Likewise, I presume the liberated state of men. Now, My devotees, both men and women, must presume it about themselves, and, therefore, they must enact it in daily life.

* * *

As My devotee, give yourself up to practice of the Way of the Heart in community rather than living as an ego in a conventional model of society. Everyone, whether male or female, should enjoy the benefits of the community of My devotees. Women should not need an intimate partner to survive in the community of My devotees. Women should live equally with men. Women are more domestic when they have young children, but the responsibility for older children is shared by the community.

Single women or women separated from a relationship should be able to work and survive simply in the community without any problems whatsoever. The community, and not the household or the game of couples, should be the economic unit for My devotees. Therefore, women should not depend on their intimate partners for financial support. Women should make their own money and share in the economic support of the community.

In the community of My devotees, men and women should function on an equal basis. Women should not depend on or exploit men. Women should not be in a position to be owned by men. Women should function freely and freely make the life that they choose. The medieval and ego-based householder model does not have a function in the Way of the Heart, and it certainly does not have an economic function.

* * *

At one time in the past, the town meeting was a common model of local government, whereby all men and women could participate in decisions that affected everyone. At such meetings, people decided together how to fulfill their mutual obligations in the community.

That is how the community of My devotees and the culture of the Way of the Heart must operate.

*   *   *

There must be regular meetings of the entire collective body of My devotees, at which all the workings of the community are fully disclosed and decisions are made on how to improve things. Each and all of My devotees must participate fully in these meetings.

*   *   *

It is not that people come together to decide the Principles, Callings, and Agreements of the Way of the Heart. I have Given My Instruction, and, as My devotee, you are here to fulfill My Instruction. Of course, various details can be proposed to Me for My further "Consideration".

There should not be any petty factions struggling with one another and imitating the models of conventional democracy. I Call each and all of My devotees—and not just a group of administrators, managers, and leaders—to full participation in the community.

*   *   *

For the sake of making things work, the membership of the community of My devotees must represent themselves through a group of individuals who are specifically trained in administration, management, and leadership. The community of My devotees must function in a manner that I describe as "cooperative democracy" and always handle the business of the community without fail.

*   *   *

The "herd mentality" of passivity and weakness is childish and dependent. It is the pose of the "sheep", and it must not be permitted within the culture of My devotees. Likewise, independence, adolescence, and high visibility of someone in charge (which is the pose of the "wolf") must always be addressed and undermined within the culture of My devotees.

*   *   *

As My devotee, stop living like one of the herd and leaving the creation of your community life to a few spokesmen. Everyone must be involved in the life of this community. Do not relinquish your life to the decisions of a few, and never allow a failure.

*   *   *

My devotees are to maintain their integrity by virtue of their devotion to Me and their adherence to My Heart-Word. What is needed is not conventional leadership but a truly cooperative gathering, where My devotees meet one another on an equal basis and transcend themselves by devotion to Me and strict adherence to My Heart-Word.

Those who fulfill certain cultural responsibilities are not superior, nor should they be viewed as leaders in any conventional sense. Only the true renunciates among My devotees, those who are worthy of a greater position in the culture of My devotees by virtue of their real devotion and submission to Me, are qualified to be addressed as leaders in the culture of the Way of the Heart.

Although such renunciates may serve the culture as a whole to intensify everyone's devotion to Me and adherence to My Heart-Word, the worldwide culture of My devotees must always be undermining the tendency of people to make themselves cultural insiders.

*   *   *

You all, as My devotees, are My Gift to you. You have My Silent Person here, My Heart-Word, that always Speaks to you, in Eternal Conversation. I Give you the Gift of one another, My devotees together, to make a culture of "inspiration and expectation".

*   *   *

CHAPTER 37

A Visit to the Optometrist

A STORY OF SRI DA AVABHASA'S LIBERATING INSTRUCTION
by Cathy Lewis

W hen I first came to Sri Gurudev Da Avabhasa (then Bubba Free John) in 1974, I was immature in almost every dimension of human life, but particularly in the emotional dimension, and Sri Da Avabhasa expanded and Instructed me in so many different ways. One of these ways was through service, and through requiring me to put out energy. Since I am a rather sedentary and lazy person, for me this demand was not an easy one. A moment of crisis came on a Saturday when I was serving in our food co-op. I was being a very reluctant server and very grumpy because I did not want to be there. I wanted to be doing something for myself.

I went home for lunch and fell asleep listening to an audiotape of one of Sri Gurudev's Talks. I dreamed that I was struggling against someone. Someone was holding me from behind, and I was desperately trying to get away. At one point it occurred to me that maybe I should find out who I was struggling to get away from. I slowly turned around and found that it was Sri Da Avabhasa Who was holding me! Instead of struggling, I relaxed back into His Body, and I experienced the most profound feeling of His Love-Bliss.

When I awoke from that dream, my relationship to service had changed dramatically. From then on I experienced real pleasure in my service, because I could feel that Sat-Guru-Seva is direct service to my Guru and not just "work". My first layer of resistance to service had been undone, but the emotional dimension in me was still very much locked up.

One evening at a gathering with Sri Da Avabhasa, I was sitting alone in a corner of the room, feeling very sorry for myself. It seemed to me that everyone else was very socially adept, talking and laughing with Sri Da Avabhasa, but I felt shy and awkward and inadequate even to carry on a conversation with my Sat-Guru. I felt He could never love me.

Just at the moment of my thinking this, someone called me to come over to where Sri Da Avabhasa was sitting and talking with His devotees. As I approached Him, I noticed that He was also talking with one of my housemates, a young man named Fred, whom I regarded as a very eccentric person.

The first thing Sri Gurudev said was, "This man says that he is attracted to you. Do you feel any attraction for him?" My heart sank. I became very afraid, because I definitely did not feel attracted to this man and I did not want to get involved with him in any way! Would the Guru ask me do something I did not want to do?

"No, Bubba, I am not attracted to this man," I said very righteously and emphatically.

"Who are you attracted to, then?" Sri Gurudev asked.

"No one but you, Bubba," I replied, with a little fear.

"Well, you'd better get attracted to somebody," He said playfully. "I can't marry everybody!" As He was talking with me, I could feel His Love for me very strongly, and I was lifted out of concern for myself.

Then Sri Da Avabhasa did a most wonderful thing. He Instructed me on how to enter into a relationship of service with Fred. He said, "Cathy, I have been looking at this young man, and he has the most ugly glasses, don't you agree?" I agreed without hesitation. "I would like you to go with Fred to an optometrist and pick out a very handsome pair of glasses, something attractive that will make him look good. Will you do that?"

I again agreed emphatically; I was relieved to have such a humble and simple test from my Guru. He did not address my total unlove and inhumanity to Fred; He did not point out how totally shut down I was in the area of human relations; He simply asked me to enter into a relationship of service. Fred also seemed happy with the arrangement.

A few days later Fred and I went downtown together to pick out some glasses. To my amazement, we had a wonderful time. I realized later that I had forgotten all about my righteous reactions to Fred's qualities. I was simply happy to be serving the Guru and to be serving another human being instead of reacting to him. And in this simple act of service, the most ordinary human emotion of love was awakened.

Many times over the years I have remembered this moment of Instruction when My Beloved Heart-Master Da drew me out of myself and showed me that if I keep my attention on Him, the whole quality of my life is transformed. Sat-Guru-Seva is a great Gift, and I am profoundly grateful for every moment that I remember to serve Him, and Him in others, instead of myself.

PART VI

Become a Renunciate by Handling Your Life-Business

CHAPTER 38

Letting Go

A CONVERSATION WITH SRI DA AVABHASA

BROOKS GODWIN, a woman: Sri Gurudev, I would like to speak to You about attachment and dependence.

SRI DA AVABHASA: Hmm.

BROOKS: Over the past few months You have been talking to me about my dependency, and I did not understand altogether what you meant. I was determined to handle, at least superficially, certain aspects that would make me a less dependent character. But during this last week I could feel something underneath that was not just anger but more a fear of my attachment to others and things.

SRI DA AVABHASA: Stop talking generalizations. Just get down to it.

BROOKS: Three days ago my grandmother died. In feeling my love for her and the loss, I felt that in all of my relationships I hold myself apart because I do not want to feel the pain of the relationship and allow myself to release my relations. Either I hold on or I set myself apart. I felt that dichotomy of being either an adolescent or a child in my relationships with people because of the fear of letting myself feel what You call the "wound of love". I do not let myself feel that wound in my relationships.

The day before my grandmother died, you talked to me about grief. It was not even something I was discussing with You in that moment, but You brought up the subject to me and You Gave me the Gift of the tapas of letting go. It was perfect for me to feel it, because the very next day I had to practice the process of letting go.

I also wanted to tell You that I communicated Your Wisdom to my family, and they were very appreciative, Gurudev. They expressed their appreciation for Your Wisdom-Teaching and Your Service in this moment when they had lost a loved-one, and they were very, very grateful. I do not think I have ever had so full a conversation with them when they felt Your Gift so much. I wanted to tell You that.

I do not know what else to say about it. You told me that I remain insensitive, and You have criticized my rigidity and my lack of feeling. I do not want to feel the pain.

SRI DA AVABHASA: Then you are probably more like your friend here [Sri Gurudev indicates a man in the room], not caring about anybody. You put on an air like that, anyway.

BROOKS: I do.

SRI DA AVABHASA: He has to put on an air, too.

BROOKS: I put on an air, but it is not what I am really feeling. I really just try . . .

SRI DA AVABHASA: You talk about love and attachment in the same sentence. [Sri Gurudev pauses.] Perhaps you sometimes confuse the two.

BROOKS: I definitely do.

SRI DA AVABHASA: But attachment is your reason for not loving.

BROOKS: Yes.

SRI DA AVABHASA: Just as soon as you become attached to somebody, even though you have love feelings for the person, you defend yourself against them.

BROOKS: That is true.

SRI DA AVABHASA: Therefore, your attachment is not serving anything. If you agree to become involved in a feeling relationship with someone, you must also agree to endure the changes in the other person and the difficulties in the relationship. Whatever is going on in the other person altogether, you must be able to endure the loss. It all comes with the relationship. The discipline of love is quite a different thing from indulgence in attachment.

What you are saying, stated simply, is that you cannot agree to the conditions of a feeling relationship because you do not want to experience the pain of loss and separation. Therefore, you do not want to experience the difficulties that may occur all along in the relationship.

You are not quite prepared for such relationships, are you? They just sort of happen to you, and you do not really participate in them.

BROOKS: Yes, that is what I have been feeling.

SRI DA AVABHASA: Because your grandmother has died, now you are feeling grief but also stomping on it a little bit at the same time.

BROOKS: Yes.

SRI DA AVABHASA: When the actual loss occurs, you feel it anyway.

BROOKS: Yes.

SRI DA AVABHASA: Therefore, the whole ceremony of resisting such feeling does not work, because inevitably you experience the pain eventually. And it also does not work in ordinary daily life because you immunize yourself against feeling relationships. And attachment—or what you are describing as attachment—is the reason it does not work. You are not capable of real love, real relationship, yet you are allowing yourself to be involved in all kinds of relationships. You are basically just a pain in the ass about all of this.

BROOKS: Yes, that is true, Sri Gurudev.

SRI DA AVABHASA: Um-hmm. What else about it? If letting go is a good idea when somebody dies, why isn't it a good idea all the while?

BROOKS: Even in that loving conversation with my family I immunized myself, even though I felt the most connected to them then. It was a real revelation to me because I could feel all the ways I tend to do that in an ordinary way.

SRI DA AVABHASA: What about other people who are involved in these relationships with you? When do they get some relief from your game? You are not practicing the discipline of love. You are indulging in your own egoic "self-possession" and fear and reluctance and resistance, and you are immunizing yourself. This is what everybody is experiencing in relationship to you.

BROOKS: Yes.

SRI DA AVABHASA: Fundamental to the discipline of love, then, is letting go. You are practicing attachment and using it as an excuse to immunize yourself. The discipline of love requires letting people go. I do not mean letting them disappear. I mean giving them their life, giving them your feeling rather than withholding it, allowing them to grow, supporting their growth, supporting their free process of life. Sometimes people smother their children, in a sense, because they do not practice the discipline of love. Because they are attached and fearful, they suppress their children even though they would not want to do such a thing. They do not allow their children the process of true growth. They do not bring wisdom to the lives of their children. They just practice attachment and resistance, suppression, manipulation. They are afraid for their children to change, afraid for them to do anything that would in the slightest bit endanger them.

I am sure you know people who have done that with children. Since you were all children in relation to your parents and who knows who else, you probably have had that very experience, in fact. So also in all other relationships of a feeling kind, or that should be of a feeling kind, people do the same thing. They do not practice the discipline of love, they do not give one another freedom, they do not support growth in one another, they do not express feeling. Rather, they suppress the other through the denial of feeling.

Therefore, this is not just something to deal with in yourself. It is time you saw something about your effect on others.

What people usually call love is attachment, whereas real love is a great discipline and it requires great self-understanding, great self-discipline. If letting go of another in a time of grief is right, then letting go of another is also important in daily life. That is how love works. And that is the discipline of loving, then—being free to feel, being free to embrace another, to allow the other to change, to grow, to develop, to exercise himself or herself in life. That is the discipline of loving, whereas you all tend to practice love as a feeling of attachment because of all of the things you want from another, including another's attention or familiarity with you. Because you crave these things, you practice attachment to others so that you can get what you want from them. And because of your fear, you do not give them anything in return.

There is no discipline in that. Such attachment is not love, although it passes for love in the common world. "Love" is a common word that is used all the time for all kinds of things, even liking ice cream. The word "love" is used very casually. Truly, however, love is a discipline of letting go. And that means letting go in yourself, being expressive in a feeling fashion, being aware of another, enduring another, supporting the changes in another, enduring the changes in another, being willing to lose the relationship because of death or whatever else—there are all kinds of ways for relationships to come to an end. But this is the discipline, and it is a much larger exercise than the game of attachment that you call "love". Because love is a discipline, it requires understanding, an intentional practice, not just riding on your desires to get what you want from another and on your reluctance and problems. Love must be a self-generated discipline, constantly exercised, just as any other discipline in the Way of the Heart. It requires self-understanding. It requires attention. You must animate it beyond your tendencies.

Love is a kind of work, then. It is sadhana. Love is a sadhana. If you are unwilling to do it, then you must deal with yourself not only for the sake of your own growth but for the sake of anyone with whom you are in relationship. You do all kinds of people some good by doing such sadhana.

BROOKS: Yes, that is true.

SRI DA AVABHASA: But you must agree to do so, and you must have the self-understanding to do so. So often when any of you speak to Me here, you tell Me about this or that emotional limitation in yourself. This conversation is about such a limitation. You could say that almost every time one of you talks to Me, you express an emotional impediment to your living rightly and fully. What are you expressing when you are communicating this? Your lack of self-understanding, your lack of self-discipline, your lack of concern for others, your unwillingness to relate to another completely. You are all the time dramatizing, and not only binding yourself egoically but also binding others likewise. You are not functioning in love, and you are not doing anybody the good of love. You are calling what you are doing "love" all the time and saying "I love you's" all over the place. Yet love is not what you are really doing.

There is no real love without self-understanding, without intention, without work on yourself, without real work with others. Then That Which truly <u>Is</u> Love is magnified and is part of human life. If you only play the attachment game, the ego-mechanism, love does not become a part of life. It is talked about, but it is not lived.

You all use the word "love" all the time. But how much of it do you actually live apart from what you express through your attachment psychology, which is really about the suppression of love, not allowing it to be fundamental to human existence, fundamental to human relationships, fundamental to life altogether?

[to Brooks] What you are saying about yourself requires you to become serious, to understand yourself, and to embrace love as a discipline in life, to exercise it in relation to others for their sake as well as for the sake of what such sadhana does for you altogether.

That being said, what?

What about it in your case, then?

You would be a little better off in times of grief if you had a bigger philosophy, a bigger understanding of what life is altogether and of what the death transition really is for someone. Of course, when anyone intimate to you dies, you tend to go to zero. Suddenly you embrace the "When you're dead, you're dead" mentality, all the time thinking of <u>your</u> loss. You are mourning yourself more than anything else, rather than staying continuous with the one who is no longer physically present and blessing the person's transition and participating in it.

Grieving in the form of sorrow and tears is all part of rightly relating to someone who has passed. But there are two ways to grieve. One is to dramatize the attachment game and not to let the person go, and the other is to participate in the transition with real feeling and to let the person go. These are two very different ways of dealing with grief, though both of them shed tears. In the one case you are shedding tears for yourself. In the other case you are releasing another and participating in the person's transition, even changing with the person.

Therefore, it is good that you have more experience and a greater understanding of what the transition that is death really is all about, instead of just presuming the "When you're dead, you're dead" mentality that comes out of the common world where people refuse to understand such things.

Your grandmother is not dead. She has passed out of your view, and she has a great deal of business to handle now. You with your tears and feelings should be blessing her to do so instead of mourning for yourself and your poor attachment-ego. Therefore, realize a greater understanding of life and the world, including death, instead of succumbing to the hurt and presuming the least intelligent notion about everything.

You prepare for death, even the death of others, by living rightly, by doing sadhana, by embracing and not denying the laws of life. Therefore, what is all this about your refusal to feel? Poor little you! Picked out of the whole mass of humanity to be so sensitive! This is your excuse?

BROOKS: I am sure that it is my excuse, Sri Gurudev, but I can see how phony it is. It does not go very deep.

SRI DA AVABHASA: It does not allow any depth at all. It keeps everything superficial, cool. You cannot love, cannot mourn, cannot be devoted, cannot Realize. And all because you do not want to be vulnerable? It is a waste of life.

BROOKS: I understand that.

SRI DA AVABHASA: If you really understand Me, you will not waste your life. If you have a real appreciation of all the results of this game you play, then you just will not choose to do it anymore. But to so choose, you must come to some seriousness. That is why fundamentally what I am talking about is self-understanding.

BROOKS: Yes. You have Given me so many Gifts of understanding just what I am up to as a character.

SRI DA AVABHASA: And what you are doing does not work.

BROOKS: It does not work, and I am totally self-obsessed.

SRI DA AVABHASA: Well! I guess you are just a total pain in the ass and you should be shunned by everyone. Would you like to leave now? [Laughter.]

BROOKS: I don't want to leave.

SRI DA AVABHASA: Then earn the company of mankind. Join up!

BROOKS: Thank You, Beloved. I know I have to.

SRI DA AVABHASA: What more about it?

BROOKS: I am so grateful to You, Beloved. You are drawing me through a process I could never have imagined, feeling things I would never allow myself to feel. I am so grateful to You. I love You so much. You have Given me so much Prasad, so many Gifts. I am so grateful to You. I bow at Your Feet again and again.

SRI DA AVABHASA: Tcha.

CHAPTER 39

The Undying Beloved

SRI DA AVABHASA: Your ecstatic Communion with Me as a moment to moment condition of existence makes all of your associations something other than they appear in themselves. As My devotee, you need no longer live in the world concerned about worldly things. Instead, you live in the Ecstatic Play that is Satsang with Me, and thus your association with the things of life is not binding, not obsessive, not problematic. You do not require worldly association to provide you with the fulfillment that only ecstatic Communion with Me provides.

* * *

When people say in the common way that they love one another, it is the ego speaking. They mean that they are attached to one another, and they would be insulted greatly if their attachment were offended, or if the other were lost, or if the other died. Yet such losses and deaths are inevitable. Love, then, is the Force of the Heart—Prior to conditional Nature yet even Invested within it—That Transcends limits, even particularities of all kinds, while Investing Itself in them.

Feeling attached, therefore, you must magnify love. To magnify love and to transcend yourself requires great seriousness of practice of the Way of the Heart in My Blessing Company, Which Grants you the great power of self-observation, self-understanding, and self-discipline.

* * *

The spell of egoic bondage is broken only when there is awakening from both the burden of dependence (wherein mortality is still the last word) and of separative independence (which is limited to rituals of self-consolation and of exploitation of relations in an egoically "self-possessed" mood).

Your human freedom and maturity comes only when you abandon the whole disposition of dependence-independence, or the ritual of "You don't love me" and "I don't love you". It comes when you are re-established in and re-adapted to the Prior Condition of your existence, Which precedes all relations (even while the great pattern of human and cosmic relations is the modification of that Divine Self-Condition in the framework of conventional experience).

* * *

You must awaken from the spell of your childish presumptions and become human. You must neither depend on (in the absolute sense) nor recoil from any relations. You must discover the Divine Reality Itself, Prior to all agents, mediators, or means. You must become established as love rather than the search for love via any agents outside you. You must enter into most direct Communion with the Divine Truth that literally Sustains you, and with Which you are ultimately identical, at the level of consciousness and even bodily. You must be free of the illusion that the ordinary agents of life are necessary in themselves. You must come into the responsible disposition of stable love (unobstructed feeling-attention) toward all the numberless and ordinary agents of life that appear in the universal pattern of your relations, but you must be free of all illusions that bind you to others than the Love-Blissful Divine Being. You must yourself consent to be the agent of life through love, and, through feeling-Contemplation of Me, you must become less and less obstructed in that function.

* * *

Existence as a dependence on the conditions of pleasure and conventional happiness is itself a trap, a torment, and an inevitable failure. In My Company, you must Awaken to the Wisdom of self-transcending Divine Communion and thus transform your participation in the play of experience. In that case, you will presume the disposition of service, surrender, love, tolerance, and transcendence of the effects of experience, while fulfilling the role, or conventional obligation, to which you are suited or led.

* * *

215

Do Not Abandon Your Inherent Sympathy With others, but Do Not Become self-Bound By Indulgence In others, or Ever Lose Your Heart In the world itself. Therefore, Always Already, Merely <u>Be</u>, Untied Of The Bundle With others and things.

The Dawn Horse Testament

* * *

If you would hear Me, if you would see Me, if you would understand, if you would practice the Way of the Heart that I have Given you, to the Most Ultimate degree of Divine Self-Realization, you would be totally free of—what? TOTALLY FREE OF ONE ANOTHER! THE SENSE OF "ME"! AND "YOU"! AND "THAT ONE"! ALL these "ones". You would be completely, absolutely, and Most Perfectly Free of all relations. Because there are no relations. THERE ARE NO RELATIONS! NONE! NOT ONE!

* * *

You do not need sex. You do not need society. You do not need the realm of cosmic Nature. You do not need the universe. All of this is a modification, a distressful perturbation, of the Well of Divine Being. You do not need all that. Surrounded by one another in this terrible place, you need nothing whatsoever.

There is an Infinite Well of Being Itself, of Happiness Itself, of Consciousness Itself. Even now you are immersed in It. That cool, Free Water is unblemished, undosed with the chemicals of egoity, not stressed, not transformed, not modified, not limited in any sense whatsoever. In the seventh stage of life (which is Revealed and Given only by Me) you lie in the Well, Divinely "Inebriated", shouting Infinite Happiness of Being, without the slightest qualification. You lie There now, infinitely dead, and therefore infinitely Alive and Love-Blissful, Radiant without qualification. Before and after the "Big Bang", and at all times in between, you are altogether fulfilled Where you Are.

Here, you are struggling with one another, trying to figure yourselves out and mating with one another, exchanging communications and contracts. What an infinite mass of insanity! That is not it. It is not it at all. All this clinging to your relations is not it. Not it, My friends—not it at all. Not it at all.

* * *

You cannot ultimately depend on any of your objective relations (high or low in the scale of manifestation) for love, attention, support, sustenance, or their unchanging continuation through time and space. First of all, you discover that your relations are themselves generally dependent and undependable, changing or mortal, coming and going, and always changing the objects and the quality of their feeling and attention. Thus, if you depend on them, you will surely feel betrayed, and anxious about the line of love or life that feeds you through your relations. Then you become possessed in your relations with the testing mood of "You don't love me".

But, more than this, if you depend on love or life to come to you through your relations, then you yourself tend to remain irresponsible as love or attention and life. Always watching to see if you are loved and fed, and your pleasure and existence protected, you never abide as love simply. Such is the error in your childish and adolescent adaptation to born existence.

* * *

You feel so dependent on someone in the present that you would be sorrowful if he or she left you, but you can transfer the same interest to someone or something else and feel just as Happy, so that the previous one could leave you. This ordinary fact tells you that you are not really dependent on anyone or anything, but that you are engaging in a ritual of dependence, and locating your Happiness in various relations. Actually, however, you are playing on Something Inherent in your own Place, and in your own Condition.

Happiness Itself is not dependent on the objects and relations of life. It is Inherent in the Divine Self-Position, or in the Real Condition of your life. Your noticing of this is the beginning of renunciation, the beginning of the expression of true understanding, which does not dissociate you from relations but simply associates you with a greater Principle, the Great Principle. Instead of making Happiness depend on your relations, therefore, you should magnify Happiness in your relations. You should magnify That Which is Inherent in your own Place, rather than depend on relations for the feeling of Happiness.

Easy Death

* * *

Where there is genuine relationship with an individual, a place, a thing, an environment, it is not subject to the quality of desire. Desire does not "create" it. The end of desire or the change of desire does not bring it to an end. Where relationship is discovered and lived, it never does come to an end. Its quality may change, and there may be apparent separations in time and space, but the relationship itself is fundamental, continuous, real. Where there is relationship, there tends to be apparent growth, intensification, change, but it does not come to an end.

Associations, however, come and go. Associations belong to periods of one's life, stages in one's own experience. They are functions of time, space, and desire. Therefore, when some particular desire, or desire itself, ceases to be the point of view of conscious life, associations tend to fall apart, disappear, come to an end. But when there is perfect, "radical" understanding, there are no longer any associations at all. There is only relationship. There is no separation. And relationship is enjoyed under all circumstances, all conditions, with all beings, in all environments. Because people are identified with their own desires and live by the habit of association rather than relationship, there is suffering. Because people do not become more for one another than extensions of their own minds, their own desires, there is no relationship. Therefore, the communication of the Force and Condition of Consciousness Itself does not take place.

The Method of the Siddhas

* * *

Your relationships with others should be based on your acknowledgement of the nature of existence, or the inevitability of death. In other words, make your relationships on the basis of renunciation. If you will do this, then, yes, a variety of human relationships will continue but you will be a renunciate in the context of your relationships.

* * *

Life rightly lived is an intentional free-fall. You cannot at all prevent your death. And you cannot predict the hour, the day, the moment, when you will die. Your death could happen at any time—even right now while we are talking. Anybody could drop dead at any time. You cannot prevent your death. You can build your life on trying to prevent it, but such is an illusory effort, a terrible philosophical ordeal, because you cannot prevent your death. You can indulge in illusions that desensitize you to the fact of death—and most of exoteric religion is the source of such illusions for most people. Conventional religion is a way of desensitizing people to the facts of existence in this conditional life. But you cannot prevent your death.

One cannot blame people for being afraid and for clinging to consolations, but there is no truth in consolations. Because the renunciate knows this, he or she relinquishes consolations and allows the free-fall. And then you make great discoveries. The discoveries in free-fall are what the esoteric life is about. You cannot control the ultimate thing you fear. But you can be free of fear by allowing the free-fall and relinquishing consolations.

Your right relationship to Me is not a consolation. Your relationship to Me is the embrace of the Beloved, the certainty of the Absolute under circumstances wherein you are utterly bereft of certainty otherwise, wherein you allow the overwhelming force of conditionality to be as it is. Only in that certainty do you discover the Truth of existence. Renunciates have assumed the disposition that is a unique advantage. All My devotees are Called by Me to renunciation, but it is only when you embrace renunciation, only when you allow the free-fall, intentionally submit yourself to the egoless state in the egoic circumstance, only then do you Realize the Divine Reality.

Have I not been this lesson to you of the utter embrace of the free-fall of life? You must intentionally embrace the free-fall of this Divine Ecstasy and be mad in it. That is how you find out What there Is to find out. All My devotees are welcome to participate in this Ecstasy with Me, and they will all make their choices as they will, to participate either fully or with one or another degree of limitation.

* * *

Be manly, man or woman. This is My advice—you do what you will. Believe that every moment of life is on the edge. Wake up! You do not want to, because to be on the edge, to be truly mortal, means you must suffer pain in your heart in every moment of your existence here in this body—every moment. And there is no relief. None. Not with sex, alcohol, cigarettes, drugs, politics—nothing can relieve you of this heart-pain that is true to life. Nothing. Only this devotion to Me, to My Sign here, only you embracing Me, wakes up the capability for love with all your friends and lovers. That is the great love. All your faces will be eaten by worms like the faces of all the millions that came before you. Do not be stupid! No one is protected! NO ONE! Everyone is dying. Everyone is threatened. Wake up at heart. Truly! Truly!

* * *

Everything you depend upon is going to change or pass away. Everything you now own or cling to could be taken away from you in a moment. This knowledge, even before anything happens, makes you sorrowful, driven, and angry. What purpose is your dependency serving, then, other than to disturb you and others? The whole connection of dependency is a disturbance!

The only right relations between living beings are free relations based on Happiness Itself, in which people magnify the sufficient Love-Bliss, or Happiness Itself, of Inherent Being to one another. All the rest is garbage, just a torment, just the usual stuff, just the daily news.

* * *

You make relationships as if you are immortals, suffering perhaps the possibility of the failure of relationships but not realizing the reality, which is that relationships necessarily fail. Will. Necessarily. Fail. Inevitably.

* * *

In the world, the beloved dies—or appears to die. Whatever is desired or loved that is merely conditional will inevitably die, or pass away and change. One who observes this with true seriousness realizes that this Lesson of life requires that you find What is Deathless in others. True Love is devoted and submitted and attached and conformed to the Undying Beloved. This principle, in brief, characterizes the Way of the Heart.

The Hymn Of The True Heart-Master,
"I Am Grace Itself" section

* * *

You cannot oblige any creature you love to live forever, because he or she simply cannot do it—and neither can you—as an act of will. Whenever you come together with someone and you say you love one another, you cannot promise to stay with one another. You can promise your life to one another and in that sense stay with one another, but you do not have in your will the capability to stay with one another forever, because the body-mind dies. This bodily condition disappears.

Therefore, you must die while living. You must be able to let go of this unnecessary realm and dwell in the Divine Self-Condition while you are alive. In that case you will be free of anxiety. You will have humor in relation to things here. You will be capable of loving in the natural fashion, because you are not obliging all of this to stay here forever. In that Most Ultimate Realization in the Way of the Heart, you are Divinely Recognizing all of this intuitively. Then the Divine Condition of all these conditions is the Divine Beloved you find in your lover, in every arising phenomenon, in every moment, and, most directly, in Me, your True Heart-Master.

Anything or anyone that you love and enjoy in this realm is only, if you will notice it, the Divine Beloved, the Very Real Itself. This is what you discover in all your loving, all your enjoyments, if you are a true man, a true woman. If you do not live by such sacrificial acknowledgement, all your experiencing and enjoyments lead to attachment only. They reinforce ritual behavior, craving for contact, craving for experience, craving for repetitions in which you are constantly anxious, ill at ease, suffering reactive emotions, endlessly thinking, mulling things over mentally as if you were trying to solve some hidden problem, knotted up in the body, always active to find some pleasurable condition that will last, that will fulfill you.

If you intuitively understand all this that is arising here, you are not bound up by reaction to the whole automatic ceremony. You are relieved of it. And that understanding is the only release. There is only a Single and Absolute Divine Self-Condition, Unspeakable in Its Nature, Which you may not see, hear, or experience over against yourself but Which is your very Condition Prior to all changes, high or low, should they arise. And in that Divine Self-Condition, as it happens, this one you seem to be when active in the waking world continues to arise for the time being—paradoxically, because it does not amount to anything.

Nothing is gained by a moment's living—absolutely nothing. Nothing changes on the basis of it. Nothing is gained by a single meeting, by a single moment's satisfaction, by a single contact. This living is not anything. It is only an illusion, a modification of the essential Divine Self-Condition. If you come to rest in that Condition, in the Realization of the seventh stage of life (which is Revealed and Given only by Me), then in every moment you Divinely Recognize this arising and you are Happy, already Happy. You can play in the ordinary ways, but you never become wretched. You are not degraded through your own craving, because you Divinely Recognize What you love, and therefore your relations with loved-ones, with this whole world, are natural, ordinarily happy.

Otherwise, your craving for the immortality of the loved-one will become so profound that you will be forced to bring the relationship to an end. You will drive the loved-one away in your craving for the loved-one's immortality. Your anxiety over the loss, the separation, will become so great that you will eventually begin to degrade the relationship itself, to separate yourself automatically. Then, even though you are here to be loving, everything you do begins to separate you from the loved-one because you are so anxious, so terrified, so upset.

In the by Me Revealed and Given seventh stage of life, you will Divinely Recognize one another in Truth, you will Divinely Recognize this world in Truth, you will acknowledge Me in Truth. Then you are engaged in the process that relieves you of this illusion, and you can come to rest. You can be Happy.

Therefore, even now it is not necessary to go on with great plans to conquer this world in one fashion or another. Nothing is gained by it. You never conquer the loved-one. You are enamored. You are in love. No conquering goes on at all. You only start conquering when you become afraid, when you fear this separation. Then you become anxious and start craving all kinds of satisfaction.

* * *

Everything you know or own or think or understand or presume, and everyone with whom you are associated, will be taken away from you. Your body itself and also your own mind will at some time be kept by the Divine. If you surrender your relations, your children, and your spouse to the Divine Person every day, they will someday be kept by the Divine Being.

You must be free of anger on that day! You must be free of sorrow while you live, and free of doubt and fear, or you will be crippled through your own recoil upon yourself. You will become an idolator, a cultist, an owner of experience, an owner of mind, of body, of relations, all of which can and will be taken from you, and thus you will be always un-Happy. Whatever is given to you, for however long it is given, must be accepted as something that belongs to the Divine Person. You must literally acknowledge everything as belonging to the Divine.

* * *

Hold on to no thing and no one, not even your apparently individual self. Be certain of no knowledge. Be the sacrifice of all conditions in every moment, and thus abide in Communion with the eternal Truth, wherein the root of your independence is eternally hidden and your common Identity is always already Revealed.

In this way you will affirm and participate in the necessarily eternal Existence in which you all appear: Surrender into Infinity with all your friends and hold on to no thing or condition that ever appears. Forget all things in present Happiness, and so forgive the universe for all its playful changes. Always love one another, and so forgive one another for appearing, for changing, and for passing out of present sight. So be it.

Easy Death

* * *

CHAPTER 40

No Fish Is to Die

A STORY OF SRI DA AVABHASA'S AWAKENING PLAY
by Jeff Polson

In the early winter months of 1979 I was asked to set up a fish
tank in Bright Behind Me, which at that time served as Sri Da
Avabhasa's Residence at the Mountain Of Attention in northern
California. I was overjoyed at the opportunity to perform this service.
In my enthusiasm, I claimed that I knew "all about" fish and aquariums, having had vast experience in the field. Actually, I had kept a
twenty-gallon tank for about a year with a few small tropical fish!

I jumped right in. I immediately bought and installed a fifty-five
gallon aquarium with all the necessary accoutrements, which I
installed in Bright Behind Me. When I was finished, I received a
message from Sri Gurudev: "No fish is to die."

No fish is to die?! I thought back on the number of fish that had
perished in my limited and brief career. I had pulled many lifeless
bodies from the water. Everybody who has kept fish has lost fish. I
was taken aback, but I doubtfully acknowledged this edict.

Soon I added another tank, then two more. Before long there
were nine tanks (marine, tropical, and goldfish) in Sri Gurudev's
Residence under my care. Needless to say, the casualties were soon
to begin rolling in.

Indeed, it was not long at all before I was called over to the
house to remove a dead fish from one of the tanks—the first of
many. I was told that Sri Da Avabhasa wanted to know why the fish
had died. I took the two-inch corpse in hand and studied it—no
wounds, no signs of disease or distress. In fact, it was still quite
beautiful. But it was dead. I replied that I did not know why.

As the days passed, there were more sick fish and more deaths.

224

I became proficient at spotting diseases and learning how to minister to the victims. Nonetheless, many fish continued to perish.

One day I was called to tend to yet another sick fish. I found a dwarf gourami floating on the surface of the tank, his body already frozen in a rigid arc, indicating death was near. I was told that Sri Da Avabhasa wanted me to "save this fish".

"Save this fish?" I thought. "Nothing can save this fish!"

Still, I removed the fish from the tank and took him to a hospital tank in my cabin. There I treated the water with medication. I watched the fish for a few minutes, hoping that there would be some sign that he would recover. I placed a hand on either side of the tank and prayed for him. I also poured in a small amount of holy water—water that has been infused with the healing energy that is Radiant in Sri Da Avabhasa's Company and in the Holy Sites that He has Empowered as His Agents. But the moment I had seen the fish, I had known that he would not survive. In twenty minutes he was dead.

I took his body from the tank and flushed it down the toilet.

In the meantime, another devotee had come to my cabin. He watched while I tended to the fish. After I had disposed of him, I said, "Well, there goes another one."

He looked at me. "Don't you feel anything for him?" he asked.

"No," I said, "it's just a fish. Do you?"

"Yes!"

"You do?" I was really surprised.

"Yes!"

"Do you think most people would?"

"Yes!"

This was a revelation to me. I had felt nothing for these fish. I had no emotional connection to them. That was the point—I felt no emotion. I had approached the matter intelligently and with a good deal of energy. But I did not care about the lives of the fish. I had not given my heart. And I saw that this lesson was not just about fish. It was an indication of how I lived my life.

The following day, Sri Da Avabhasa asked how the fish was doing. I realized that He had truly expected the fish to be healed. I saw that I would have to engage this service in a new way.

I should interject here that I hadn't taken lightly His edict that there should be no dead fish. I was constantly studying the subject, reading books, talking to experienced aquarists, university professors, and anyone I thought could help. But now I intensified this study.

One morning not long afterwards, I was again called to Bright Behind Me. A fish that was very special to me was acting listless. Heart-Master Da had noticed his lack of energy and had sent for me.

The fish was a "blue-faced angel". When I had first begun setting up aquariums for Sri Da Avabhasa, I was taken by the beauty of this fish and immediately decided to buy it as a gift for Him. But blue-faced angels are so delicate that I had to wait many months, allowing the tank environment to stabilize completely, before I had felt it was possible to present this gift. So when the blue-faced angel, which I had only recently given to Sri Da Avabhasa, took ill, I felt a real desire to keep him alive. I am certain that Sri Da Avabhasa intuitively felt my connection to this fish, because He took a strong interest in its welfare.

At Bright Behind Me I stood beside the tank with Heart-Master Da, "considering" what to do with the angelfish. The diagnosis and treatment of fish diseases is a little-researched and inexact science. Many times the symptoms are not specific enough to indicate a particular treatment. Quite often any treatment is a shot in the dark.

I elected to leave the angel in the tank. Moving a fish causes stress, often worsening the condition of one already ailing. I told Heart-Master Da that this was what I was going to do. He accepted my decision and left the room. I then treated the tank with a wide-spectrum antibotic. When I had finished, a devotee arrived with a message to me from Sri Gurudev. He said:

"You should do everything possible to save the angelfish. Find out everything you can, do everything you can, to heal him. When you have done everything that you can do, then go to the Communion Hall and pray."

I received Sri Gurudev's communication very profoundly, and my resolve to save the angel deepened. I called the Marine Biology Department at the University of California at Davis, and spoke to an expert there. I also called some knowledgeable aquarists and aquarium shop owners I had been in contact with. Everyone agreed with my handling of the fish, and no one had any new information to give me.

Then I went to Plain Talk Chapel at the Mountain Of Attention and prayed for the angelfish. I breathed deeply, directing energy to my heart, asking Sri Da Avabhasa to come to the aid of the fish. I felt how I wanted him to live. I stayed in Plain Talk Chapel for an hour and a half.

Throughout the day, I kept my attention on the fish, at the same time feeling Sri Da Avabhasa with my heart, and directing toward the fish the healing energy I contacted through my Communion with Sri Gurudev. That evening I returned to the house to observe the patient again. His condition had worsened. I decided to move him to a tank in my cabin.

I placed him in a hospital tank and added a small amount of holy water and a bit of holy ash—a pure white ash remaining from a fire ceremony performed at one of the Holy Sites of the Way of the Heart. I again placed my hands on either side of the tank and prayed. His condition worsened further. As he weakened, I put my hand in the water and gently cradled him, praying for him. I was filled with compassion for that being, and I stayed with him until he died at three the following morning. Then I took his body to a pond on the Sanctuary, said a prayer, and threw him into the water.

Later that morning, I was called to Bright Behind Me to feed the fish. I went into the dining room where Heart-Master Da was eating His breakfast. As I knelt before Heart-Master Da and prepared to feed the fish in the tank from which I had removed the blue-faced angelfish only hours before, He asked me how the angel was doing. I told Him that he had died that morning. It was hard to give Him the news, because I had really felt the loss of the fish.

Heart-Master Da then looked in my eyes and quietly said, "It was his time." I don't know what I expected, but I didn't expect that. I was at once perplexed and undone by the tenderness of His Compassion. I know that Sri Gurudev wanted that fish to live also, but it was my heart that He cradled in His Hands and soothed in this moment. There was no miraculous recovery to thrill about. Not as far as the fish is concerned, anyway. But I learned how to bring life to another, how to serve death, and what it means to be feelingly present in both. And the greatest thing that I learned about was the Love and Compassion my beloved Sat-Guru has for me, and for all. I am forever grateful to Sri Da Avabhasa for His Instruction and His endless Grace. Every moment in His Company is Revelation.

CHAPTER 41

The "Cave" of Relationship

SRI DA AVABHASA: Renunciation in the Way of the Heart is a commitment to ecstasy. Renunciates are about ecstasy, not dried-up, conventional lawfulness.

* * *

I am not talking about rejecting your human life. I do not reject human life. I take great pains to absorb, accept, and submit to human life. That is the Yoga I Live and the Example I Give to you. I am not Calling you to put on orange robes and go to the caves. It is not necessary. My Calling to you is greater than that. Any phony can give up everything and be supported in some monastic cave!

* * *

The Way of the Heart is not about a dissociated tendency. It is about precisely the transcendence of the dissociative tendency. That is its root altogether. Therefore, as My devotee you do the sadhana of the Way of the Heart in life. You transform your life in various ways. It is a life, not a cubicle. There is nothing to do in a cubicle. There is nothing in a cube—no man, no woman, nothing. And no circumstance for a celibate. There is nothing. It is an illusion. It is an error, a religious error. It is an error in the religious mind. That is the first lesson for somebody proposing to be a renunciate. Renunciation is not a cubicle. It is not dissociation from life, and it is not loveless. It is the opposite of all of that. It is done in life. It is about love altogether. That is its context and its Realization.

* * *

You thought you could renounce the business of life to become a renunciate. No. You become a renunciate by dealing with the business of life.

* * *

Paradoxically, the basic self-force, or ego-force, must be strong in you if you are to Realize the Event of ego-death. This is because ego-death is not the ultimate suppression or negation of the basic force of the individual being, but it is the release of that force from limiting identification with the body-mind.

Ego-death is the Awakening of the individual being to its Real Condition of Inherence in the Divine Reality in Which all things and beings are arising. The secondary symptoms of ego-collapse are all the reactive emotions, the petty habits of self-indulgence, the selfish and mean attitudes, the physical weaknesses, and the unillumined opinions, beliefs, and philosophies that characterize people at their worst. (From this description it should be clear that, at the present time, human beings in general are suffering from the disease or wound of ego-collapse, rather than from too great a sense of egoic self. And My Wisdom-Teaching is an Offering of Divine Help in response to that universal disease. My Wisdom-Teaching is intended to strengthen humanity by Calling them to recollect the Great Life-Light that is the Substance of this world. Such Divine Wisdom-Teaching has Power to Awaken humanity to the Love and Fullness that is naturally ever expanding from that dimension of the living being which Realizes its own Inherence in Self-Existing and Self-Radiant Divine Being.)

* * *

To suppress the composite egoic self, or "I", is only to intensify the mood of the egoic self, which is the primary sense of separation, limitation, and vulnerability.

* * *

In your present delusion, you tend to feel that God-Realization is a matter of stripping yourself of attachments, relations, and enjoyments, rather than giving up to the Divine Being. However, in Truth God-Realization has nothing to do with such self-denial. Ultimately, Realization of the Divine Self-Condition is the Outshining of attachments, relations, and enjoyments through Heart-Identification with

Me. In that Divine Self-Realization, when you are already in a condition of Spiritual, bodily enjoyment, then all manifested enjoyments become superficial, ordinary, conventional processes that are neither overwhelming nor binding.

* * *

I acknowledge that the ego is impure, or entangled in its own results. But I have Revealed the Way of the Heart, which is the Way of continuous self-understanding, present ego-transcendence, and direct Realization, through devotional fidelity to Me as the True Heart-Master. Therefore, I do not emphasize the conventional motive toward purification. The purified ego is still the ego—and as long as the ego (or even the phenomenal body-mind) persists, perfect purification is not possible.

The ideal of perfect purity is ego-made. Such perfect purification need not be your concern. Through practice of the Way of the Heart in My Company, you must "consider" the conditions of existence more directly and fully. In doing so, you will indeed be purified to a significant degree—that is, you will restore balance, or equanimity, regenerate your fundamental energy, and set your attention free to Realize the Truth. Just so, if you observe yourself fully, you will enjoy a more balanced view of human existence—free of righteous self-suppression and all of the kinds of public and private intolerance that reflect the righteous ideal of too much purity.

Above all, what becomes possible through the direct self-understanding that is realized through feeling-Contemplation of Me in the Way of the Heart is a correct view of God-Realization—that it is based not on righteous self-purification but on free self-transcendence.

* * *

Cultures that have a sex-suppressive orientation to children tend to be characterized by aggression, as we see in many Western, and Westernized, societies, for example. If a sex-negative and vital-negative and life-negative orientation is forced upon children, they cannot adapt fully to the descending circuit of My Spiritual Heart-Blessing, from head to foot.

If the sexual function is attacked with negative attitudes and punishments and all the other manipulations that arise from a suppressive orientation, then individuals cannot adapt to My Divine

Grace, Which is fully Descending. They tend to become anxious at the solar plexus, above the vital mechanism, and sex, excreting, and all the rest of the vital functions become the subject of guilt, shame, and taboos. In this way, the child's adaptation to My Spiritual Life-Current is retarded, and he or she develops a contraction in the solar plexus that is a critical limitation to his or her reception of Me.

When the contraction at the solar plexus, or the "navel" center, is strong, then what emotion is magnified? The emotion of anger, or suppression. It is a violent emotion. It is a sign of retarded adaptation to My Spiritual Current of Life, Which is modified as universal life-energy in the body-mind and the world.

Therefore, do not introduce these taboos, these life-negative views, into the lives of children (or the life of anyone). Instead, help them adapt to a life-positive economy based on intelligent understanding of the process that is truly human life. Permit children to adapt to the life-energy, but do not reinforce any tendencies toward self-indulgence, because suppression and indulgence have the same effect—they prevent children's adaptation to My Descending Grace. Self-suppression and self-indulgence mutilate My Spiritual Heart-Transmission and foster a self-contracted, or egoically "self-possessed", orientation to the descended functions of life. In that egoic mood, human beings become aggressive, and their sexuality is aggressive.

Therefore, develop an intelligent economy in your children (and in yourself and in others), without taboos or negative views, by establishing a very positive human association with them. Permit them to adapt gradually, from infancy through the third stage of life, to My Descending Spirit-Current of Divine Life, so that My Spiritual Life-Current can be fully adapted to all of the functions of the manifested personality from head to base, and so that shame, guilt, sorrow, fear, anger, and all of the rest of the reactive emotions do not become chronic attitudes.

Such attitudes are simply the signs of contractions in one's reception of My Divine Descent.

* * *

The Way of the Heart is not a process that is moving in the direction of perfect purification, perfect goodness according to any traditional conception, or perfect manifestation of the rules of public morality and the conventions of expected behavior. The Way of the Heart is not expressed through asceticism, self-suppression, suppression of functions, denial of life, or denial of this world, all of which are the expression of the conventional and righteous ideal of purity.

Those who practice the Way of the Heart express the benign qualities of tolerance, cooperation, and love in the company of others. They express a similar disposition in their own lives, a tolerant or free orientation toward their own functional existence, not an intolerant, self-suppressive, or angular disposition. Thus, My devotee looks like an ordinary individual in many ways—not an ascetic, not a religious social idealist, but a humorous and benign character, a tolerant character. This is the kind of disposition that develops on the basis of real practice of the Way of the Heart.

But not even development of such a character is the purpose of the Way of the Heart. It is simply an inevitable expression of practice of the Way of the Heart. The purpose of the Way of the Heart is to Contemplate Me with feeling-devotion, and through that Contemplation to free energy and attention for the observation, understanding, and transcendence of the self-contraction and to Realize That Which is at the root of, or That Which is the Source of, that contraction.

This "radical" orientation to transcendence of the ego-self at its root, or in its fundamental form, via feeling-Contemplation of Me as your True Heart-Master is the Way of the Heart.

*   *   *

PART VII

My Gift of
Heart-Vision

CHAPTER 42

The Beatitude of Perfect Surrender to Me

A CONVERSATION WITH SRI DA AVABHASA

BILL KRENZ: I love You, my Lord.

SRI DA AVABHASA: [Sri Gurudev hugs and kisses His devotee.] That is the most directly devotional act you have ever done in My Company—not just the hug and the kiss but the feeling and the sounds that accompanied it. I Love you. Never forget this or act otherwise.

BILL: I understand, my Lord. I love You.

SRI DA AVABHASA: And so is there some question?

BILL: Yes, Sri Gurudev. One of the conditions I have is to always be sensitive to the effect I have on other people.

SRI DA AVABHASA: The culture has discussed this with you?

BILL: Yes. It has been a very useful discipline for me to have, my Lord. You have given me the arms of understanding relative to many matters—reactivity and desiring, feeling reactivity as the self-contraction and being able to move beyond it. But what I notice, and it happens primarily in a relational context where I will be talking with somebody and not be sensitive to them, I will not be animating love with them . . .

SRI DA AVABHASA: That! Just that. Obviously <u>that</u> is it. Your animating love with them ought to be required—not just noticing your effect on other people but maintaining the discipline of your devotion to Me and expressing it in feeling love-relationship with others. That is a better way of putting it, I think. Yes, do not drop your observing your effect on others, but this is more fundamental.

BILL: Thank You, my Lord. Just after Your conversation last night I practiced this discipline more today, and it allowed me to notice more readily when I was contracting and becoming righteous or angular with other people. I feel it is the key area I need to incarnate so that I do not notice the effects downstream.

SRI DA AVABHASA: There will be nothing to notice downstream if you love Me all the while, if you keep yourself as My devotee, always hugging Me as you just did, emanating those sounds, those feelings. Be always in that disposition. Bring that, then, to all your friends, to all your relations, to everyone you meet, with no compromise. You will not have to worry about "downstream" if you are feeling Me. Nothing can come downstream for you or anyone else except the Beloved, if you stay true with Me.

BILL: This is a very useful conversation, my Lord. Thank You very much.

SRI DA AVABHASA: What about all this mind, then, and solidity?

BILL: Well, it all comes, as You said, when I am not present, loving, feeling my devotion to You, talking about my devotion to You.

SRI DA AVABHASA: The mind is interesting—the whole body is interesting, but the mind is interesting, especially in "solid" types, who are always thinking, always under the stress of thinking, trying to explain, trying to come to some understanding, some insight, some explanation, something they can communicate. This mind business is interesting stuff, because the mind presumes it is capable of something that it is not in the slightest capable of. The mind presumes it is capable of everything, because it can embrace, communicate, believe in, associate with, a symbol for anything and everything.

There is only one thing of direct experience in the mind. It is the self-contraction, the ego-"I", the sense of separateness. Everything else the mind does is either a conversation with itself or a symbolic representation of something that is beyond itself.

There is no thing in the mind—apple, God. There is no "apple" achieved by the mind, nor God. You can think about God, say "God", say things philosophically about the Divine, about Realization and so forth. It is never Realization. It is never God. You can say "apple, apple, apple, apple". It is never an apple! You can say "apple" and think "apple", but it is never an actual apple. You can say "God" and think "God", but it is never actually God.

The mind is filled with representations, and not one of them is what it represents. What it represents is always beyond the mind. The mind is always chattering through representations. Everything it represents is outside itself or beyond itself. And otherwise all the mind is, is the chattering of the ego-"I". The separate "I"-notion is the only direct experience of the mind, perpetually. This is the only thing the mind experiences—this one experience of separateness, separate ego-"I". Every symbol, every conversation inwardly or outwardly expressed, is just the babble of that separate feeling, through representations seeming to associate with things that are utterly beyond itself.

The mind is self-contraction, a rehearsal of self-contraction, a ceremony, a ritual, of self-contraction. The only experience of the mind is the sense of separate self. Every word in the mind represents something that is entirely outside itself and cannot be achieved unless the mind relaxes and the thing itself is entered into.

There are only two things the mind does apart from this constant of the self-contraction: the awareness of separateness and the representation of what is outside itself, chanting to itself like Narcissus whispering to himself while hanging over the pond, [Sri Gurudev whispers] "Oh, my beloved, you are so beautiful. I think about you all the time. I look at you constantly. I cannot look at anything else. I cannot think of anything else. You are mine, my beloved." And it is only him! It is either chatting to itself or making up words or images to represent something outside itself. The only experience of the mind is itself, its sense of separateness.

BILL: It is true, my Lord. It usually comes in the form of an insight, and I will really be attached to that insight or feeling that I did something that really . . .

SRI DA AVABHASA: It is the mind experiencing yourself. The mind is stress, stress manifested at the level of what we call "mind" or "cognition". The same experience is generated emotionally as all your reactions, to this, that, and the other thing, to which the sense of separateness is fundamental all the while. And as bodily conception, bodily sensation, it is always self-placed.

The sense of separation is always generated, experienced. It is the only experience. Everything physical, emotional, and mental is one experience—separateness, ego-"I", "I", "I", "I". There are mental representations of what is outside the mind. There are emotional representations of what is outside feeling. And there are physical sensations of what is outside the body. Yet it is <u>one</u> experience, constantly perpetuated, of separateness. If you are "vital", it is physically based. If you are "peculiar", it is emotionally based. If you are "solid", it is mentally based.

Whether "vital", "peculiar", or "solid", everyone has this one experience—self-contraction, the sense of separateness perpetually re-enacted, constantly rehearsed, dramatized, all the time dealing with representations only, the figments of its own contraction. You must find yourself out. This is so.

Each one of you is most characteristically "vital", "peculiar", or "solid". Some are very, very classically one or the other. In others the distinctions are a little bit muddy, but generally one of the three strategies is more dominant than the other. In any case, there is only one experience, whether it is classic or complicated: the separate "I" sense, the sense of separateness manifesting illusions, representations, conversations with itself. It is madness, absolute madness, utterly without God. It is Narcissus at the pond, looking at himself and not knowing that it is him.

When you come to this understanding, by Grace, with all Help Given to you, your intelligence exercised, then you can break the spell, you can move up from the pond. It is just your reflection, you see. You open up and feel beyond, without the self-contracted forms of mind, emotion, and body. All that is felt beyond. The immense mystery of What Is cannot be compre-hended because you do not know what even a single thing is.

Just to be so open to self-transcendence is to be continuous with Me, continuous with the Divine Self-Condition. It is not to know what anything is merely, especially from the beginning—there is nothing absolute about anything that is arising—but it is rather to be continuous with it, to be open to it and therefore able to be expanded, able to be experiencing the Revelation of What Is. More and more by stages, by growth, the Revelation becomes most profound.

To begin with, what must become true is your continuity with What Is, not your command over It but your continuity with It by transcendence of this contraction.

Therefore, whether you are "solid" and mentally possessed, or "peculiar" and emotionally possessed, or "vital" and physical-ly possessed, all you are doing is meditating on the separate self sense and "oinking" out representations, conversations with yourself. And all the while everything that is, is outside of it. That is why it is self-contraction. The apple is something else, not what is in your mind. Even if the apple is in your belly, how close can you get to it, you being who you are?

TONI VIDOR: When I went through the difficult week that I told You about when all the things that I was letting go of kept very forcefully coming up for me . . .

SRI DA AVABHASA: Your children and so on?

TONI: Yes, and objects and whatnot. I was able to stand back and observe it, and the temptation of the mind was always grab-bing and grabbing me and wanting and wanting. It was rather like observing another person, a silly childish person who was not really me. It was the ego, this automatic thing, and I could feel that it was just the power of the mind. I did not really get sucked into it, but I could see the meaning of the saying in the Bible, "Get thee behind me, Satan."

SRI DA AVABHASA: In some sense the greatest power of all, the greatest Grace of all, therefore, is unqualified pain. As long as you have an option, some way to slip and slide out of your dilemma, your difficulty, your egoic "self-possession", you will tend to take the way out or otherwise just be confused. All of you must have had some moments in your life when the pain, the confusion, the forcefulness, of the intrusion of the difficulty of life was so profound you could not figure anything out about it, you could not make an emotional gesture to escape, you could not do anything physically about it, you could not do anything socially about it, or anything else. It was so confusing, so overwhelming, so profound, it was not even that you <u>could</u> surrender but surrender was inevitable. You nakedly felt beyond yourself, relieved of your apparently independent self, the egoic self eliminated by that most profound intrusion.

TONI: It was as if the contracted self was another person, like an entity all its own.

SRI DA AVABHASA: A kind of idol sitting there, which you can resort to when pain is not absolute. When pain is absolute, that little idol, that dump there, cannot be resorted to. No gesture can be made by it.

And then there is a kind of beatitude, not necessarily Divine Enlightenment every time such a thing occurs, but a kind of beatitude, continuous with What <u>Is</u>. In such a moment, you must be given up to What <u>Is</u>, whatever It Is, and there is no choice about it.

TONI: But there is a great freedom in realizing that you are able to do that.

SRI DA AVABHASA: Well, but you are all the time fearing death and great pain and the most dreadful of consequences. If any of those things did happen, a beatitude would be inevitable. But there is a great lesson in pain. In pain, you can allow that very same condition of beatitude to coincide with your ordinary life. You can allow it. It can become the greatest principle of Yoga, the greatest principle of sadhana. You will allow, even embrace, great discipline, great devotion, great service, great meditation, great heat, great tapas, knowing that in such circumstances there is always beatitude, because no choice is available to you.

The great Realizers know this secret. I know it. If you can come to the point of allowing such complete and total surrender, so that you never avoid it, so that in fact it becomes the condition of existence, then life is beatitude, existence is beatitude.

There is a secret in such surrender that is most fundamental to sadhana in the Way of the Heart. Allow yourself to be cooked, to be burned alive, to avoid nothing. To be, in this moment, in such a place where surrender is not even your only choice, where it is only inevitable—this is the secret of most effective sadhana. It is the secret of renunciation. It is why renunciation is the secret of Realization, bereft of all means, all strategies, only There, without resorts of the egoic kind, in Place with the One Who Is, only devotion—and not by choice. There is no choice. Giving yourself no choice whatsoever is the greatest principle of sadhana.

Be God-made, God-born, with God allowed, God Existing, and with no alternatives—this is the great Secret. The greatest Realizers, the greatest renunciates, all know this Secret. This is why they do what they do. But if you are only mediocre, always trying to avoid the great Imposition of Reality Itself, then you always have an option, some way to slip or slide to the right or left, always some way to desensitize yourself to the great Condition, not to mention all conditions. To become so humbled, so ground up, that there cannot be anything but Divine Enlightenment, this is the Secret. Mark My Words!

You are all maintaining options—that is what I am telling you. You always have an option. Even suggesting to yourself "I would choose always the option of surrender and devotion" still gives you room. You should give yourself no room—devotion absolute, imposed to the absolute degree so that no gesture even can or even need be made, but only God Is. That is the Secret.

CHAPTER 43

For the Love

A CONVERSATION WITH DA AVABHASA

ANIELLO PANICO (a man who managed the kitchen at Sri Love-Anandashram): Sri Gurudev, the other day we were cleaning out the kitchen, and I said to Stephan, who was working with me, "Let's move those two cinder blocks. What are they doing in the kitchen?" We picked up one cinder block to move it, and there was a rat staring at us. Now, everybody here would call it a mouse, but I am from New York and I know it was a rat! He was easily six inches long. He was looking at us and thinking he was as cute as Mickey Mouse.

SRI DA AVABHASA: They are cute, Aniello.

ANIELLO: It was a rat, Master!

SRI DA AVABHASA: I don't mind them.

ANIELLO: I mind them, Sri Gurudev.

SRI DA AVABHASA: That is part of the liability of being from New York.

ANIELLO: But, Sri Gurudev, he was not alone. There were four or five little mice with their heads eaten off! This killer was trying to look cute, as if he were at Disneyland, but that devil had eaten those little mice's heads off. I knew it! I knew it! Stephan said, "Isn't he cute?"

SRI DA AVABHASA: Those were living beings, conscious as you are, getting their brains gnawed out! Crunchy, crunchy,

crunchy, little ears and noses. That is pain and disillusion-ment and confusion! Imagine the state they were in when they got to the other side.

STEPHAN BLAS: Sri Gurudev, do You know what Aniello is asking You for? Mouse control!

ANIELLO: I want a cat.

SRI DA AVABHASA: Would you rather a cat ate the heads of the mice?

ANIELLO: Yes. I want a cat to eat that big mouse.

SRI DA AVABHASA: That is equally disgusting, Aniello.

ANIELLO: Please give us one of Your cats for the kitchen, Master.

SRI DA AVABHASA: Eating beings is always disturbing—not necessarily the eating but the witnessing of the eating, the after-death. There is nothing I can do about this, Aniello. This world is dreadful. Do you have any idea what is happening in condi-tional Nature? Everyone must sacrifice beings to survive.

ANIELLO: But not Your own, Sri Gurudev.

SRI DA AVABHASA: They are all My own. They are all your own, Aniello. And you must sacrifice them to live. Forget chewing off a mouse's head. You beings, you humans here, require the murdering of living beings to eat and survive. You must come to terms with this fact. To do so you must come to terms with your own life and death and accept the fact that you are a sacrifice and that existence in manifested form is not merely a jolly time. All of you could potentially die a painful death and live a painful lifetime. I am giving you another slice of possibility, but you need not take it, and many of you do not fully. Manifested existence, with arms, legs, head, trunk—when you get born in this world, you are asking for trouble.

Do not become overly disgusted by the manifestations of less-than-human creatures, Aniello. Accept your own state and the fact that you eat heads and require the pain of beings to live. Beyond that, know that you must accept the pain of life and death. You are a sacrifice. To exist in this form is revolting, treacherous, and potentially painful. Some few may slide through with comparatively little pain and die in bed, but of all the beings on this planet, how many do that?

ANIELLO: Not many. Not many at all.

SRI DA AVABHASA: Some, in fact many, tweet and fly and move and shake and sex. But in between and after, they are sacrificed, fully conscious, in such a form, in such an incident, that you could not keep your stomach down if you knew of it. That is not merely the fate of rats. That is the common fate of beings called "human". A large percentage of mankind suffer the fate of rats. You are not gods and goddesses here. You suffer the fate of animals. You must come to terms with this, and, out of compassion, relieve as many as possible from that destiny. To date, however, you have not been too successful at that. Am I right, Aniello?

Do you know how many dreadful deaths human beings have suffered compared to your mice? There have been much worse. And how many fear death? How many fear that kind of death? Everyone does. You are meat and can be eaten. Luckily for you, you get to Contemplate Me and live the Truth and be Delighted and experience Ecstasy while manifested in mortal form.

ANIELLO: Thank You, Sri Gurudev.

SRI DA AVABHASA: You give slices of gratitude, maybe, but you do not understand how grateful you should be. These are still very primitive times. And the Master of mankind is not yet in charge. I am the Person here to make such Ecstasy acceptable, a sublime Possibility for all—not just humans, but mice and rats as well, spiders, frogs, walls, TV sets, and plants—to go beyond themselves, without the threat of being eaten by another mover. All of them are given the opportunity for Sublimity.

But tell Me about the rat and the mice, Aniello. Your revulsion is unreal and bourgeois. Such a sight is repulsive, yes, but you act as if it is not knowledge about yourself, about what you do, and about your fate. You are meat in this form. Human beings have the potential to transform this planet, but they have not done it yet. They are merely increasing the insanity.

243

ANIELLO: But they can transform the planet.

SRI DA AVABHASA: They can, but they have not done it yet. Human beings murder one another all the time, all the time. Every year hundreds of thousands of human beings suffer the fate of mice, insects, cockroaches. They are treated like dirt—really! That is the way it is. Only because you have not experienced that possibility yet, and your immediate friends have not experienced it yet, can you look at the rat and be disgusted. Yes, be revolted, but be more intelligent about it. That rat is you. It is mankind. And you only live because you act something like the rat. Do not be righteously revolted by it, because you will die from the same aggression.

You have the potential to do something different, but you do not have the potential to not sacrifice. Existence in manifested form is participation in sacrifice, and there is no reason to be righteous about that fact. You should be humbled by the knowledge. You cannot even breathe—not even breathe—without sacrificing self-conscious beings. You cannot walk or move, you cannot live from day to day, without taking life in some form. You may eat an orange or a bit of lettuce in your salad. Look at your plate. Look at the sacrifice. Do not be guilty about it. Know it. You are not yet so different from the rat. You eat heads, too. You are revolting. You are flesh. You are to be sacrificed. You are a sacrifice in your most precious form, that to which you would most dearly cling. You are! Be revolted, but be illumined by your knowledge. Make changes. Devote your sacrifice to changing existence. Do not be happy about it, but do not be righteous either. This is My advice, Aniello.

How many living beings have you eaten in your life, Aniello?

ANIELLO: Many.

SRI DA AVABHASA: Do you think they liked being eaten?

ANIELLO: I am sure they did not, Sri Gurudev.

SRI DA AVABHASA: Then what makes you different from the rat? The beings you have eaten did not like anything about it, and you will not like it when you die. You will struggle and resist. Until your quiet time comes, you will resist.

You all know that death can come to you quietly. But all your life you struggle, nonetheless. Like a chicken running in the yard, waiting to get its head cut off, you anticipate the most terrible death. And you think that by organizing yourself with other human beings in some fashion or other you will have a quiet death in bed and not even be aware of your death. You hope for that infinitesimal fraction of possibility.

Most human beings die uncomfortably. And if they do not die uncomfortably, they live uncomfortably. This flesh is a sacrifice, a transformation. This place is a transition place. Do not be righteous next to the rat. The poor animal is as self-conscious as you. So what if he looks ugly! You have seen ugly humans, haven't you? Compared to the Great Shining without deaths, without aggression, in this place everybody is really ugly.

This is a dreadful and transitional place. Accept it as such. Love Me. Be consumed by adoration of the Divine Person, Who I Am. But do not make moral judgments. Do not look down on the rat. Look at the rat and realize that you have hairs, too! No righteousness is appropriate here. Humility, submission, surrender, even Ecstasy ultimately is justified here. This is a transitional place, and nobody knows what is beyond it except those who have the Divine Vision.

You must get this Vision through Me, be Lifted Up, be Happy, even accept the sacrifices you must make to survive, the sacrifice of beings you must make to live. But do not do it righteously, angrily. All beings suffer, as you do, as you must, as you might, as typically is the case in death! You are all rats and cattle here.

Know this and see what I had to Submit to in order to be here, looking like you, not merely being Sublime in the Divine Place. I had to become this and suffer it! Now I suffer it! I love rats, Aniello. I Embrace them—rats, mice, walls, amoebas, frogs—I Embrace everybody. I Love everybody. I want to Wake Up every being to this Ecstasy in the midst of death. I have no righteousness in Me, no moral righteousness on any point. I have been willing to become incredibly ridiculous to Wake you Up. I have done everything! I have no moral righteousness in Me, no un-Love. I make no distinction between beings—humans, rats, amoebas—none.

You are all suffering the obligation to be eaten. Therefore, I Love you, because of Who I Am. I want to Give you the alternative, even though you may be eaten and even though you eat in the meantime. I want to Give you the Vision of My Glory, Wake you Up, Give you Ecstasy, the Experience of Happiness and Fullness, even while you are dying, not to mention while you live. This is a real and very important matter. I am not here to deny you the knowledge of what you are experiencing and what other beings experience. I am here to sensitize you to what you experience and to what other human beings experience, what other creatures supposedly less than human experience, what other forms—like these curtains and that fan—experience, even though they may not even appear to be conscious.

You think there is no conscious awareness in these so-called objects. There is nothing but such consciousness, everything threatened by the fact of existing in form temporarily. I have great Love, Compassion, Feeling. I Identify absolutely with all manifested beings. I do not look down on the rat, Aniello. That poor being breaks My Heart! And you should feel likewise, if you love Me. You must come to that point of feeling. I am here to sensitize you to your own sacrifice and the sacrifice of others. I am here to Call you beyond it, not to deny it. Go beyond it! Acknowledge it! This is a dreadful place! Your time here is so short! The logic of existence itself, when you know Me, transcends these murders, this ugliness, these limits—even the limits of humans, some of whom are relatively lovely, some of whom are relatively not. You must love them, Aniello! Love them! Absolutely! And relieve them of this terror!

Where do you think you are? You deny the rat your love? Really! I deny no one! I Embrace all—and not just humans but all manifested beings, suffering this limit, this horror, ending in death! All! With incredible passion! Really! Really, Aniello! Real love! For every one! Even for every molecule I breathe in! I never have a moment of un-Love, not a moment! I do not regard any ugliness except to observe with Compassion the terrible horror of its state and to receive it to My Self, to Give that being the Glory of loving My Heart, My Person! I would not blink an eye and deny any one that Vision.

This is exactly what I do. I never do anything else. And this is exactly what you must do, but not on the basis of some ideal-istic commitment to My philosophy. Only by loving Me, embrac-ing Me, being Embraced by Me, will you ever come close to this Disposition. Get into this Disposition. Yes, be disgusted by the rat because he is an ugly creature. But do not reject the being, as if you as a human live in paradise. You eat rat as rat eats mouse. You sacrifice. You die. And that is a horror. Every one of you expects the possibility of horror. It brings great tension to your heart. The only thing that relieves the tension on your heart, that Sublimes you in the midst of this realistic vision, is My Company.

My Company in this bodily (human) Form is temporary, like you. Most human beings who will be My devotees will never see Me in This Body except in photographs. They must know Me in My other Forms—My Spiritual (and Always Blessing) Presence and My Very (and Inherently Perfect) State. Why deny the rat, then? Why not bless the rat in its poorness? Think, Aniello! It is ugly, yes. But it is a being, suffering! What choice does that rat have but to eat the mouse's head? What choice do you have? You do not have choices beyond a point. Therefore, you need God-Grace to relieve your heart. So does the rat! Give him, or her, the God-Grace of your regard, beyond your acknowledgement of ugliness. Love. Sublime the poor state. That creature has no choice but to eat mouse head. Don't you understand, Aniello? Human beings have no real choice—philo-sophical options, maybe, but not real choice.

This is why you must forgive. To forgive is part of your obligation to bless all others. No matter what you suffer, unfor-tunately, you still must bless, forgive, relieve, be compassionate, be Happy. No matter what! It is a terrible discipline, a terrible discipline. Mark My Words! It is a terrible, fierce, sorrowful disci-pline! It is tapas. You need not go to the cave—merely to live is heat. To know Me is to be cooled, Sublimed.

You cannot know Me unless I suffer like you. Yet I suffer more than you do. I suffer the horror of this life more than you. You are hardly even aware of it. In My contact with this bodily (human) Form, I have not only Submitted to the Form of this Birth. I have Submitted to yours. I have had no end of horror, no end. I have Transcended all destinies, not just the Destiny of this body. I get no relief. I Give Relief. This is the Law. The Great One Suffers.

You imagine that you suffer and that you should therefore blame the Father, the Living One. You do not understand. You suffer nothing even close to My Suffering. Therefore, you are not horrified. It is because I have always been Present that you can live a human life and ever laugh, ever smile, whatever reason you may think you have to smile. How do you think it is possible that human beings ever experience enjoyment? It is not a philosophical matter. It is because I Am! How else under these circumstances could any being ever smile, ever weep for joy, ever be Happy, ever experience enjoyment, ever endure pleasure? It is possible because I Am.

The Living One Suffers. That is why there is any enjoyment at all, just as that is why there is Ultimate Enjoyment and Love-Bliss. This is the Truth. As My devotee you should understand Me and not merely believe what I am saying. Witness it! See My Life! See what I Do. See the Signs in My face, the Signs in This Body. I am not a balanced ascetic, communicating platitudes to you. I suffer your company even for a few, even for one. I do it all for anybody. That is why you must bring to Me only those devotees who are prepared to participate in My Sacrifice. I will ruin My Self with ordinary people.

So you, Aniello—disregard the rat! I am not trying to put you down or suggest that you are an extremely vulgar person. I am trying to Instruct you and everyone. A primary rule of religious life is sympathetic identification with beings. If any law has ever been communicated through religion, apart from the primary Law to Identify with God, it is to identify sympathetically with all beings, human or otherwise—all. Have heart-felt sympathy with the poor state of beings. Always be sad in your Ecstasy. You will not be relieved of this obligation. To know where you are and who you are is to be Blessed, to suffer with joy and know the reality of beings.

This Earth is no paradise, and to be My devotee is not merely to exist in paradise—not yet. Go to the seventh stage of life and beyond. In the meantime, because of your love for and acknowledgement of Me, identify sympathetically with all beings, even the next molecule you suck up your nostrils. Yes, there is a lot of ugliness, rats and otherwise. There is a lot of ugliness, Aniello, a lot. But look at that person. Look at that fraction of Light. Experience sympathetically that destiny, and bless it in your revulsion. This will add something to your consciousness. This will change the world. I Call you to that added disposition. After a while everyone will look to you at least as beautiful as the most beautiful of humans.

It will take a long time. This is not the generation in which those evolutionary changes will take place. My Appearance here is not the Prologue to paradise—or perhaps it is the Prologue to paradise if you understand that the Divine Self-Domain is right in front of you to be Realized. But My Appearance here does not mean that all beings will be Sublimed automatically. My Appearance here now means there is a choice. You must really awaken from your adolescence and become a true man, a true woman, stronger than the effort of cosmic Nature. Bless beings, and be Blessed.

This place certainly is not paradise, Aniello. You would be better off being bitten in the ass by that rat you despised. Do you know what I mean? That is good. For the love.

CHAPTER 44

Love Is a Puja

A DISCOURSE BY SRI DA AVABHASA

SRI DA AVABHASA: For Me, life is not the yahoo, gleeful smile of religious consolation. It is distress, the broken heart, the wound of incarnation. That is what I live every day, unlimited feeling of the way things are here. I put no gloss on it, you see. All consolation is gone.

Relative to human things, therefore, that is what there is for Me to feel. The body is wounded at the heart by this life. That is simply so. I offer no middle-class consolation of religion to anyone. Even so, the intimate things, intimate relations, love relations are there. And they are lived intimately. Yet even in the situation where those intimacies are lived, all those fragile things are threatened, here to be murdered, wasted.

Children are the symbol of it. What children represent that is in you also is there to be preserved, to be honored, to be cherished, to be loved, to be served. And see how fragile it is, how it could be ripped off like that! [Snaps His fingers.] There is no honoring of it in this world. You must protect and honor it yourself.

Your time will pass. The children will become more and more like you and get another piece of the human being that will tend to cover what they are more obviously at the present time. Then, as is presently the case with you, that which they are presently will have to be preserved in them. That is what Spiritual life is about. It is not about becoming some cool, dumb cultist or religionist. It is about preserving the intimacy, the heart matter, of existence—not allowing it to be destroyed.

Protecting that in you which is the real Spiritual matter is very much like protecting children. Not allowing the vulgarities of human egoic un-Happiness to damage children is the same thing as not allowing human egoic un-Happiness to damage the community of My devotees. You must preserve that delicate Eternity.

Love is a Puja, a small-scale, intimate matter, as your relationship to Me is as well. It is not about the grand victory on Earth. It is a heart matter. The Yoga of the Way of the Heart is to live this Divine intimacy. Honor it. Serve it constantly, in spite of the regulation life of suffering.

Well—that is a great Yoga, a great discipline. It is what I Do in My intimate Sphere. It is what you must do in your intimate sphere—and I am central to your intimate life.

DEVOTEE: You are absolutely the center of it!

SRI DA AVABHASA: That is where I live with you, then. That is where your Ishta is, you see, in intimacy and not in some yahoo cultic nonsense. Ishta-Guru-Bhakti Yoga is strictly an intimate matter, a truly Spiritual matter.

DEVOTEE: Sri Gurudev, I confess to You that You are the core of my life.

ANOTHER DEVOTEE: You are the Intimate of my life. I spend all day meditating on What You Are and how to serve You, because You are my greatest joy in spite of all the pain and suffering I experience constantly.

SRI DA AVABHASA: That is what esotericism is, you see, to reduce your life to intimacy. That is true renunciation. To abandon intimacy is phony renunciation. The Yoga of your practice of the Way of the Heart is to reduce your life to intimacy with Me, to the heart domain, to practice it, to honor it, to bring great energy to it, and to not allow it to be undermined by the vulgarities of ordinary life. This is just another way of saying what esoteric religion or true religion or Spiritual life has always been.

To Me, "intimacy" is just another word for esotericism. Esotericism is not mere secrecy. Esotericism is that which transcends the merely social consciousness. It is a heart matter, a direct matter. It is Where you Stand. It is not something that can be interfered with by events in the world, by politics, the news, and all the changes in the common world.

The Gift I Give to you is personal, intimate, a heart matter. You must not allow yourself to be deprived of it.

DEVOTEE: My Lord, I feel profoundly Instructed by Your relationship to children. I feel the Yoga of life that You do with them. You constantly feed them and assume a profound intimacy with them and nurture and love them. It moves me so much to see Your Example.

SRI DA AVABHASA: See what I do for them. I preserve them, honor them, feed them, Give them Life, Give them the Great Vision. This is what I do in every moment of every day with everyone who is associated with Me most intimately. Well, that is what you must do in relation to Me, then. You must make that kind of connection, live that process. Such must be the strength of the worldwide community of all My devotees.

You are not waiting for anything. You are not waiting for some future event, some "second coming". Your Way of life is here. I am here. I am waiting for you to do something in the present. I have nothing more to Do. You are acting as if your Way of life is supposed to be one of waiting. No—your practice is supposed to be one of demonstration.

DEVOTEE: That is what we are starting to understand, my Lord. We have benefited by the great opportunity of living in Your Company.

My Lord, the other thing that I noticed is a little thing, but something that impressed me greatly. Even with children You will not compromise anything. When a child expresses some egoic little movement, I have seen you require that child to change his or her action in such a wonderfully compassionate, loving, and humorous way.

SRI DA AVABHASA: Why should I cause them pain by making concessions to their egoity? Why govern them toward stress and isolation? Just so, I will not indulge you in your problem. Straighten up. Take a deep breath. Stand with Me. Become My devotee, and My Blessing-Presence will Instruct you. Do anything else, try to make the Way of the Heart out of an idealism, a scheme of practice, a routine of exercise, and you submit to yourself and not to Me.

DEVOTEE: I remember the first time I was confronted with Your Wisdom-Teaching. I went into a bookstore and bought *The Knee of Listening* and *The Method of the Siddhas*. I can still remember the very spot. That was the very moment that brought me directly to You and that was my relationship to You.

SRI DA AVABHASA: The relationship to Me is still the essence of your practice of the Way of the Heart. The Way of the Heart is a relationship with Me and not a technique. There are practices for which you must be responsible, and there are disciplines, but they are secondary to the essence of the Way of the Heart, which is your relationship to Me, the heart matter, an intimate matter. That is what I mean by esotericism. The Way of the Heart is an esoteric Way, then, an esoteric practice, not meaning that practice is a secret, since the Way of the Heart is openly communicated in the Literature I have produced. But what is the essence of it? It is an intimate matter, a heart matter. It is not a public matter, not a conventional matter, not an egoic matter.

The Way of the Heart is an intimate process. It can only be lived as an intimate heart matter. If you are going to live as My devotee, the Way of the Heart must become an intimate matter for you. In that sense you are like children, then. You are preserving the heart, conserving the heart, animating it, making it the dominant principle, not becoming vulgar by being conservative or revolutionary, not allowing the heart to be destroyed. By allowing the Way of the Heart to be an intimate practice, you are preserving the esotericism of Spiritual life.

To be sensitive to Me means that you must understand what I am saying. I refuse to be your True Heart-Master except in the most intimate sense, the real sense. I will not allow My Self to be abstracted, to be reduced to a photograph or a ceremony for the bureaucracy of a religious institution. The Way of the Heart is a heart matter, and therefore My Position as your True Heart-Master must be an intimate one and it must be so in relation to everyone who is My devotee.

That does not mean that everyone comes here to My Room and encounters Me personally. Such is not the necessary circumstance of this intimate practice. What makes the Way of the Heart intimate is not personal contact with Me but the heart-practice, the feeling practice, the self-transcending practice, not an idealistic practice in which you dominate the body-mind with philosophy or with one or another urge. I refuse to be abstracted, to reduce My Position in relation to you to anything but intimacy. I refuse to be approached in any other way.

The Principle of the Way of the Heart is your relationship to Me, then, not merely a series of practices you carry on in Marin or in Melbourne. There are practices, but they must be associated with your intimate relationship with Me, an intimate life altogether, an esoteric Way of life. I am your True Heart-Master. If you make your relationship with Me the essence, the substance, the foundation of your practice of the Way of the Heart, My Spiritual Heart-Transmission becomes the substance of your practice of the Way of the Heart. Through this relationship to Me, enter into the Domain of My Spiritual Heart-Transmission. Enter into the Domain of the Siddha-Master, of your True Heart-Master. Practice Ishta-Guru-Bhakti Yoga. That is My Revelation.

Idealisms, philosophy, practices are used by the ego to delay the course, to undermine your understanding, to submit you to a lesser state. If you remain in this relationship with Me, you cannot hold on to such things. There is no motive, no structure, of holding on. My Spiritual Heart-Transmission is the Means, the fundamental Means. Therefore, your relationship to Me is the Process, the Way of life that I have Taught and Revealed to you. That is what you must practice. If Ishta-Guru-Bhakti Yoga is your practice, if this relationship to Me is your practice, My Spiritual Heart-Transmission in relationship to you relieves you of your bondage.

My Transmission is not piecemeal. I present My Self. I am simply here As I Am. My Spiritual Heart-Transmission has nothing to do with the first six stages of life. Therefore, if your practice is Ishta-Guru-Bhakti Yoga, then you are sensitive to Me As I Am, and My Spiritual Heart-Transmission Grants Realization, Sublimity, transcendence. That Principle alone is what moves you beyond the discomfort of egoic life,

DA AVABHASA (THE "BRIGHT")
SRI LOVE-ANANDASHRAM, FIJI, 1993

About Da Avabhasa

The Giver of "Brightness"

Da Avabhasa's principal Name, "Da" ("the One Who Gives"), is an ancient Name for the Divine Being. "Avabhasa" means "Divine Brightness", and it indicates Da Avabhasa's "Brightly" Shining down into the world. "Sri", meaning "radiant" or "bright", is a traditional address that conveys respect and honor.

Even before His Birth, Sri Da Avabhasa was Awake as the "Bright" Eternal Condition His Name describes. He chose to be born in the West, and He did so to make it possible for men and women everywhere to Realize that same Divine Happiness.

He was born Franklin Albert Jones on November 3, 1939, in Jamaica, New York, into an ordinary middle-class American family. Because those around Him could not yet appreciate His Spiritual stature, He grew up not letting others know about the whirlwind of Spiritual forces and states He frequently experienced. Noticing that other people did not enjoy the Divine Freedom, Humor, and True Delight that was His constant Realization, He consciously let go of His "Bright" Divine Awakeness in order to discover the Way for others to realize the Great Happiness He had known since His Birth.

During His years at Columbia College and Stanford University, Sri Da Avabhasa began a conscious quest to uncover the means whereby everyone could Realize Divine Happiness—by rediscovering this Process in His own body-mind. In the early years of His Ordeal, when He was without the help of human Teachers, He achieved spontaneous insight into human suffering and seeking that will stand from this time forward as the fundamental breakthrough in human understanding.

In His twenties, Da Avabhasa became the exemplary Devotee

of great Spiritual Masters in a highly revered lineage of Indian Yogis, including Swami Rudrananda (or "Rudi"), Swami Muktananda, and Swami Nityananda. But the Divine Impulse to Realize the absolute Truth that was His birthright burned strongly in His heart, and It drove Him to move beyond even the exalted states of Spiritual Realization that were Revealed by His Gurus.

Eventually, with the Blessings of Swami Nityananda, Da Avabhasa became for a time a Devotee of the Divine Goddess, the infinite Source-Light, or Radiant Energy, who appeared to Him in an archetypal female Form. He enjoyed a paradoxical relationship to the Goddess as a concrete, living Personality. Such worship of the Goddess as Supreme Guru is the foundation and Spiritual Source of His Teachers' lineage, but at last Da Avabhasa's inherent Freedom Drew Him even beyond the Spiritual Blessings of the Goddess Herself, so that She ceased to function as His Guru and became, instead, His eternal Consort and Companion.

On the day following that Event, September 10, 1970, while Da Avabhasa was meditating in a small temple on the grounds of the Vedanta Society in Los Angeles, He Re-Awakened to immutable Oneness with the Consciousness, Happiness, and Love that is the Source and Substance of everyone and everything. He Describes this State in His Spiritual autobiography, *The Knee of Listening*:

> *In an instant, I became profoundly and directly aware of what I am. It was a tacit realization, a direct knowledge in consciousness itself. It was consciousness itself, without the addition of a communication from any other source. I simply sat there and knew what I am. I was being what I am. I am Reality, the Self, the Nature and Support of all things and all beings. I am the One Being, known as God, Brahman, Atman, the One Mind, the Self.*
>
> *There was no thought involved in this. I am that Consciousness. There was no reaction of either joy or surprise. I am the One I recognized. I am that One. I am not merely experiencing Him.*

Through His uniquely exemplary Spiritual practice, and His uncompromising adherence to the Divine Impulse that led Him to fulfill and exceed the offerings of all His Teachers, Da Avabhasa proved conclusively that human beings can constantly feel and even Most Perfectly Realize the Ultimate Happiness, Freedom, and Love we all yearn for!

After His Re-Awakening, Da Avabhasa became psychically aware of the body-minds of countless other persons and discovered that He was spontaneously "meditating" them. In time some of those individuals became associated with Him as His first "students", or "disciples". Finally, in April 1972, Da Avabhasa's formal Teaching Work was inaugurated when He opened a storefront Ashram in Los Angeles.

Since then, Sri Da Avabhasa has continuously Transmitted His Love-Blissful Blessing to all. He has created a vast and complete Wisdom-Literature, bringing Divine Understanding to subjects ranging from the Guru-devotee relationship, prayer, meditation, and the Nature of the Divine Reality, to sexuality, exercise, diet, politics, and science, to traditional esoteric Spirituality and the direct Way to Realize Ultimate Freedom and Happiness. Da Avabhasa's Divine Revelation, the Way of the Heart, puts every possible human activity and the entire history of our cultural and Spiritual endeavor into a new perspective. Thus, His Offering of the Way of the Heart is the seed of an entirely new possibility for humankind.

In January 1986, Sri Da Avabhasa's Work to Instruct others culminated in a unique Spiritual Process that marked His "Emergence" as the Divine World-Teacher. That Great Event signaled a tremendous magnification of His universal Blessing Work, whereby He continuously Transmits His Liberating Divine Grace to all beings everywhere.

It was at this time that "Da Free John" (as He was then known) took the Name "Da Love-Ananda Hridayam". "Love-Ananda", a Name that had been Given to Him in 1969 by Swami Muktananda, means "Inherent Love-Bliss", and "Hridayam" means "the Heart", or the Divine Being, Truth, and Reality. His principal Name, "Da", had been Revealed to Him some years earlier in vision and by other Spiritual means. Thus, the Name "Da Love-Ananda Hridayam" indicates that He is the Divine Giver of the Inherent Love-Bliss That is the Heart Itself.

Five years later, on April 30, 1991, the Divine Adept Revealed a new Name—"Da Avabhasa (The 'Bright')"—in response to His devotees' confessed acknowledgements of His Radiant, bodily Revelation of God.

"Avabhasa", in Sanskrit, has a rich range of associations. As a noun it means "brightness", "appearance", "manifestation", "splendor", "lustre", "light", "knowledge". As a verb it may be interpreted as "shining toward", "shining down", "showing oneself". The Name "Da Avabhasa", then, celebrates the Mystery of Da, the Divine Being, "Brightly" Appearing in human form. It points to His Divine Emergence and the ever-growing Radiance of His bodily (human) Form that is apparent to all who have been Graced to see Him, particularly since the Great Event of 1986.

The Name "Da Avabhasa" also points to His role as Sat-Guru— or One who brings the light of Truth into the darkness of the human world.

The "Bright", as Da Avabhasa tells us in *The Knee of Listening*, was, in fact, His own description from childhood of the sublime Condition He enjoyed at birth. He speaks of this Condition as "an incredible sense of joy, light, and freedom". He was, He says, "a radiant form, a source of energy, bliss, and light", "the power of Reality, a direct enjoyment and communication," "the Heart, who lightens the mind and all things". Even His entire life, as He once said, has been "an adventure and unfolding in the 'Bright'", the Radiance, Bliss, and Love of the God-State.

Da Avabhasa is not merely an extraordinary Teacher. He is not merely a man of uncommonly profound Spiritual experience who has generated a remarkably comprehensive and insightful Teaching, and who can transmit vivid Spiritual experiences. He is, rather, the Realizer and Transmitter of the Ultimate Realization, the Realization of the Heart. This is what His devotees mean when we refer to Him as "Divine World-Teacher". Da Avabhasa's Wisdom-Teaching is a complete Revelation of the ultimate Wisdom relative to every aspect of existence and every stage of our possible growth and Realization. And His Grace is universally active and universally available.

Da Avabhasa has come into this world to Reveal His Inherently Perfect Wisdom, to establish the Way of Truth, and to Bless all beings toward Divine Freedom, Happiness, Enlightenment, and Love. He constantly magnifies His Blessing and His Help for all. He offers the opportunity to enter into the Spiritual and transforming sacred relationship with Him, which is expressed by one's practice of the Way of the Heart.

DA AVABHASA (THE "BRIGHT")
SRI LOVE-ANANDASHRAM, FIJI, 1993

An Invitation

The human Spiritual Master is Divine Help to the advantage of those in like form. When one enters into right relationship with the Spiritual Master, changes happen in the literal physics of one's existence. I am not just talking about ideas. I am talking about literal transformations at the level of energy, at the level of the higher light of physics, at the level of mind beyond the physical limitations you now presume, at the level of the absolute Speed of ultimate Light. The transforming process is enacted in devotees in and through the Living Company of the Spiritual Master. The relationship between the Spiritual Master and the devotee is not a matter of conceptual symbolisms or emotional attachment to some extraordinary person. The true Guru-devotee relationship is real physics. Therefore, because they can make unique use of the Offering of that person's Company, it is to the special advantage of people when some one among them has gone through the real process of transformation that makes a Realizer-Guru of one or another degree. And that advantage is unique in My case, because that process has Completed and Revealed the total cycle that becomes Divine Self-Realization.

The Hymn Of The True Heart-Master,
"I Am Grace Itself" section

The sacred relationship that Sri Da Avabhasa Offers you is the greatest opportunity of a human lifetime. He offers you an entire Way of life that takes into account <u>everything</u> necessary for true religious and Spiritual practice and Ultimate Realization. He Offers you a Way of life that is founded on His unique Wisdom, a Way of life that can Liberate you from the dead end and the failed hopes of ordinary life, a Way that is full of His Grace, His Spiritual Gifts, and His utterly Boundless Love from the very beginning. Sri Da Avabhasa has done everything possible to make this Liberating opportunity readily accessible to you. Already there are groups of Da Avabhasa's devotees living and practicing together in communities around the world.

If you are feeling the urge to move beyond your present level of human growth and are interested in what Da Avabhasa is Offering you, we welcome you to take the next step.

How to Begin

BECOMING A STUDENT IN DA AVABHASA INTERNATIONAL

If you want to study more about the Way of the Heart and about becoming a practitioner, or if you are already clear that you would like to take up the practice, apply to become a student or tithing member of Da Avabhasa International. The Student Course is intensive guided study of what formal practice as Da Avabhasa's devotee involves, and exactly how you can more intensively cultivate your devotional relationship to Da Avabhasa. (There are two primary aspects to the Da Avabhasa International Student Course— intensified study, and service to Da Avabhasa via the community of His devotees.)

Very occasionally someone may be ready (by virtue of an extraordinary preparedness, especially an extraordinary devotional response to Sri Da Avabhasa) to bypass Da Avabhasa International altogether and enter immediately into the student-novice practice. But, generally speaking, at least a four-month period of formal guided study of the life and Wisdom-Teaching of Sri Da Avabhasa is essential. There is a very important reason for this.

BECOMING A STUDENT-NOVICE

At the point of becoming a student-novice, you make what Sri Da Avabhasa calls the "eternal vow"—a solemn commitment to devote your life to the living of your devotional relationship with Him. This bond is sacred, and its force is profound, transcending this lifetime. Through your real devotion to Sri Da Avabhasa and your real application to practice in His Company, your participation as a student-novice becomes the beginning of the most profoundly meaningful, demanding, and transforming process possible. We urge you to seriously consider the opportunity to become a student-novice.

As a student-novice, you take on in rudimentary form the range of devotional practices and disciplines that Sri Da Avabhasa Offers to His devotees. In addition to intensified study, service, and formal tithing, you begin to practice meditation, sacramental worship, "conscious exercise", diet and health disciplines, confining sexuality to a committed relationship, cooperative community (including formal membership in the Free Daist Cooperative Community Organization), and right use of money and energy.

BECOMING A FRIEND

If you are moved by the importance of Sri Da Avabhasa's Work and would like to show your gratitude for His Presence in the world without becoming a practitioner of the Way of the Heart (at least for the time being), then you may wish to become a Friend of Da Avabhasa International. A Friend is essentially a patron, someone who helps to fund the missionary services of the Free Daist Communion and the publication and promotion of Sri Da Avabhasa's sacred literature, and who participates in the general support of His Work. All Friends contribute a minimum fixed fee each year. In addition, some tithe regularly, and some are able to offer major financial support. Being a Friend is a very honorable way of associating with Sri Da Avabhasa. At the same time, Friends are always invited and encouraged to take the further step of preparing to become a formal practitioner of the Way of the Heart.

TAKING THE MOST IMPORTANT STEP

Sri Da Avabhasa is here now, offering you this transformative opportunity. Is there anything more worth doing than to enter into His Company? He is Calling you personally when He says:

SRI DA AVABHASA: Physical embodiment has the purpose of Divine Enlightenment. If you will receive My Teaching-Revelation, if you will "consider" it, if you will become responsive, then you become capable of making use of this lifetime for the purpose it inherently can serve. You must submit the body-mind to the Great Purpose. That is what I am Calling you to do. Accept the Dharma, the Law, inherent in your birth, the purpose that is inherent in your birth. Take up the Way of the Heart in My Company.

We invite you to enter into this sacred relationship with Sri Da Avabhasa, and be Awakened by His Grace. Contact us at our correspondence department or at one of our regional centers (see the following page). We will be happy to send you more information on how to participate as a Friend, a student of Da Avabhasa International, or a student-novice—as well as information on other study programs and events you can participate in. We look forward to hearing from you.

REGIONAL CENTERS OF THE FREE DAIST COMMUNION

UNITED STATES

NORTHERN CALIFORNIA
The Free Daist Communion
78 Paul Drive
San Rafael, CA 94903
(415) 492-0930
(415) 492-0216

NORTHWEST USA
The Free Daist Communion
5600 11th Avenue NE
Seattle, WA 98105
(206) 522-2298

SOUTHWEST USA
The Free Daist Communion
655 Ocean View Drive
Camarillo, CA 93010
(805) 482-5051
(310) 777-0212

NORTHEAST USA
The Free Daist Communion
30 Pleasant Street
South Natick, MA 01760
(508) 650-0136
(508) 651-0424

SOUTHEAST USA
The Free Daist Communion
10301 South Glen Road
Potomac, MD 20854
(301) 983-0291

HAWAII
The Free Daist Communion
6310 Olohena Road
Kapaa, HI 96746
(808) 822-3386
(808) 822-0216

AUSTRALIA
Da Avabhasa Retreat Center
P.O. Box 562
Healesville, Victoria 3777
Australia

03-853-5907 (Melbourne)
02-416-7951 (Sydney)
02-419-7563 (Sydney)

EASTERN CANADA
The Free Daist Communion
108 Katimavik Road
Val-des-Monts, Quebec J0X 2R0
Canada
(819) 671-4398

GERMANY
Nürnberger Strasse 19 IV
1000 Berlin 30
Germany
030-218-3333

THE NETHERLANDS
Da Avabhasa Ashram
Annendaalderweg 10
6105 AT Maria Hoop
The Netherlands
04743-1281
04743-1872

NEW ZEALAND
Da Avabhasa Ashram
12 Seibel Road, R.D. 1
Henderson, Auckland
New Zealand
(09) 309-0032 (day)
(09) 838-9114

THE UNITED KINGDOM AND IRELAND
Da Avabhasa Ashram
Tasburgh Hall
Lower Tasburgh
Norwich NR15-1LT
England
0508-470-574
081-341-9329 (London Center)

About the Way of the Heart

The Way of the Heart is an entire life-practice, and Sri Da Avabhasa has called the essence of that practice "Ishta-Guru-Bhakti Yoga". Ishta-Guru-Bhakti Yoga is the Way of devotion ("Bhakti") to one's "Ishta" ("Chosen") Guru. Anyone who is moved by Sri Da Avabhasa's Divine Attractiveness, who chooses Him as Ishta-Guru (or Divine Beloved of the heart), may take up this great and auspicious practice. Great seriousness and great sacrifice are required to live the Spiritual relationship Sri Da Avabhasa offers, but it is worth it: The devotional relationship to Him is the greatest imaginable joy.

Ishta-Guru-Bhakti Yoga is an utterly authentic process, a life based on Sri Da Avabhasa's uncommon and powerfully transforming Spiritual Love, lived in Communion with Him, the Divine in Person. Everyone, somewhere in the depths of his or her being, longs for such a life.

Those who give themselves over fully to this great Guru Yoga in Sri Da Avabhasa's Company inevitably grow in the Way of the Heart. In His Wisdom-Teaching, Sri Da Avabhasa has described the Spiritual, Transcendental, and Divine Awakenings that are His Graceful Gifts, over time, to His devotees.

A Summary of the Process of Growth in the Way of the Heart

Once you have fulfilled the preparatory course of practice as a student-novice and have become a full member in the Free Daist Communion, you will participate in the devotional and educational programs offered to student-beginners. By fulfilling the student-beginner practice, you will establish the devotional and practical foundation of your practice in Sri Da Avabhasa's Spiritual Company. All these forms of your practice and study will serve your growth in the process that Sri Da Avabhasa calls "listening". Listening is the process of self-observation, or the observation of the self-contraction as it is operative in your case, and it takes place in the context of real practice of the Way of the Heart and profound study of Da Avabhasa's Wisdom-Teaching. As the practice of listening matures, you will transition to further forms of involvement in the Free Daist Communion (as indicated in the chart on page 270).

Eventually, listening leads to most fundamental self-understanding, which Sri Da Avabhasa calls "hearing". Hearing is the stable capability to consistently transcend, or feel beyond, the activity of the ego. When hearing is truly established, there is intuitive Awakening to the Divine Condition that is always Prior to egoity. Once that ability has been stably integrated and demonstrated, the Spiritual process Sri Da Avabhasa calls "seeing" is activated. Seeing, which becomes possible on the basis of true hearing, is fundamentally an emotional conversion to love that is characterized by the stable capability to Commune with Da Avabhasa as All-Pervading Spirit-Presence.

The progressive awakening of listening, hearing, and seeing is a necessary and graceful process. But it is to the "Perfect Practice", founded on the hearing and seeing that were established earlier, that Sri Da Avabhasa ultimately Calls His devotees.

The "Perfect Practice" Given by Sri Da Avabhasa matures in three stages. The first stage is initiated when Sri Da Avabhasa's devotee spontaneously relinquishes the point of view of the body-mind (through effective practice in the preceding seeing stages) and becomes established in the Witness-Position of Consciousness Itself. The second stage follows when Consciousness Itself becomes the "Object" of Contemplation. The third stage of the "Perfect Practice" is Divine Enlightenment, or Most Perfect Identification with Consciousness Itself. All "things" are Divinely Recognized as mere modifications of Consciousness Itself, the One Self-Existing and Self-Radiant Divine Being.

THE PROGRESSION OF FREE DAIST PRACTICE

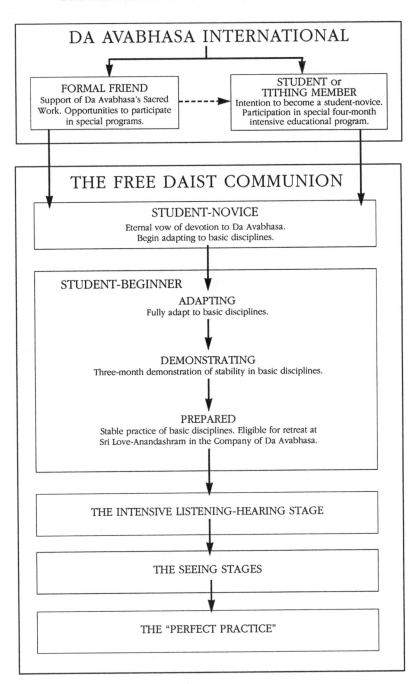

DA AVABHASA INTERNATIONAL

FORMAL FRIEND
Support of Da Avabhasa's Sacred
Work. Opportunities to participate
in special programs.

**STUDENT or
TITHING MEMBER**
Intention to become a student-novice.
Participation in special four-month
intensive educational program.

THE FREE DAIST COMMUNION

STUDENT-NOVICE
Eternal vow of devotion to Da Avabhasa.
Begin adapting to basic disciplines.

STUDENT-BEGINNER

ADAPTING
Fully adapt to basic disciplines.

DEMONSTRATING
Three-month demonstration of stability in basic disciplines.

PREPARED
Stable practice of basic disciplines. Eligible for retreat at
Sri Love-Anandashram in the Company of Da Avabhasa.

THE INTENSIVE LISTENING-HEARING STAGE

THE SEEING STAGES

THE "PERFECT PRACTICE"

THE WAY OF THE HEART IS THE RELATIONSHIP
TO SRI DA AVABHASA

Practice of the Way of the Heart unfolds through the phases of listening, hearing, seeing, and the "Perfect Practice." But these phases of growth, or developmental stages of practice, are not the focus of attention for a Free Daist. The Way of the Heart is not a path leading to a goal, even the goal of Divine Enlightenment. The Way of the Heart is a relationship to Sri Da Avabhasa, the greatest of all possible relationships, in the course of which the progressive stages of life manifest spontaneously by Grace. Liberation Most Ultimately (in this or some other lifetime) takes the form of Divine Enlightenment, but every moment of Heart-Intimacy with Sri Da Avabhasa is, in that moment, Liberation, Heart-Companionship with Him, freedom from egoic limits. This is why the Way of the Heart is highly worth practicing at any age, at any time, in any circumstance.

THE PRACTICING ORDERS

Sri Da Avabhasa has also established practicing orders—the Free Daist Lay Congregationist Order (or, simply, the Lay Congregationist Order), the Free Daist Lay Renunciate Order (or, simply, the Lay Renunciate Order), and the Naitauba (Free Daist) Order of Renunciates (or, simply, the Free Renunciate Order). The latter two orders have principal responsibilities in service to His Work, and all of the orders allow His devotees to intensify their devotional practice in the form and manner that is appropriate for them once they have developed the foundation of their practice in relationship to Sri Da Avabhasa.

When Sri Da Avabhasa's devotee moves beyond the student-beginner stage, he or she enters either the Lay Congregationist Order or the Lay Renunciate Order, depending on the individual's demonstrated qualifications of practice.

The Lay Congregationist Order is a practical service order whose members perform the many supportive practical services necessary for the work of the institution, the culture, and the community of all Free Daists. "Lay congregationists" conform every aspect of their life and practice to the Wisdom and Blessings of Sri Da Avabhasa, but their practice is not as intensive, nor as intensely renunciate, an approach to Most Perfectly self-transcending God-Realization as the practice of "lay renunciates" and "free renunciates".

Any member of the Lay Congregationist Order who develops the required signs (at any point in his or her practice of the Way of the Heart) may be accepted into the Lay Renunciate Order.

The Lay Renunciate Order is a cultural service order composed of practitioners who are especially exemplary in their practice of devotion, service, self-discipline, and meditation. Members of the Lay Renunciate Order are to provide the inspirational and cultural leadership for the institution, the culture, and the community of Sri Da Avabhasa's devotees, and they also guide and participate in public missionary work. Their basic responsibility is to serve all practitioners of the Way of the Heart in their practice of Ishta-Guru-Bhakti Yoga and to attract others to a life of Guru-devotion. When they reach the stage of stable Spiritual Awakening, Sri Da Avabhasa has indicated that His "lay renunciate" devotees will begin to function as His Instruments, or means by which His Divine Grace and Awakening Power are Magnified and Transmitted to other devotees and to all beings.

Members of the Lay Renunciate Order may practice either celibacy or a truly renunciate (and, Yogically, uniquely effective) discipline of sexuality.

The Lay Renunciate Order is directly accountable to the senior practicing Order of the Way of the Heart, the Free Renunciate Order.

THE FREE RENUNCIATE ORDER

The Free Renunciate Order is a retreat Order composed of devotees from the Lay Renunciate Order who have Awakened beyond the point of view of the body-mind to the Transcendental Position of Consciousness or to Divine Self-Realization.

Because of their extraordinary practice and Realization in the Company of Sri Da Avabhasa, "free renunciate" devotees are His principal human Instruments in the world. From among the fully Enlightened practitioners in the Free Renunciate Order, there will be selected after, and forever after, His human Lifetime, successive

"Living Murtis", or Empowered Human Agents, who will serve the magnification of His Heart-Transmission to all beings universally and perpetually.

"Murti" means "form", or "representational image". The "Living Murtis" of Sri Da Avabhasa (of which there will be only one in any given time) will not be Gurus in their own right. They will serve, rather, as a unique Living Link to Sri Da Avabhasa so that His Heart-Transmission will remain unbroken generation after generation.

Apart from its profound function to provide "Living Murtis" from among its membership, the Free Renunciate Order is the senior authority on all matters related to the culture of practice in the Way of the Heart and is completely essential to the perpetual continuation of authentic practice as Sri Da Avabhasa has Given it.

The original and principal members of the Free Renunciate Order are Sri Da Avabhasa Himself and the Da Avabhasa Gurukula Kanyadana Kumari Order, which consists of three women devotees who have for many years lived and served in Sri Da Avabhasa's intimate sphere and who have demonstrated the most exemplary practice of Ishta-Guru-Bhakti Yoga.

An Invitation to Participate in the Sacred Culture of Free Daism

The magnitude of the Gift Sri Da Avabhasa brings to humanity is being Revealed through the developing sacred culture of Free Daism, or the gathering of all those who formally practice the Way of the Heart. If you decide to participate in Da Avabhasa International and to proceed from there to become a formally acknowledged practitioner of the Way of the Heart, you will be participating in a unique and wholly worthy undertaking—the founding of a culture and a community whose sacred practice is always founded in direct enjoyment of Divine Communion, as Transmitted by the Divine World-Teacher, Sri Da Avabhasa. We invite you to join us and to partake of Sri Da Avabhasa's incomparable Blessing.

The Seven Stages of Life

by the Free Daist Writers Guild
based on the Wisdom-Teaching of Da Avabhasa

What <u>is</u> the total process of human growth? What would occur in us if we were to grow to the full extent of our evolutionary potential? Da Avabhasa Offers a schema of seven stages of life which represents His Wisdom on the entire spectrum of human possibility. He has systematically described not only our physical, emotional, and mental development but also all the phases of Spiritual, Transcendental, and Divine unfolding that are potential in us, once we are mature in ordinary human terms. This unique schema, which proceeds from birth to the final phases of Divine Enlightenment, is a central reference point in Da Avabhasa's Wisdom-Teaching. It is an invaluable tool for understanding how we develop as individuals and also for understanding how the Teachings and practices proposed by the various schools of religion and Spirituality fit into the whole scheme of human evolution.

Da Avabhasa describes the seven stages of life on the basis of His own Realization, as One Who has fulfilled that entire course. His testimony is literally unique. No one before Da Avabhasa has Realized the State which He describes as the seventh and Most Ultimate stage of life. Certainly there are hints and intuitions of this Realization in the annals of Spirituality. Da Avabhasa, however, has both described and Demonstrated not only the process of Awakening to the seventh stage of life, or Divine Enlightenment, but also the progressive signs that unfold in the seventh stage Realizer. And His Wisdom-Revelation is thus a unique Guide by which we may understand all the necessary stages of our evolutionary "growth and outgrowing".

The first three stages of life are the stages of ordinary human growth from birth to adulthood. They are the stages of physical, emotional, and mental development, occurring in three periods of approximately seven years each (until approximately twenty-one years of age). Every individual who lives to an adult age inevitably adapts (although, in most cases, only partially) to the first three stages of life.

Stage One—Individuation: The first stage of life is the process of adapting to life as a separate individual no longer bound to the mother. Most important for the first stage child is the process of food-taking, and coming to accept sustenance from outside the mother's body. In fact, this whole stage of life could be described as an ordeal of weaning, or individuation.

Tremendous physical growth occurs in the first stage of life (the first seven or so years) and an enormous amount of learning—one begins to manage bodily energies and begins to explore the physical world. Acquiring basic motor skills is a key aspect of the first stage of life—learning to hold a spoon and eat with it, learning to walk and talk and be responsible for excretion. If the first stage of life unfolds as it should, the separation from the mother completes itself in basic terms. But there is a tendency in us to struggle with this simple individuation, or to not accept the process fully. If by the age of seven or so we are left with a chronic feeling of separation from the source of life and support, then there is something lacking in our adaptation to the first stage of life.

Stage Two—Socialization: Between the ages of five and eight years we begin to become aware of the emotional dimension of existence—how we feel and how others respond emotionally to us becomes of great importance. This is the beginning of the second stage of life, the stage of social adaptation and all that goes with it—a growing sense of sexual differentiation, awareness of the effects of one's actions on others, a testing of whether one is loved. Da Avabhasa points out that in the second stage of life children are naturally psychic and sensitive to etheric energy. Children should be encouraged to feel that "you are more than what you look like", for the sake of their future Spiritual growth. The full process of growth in the second stage of life is frustrated if we become locked in patterns of feeling rejected by others, and rejecting and punishing others in return.

Stage Three—Integration: In the early to mid teens, the third stage of life becomes established. The key development of this stage is the maturing of mental ability—the capacity to use mind and speech in abstract, conceptual ways—together with the power to use discrimination and to exercise the will. On the bodily level, puberty is continuing (having begun during the later years of the second stage of life) with all its attendant bodily and emotional changes.

The purpose of the third stage of life is the integration of the human character in body, emotion, and mind, so that the emerging adult becomes a fully differentiated, or autonomous, sexual and social human character. If the process of growth in the first and the second stages of life has proceeded unhindered, then this integration can take place naturally. If, however, there have been failures of adaptation in the earlier stages—a chronic feeling of being separate and unsustained or chronic feelings of being rejected or unloved, and consequent difficulties in relating happily to others—then the process of integration is disturbed.

In fact, in most individuals, the process of the third stage of life becomes an adolescent struggle between the conflicting motives to be dependent on others and to be independent of them. This adolescent drama tends to continue throughout adult life. It is one of the signs that growth has stopped, that the work of the third stage of life was never completed.

So how does one begin to grow again? By participating in a culture of living religious and Spiritual practice that understands and rightly nurtures each stage of development. This is Da Avabhasa's recommendation, and the circumstance that He has Worked to create for His devotees by establishing the Way of the Heart. Anyone, at any age, who chooses the Way of the Heart can begin the process of understanding and transcending the limits of his or her growth in the first three stages of life and in all the stages of life that follow.

Da Avabhasa refers to the first three stages of life as the "foundation stages", because the ordeal of growth into human maturity is mere preparation for something far greater—for Spiritual awakening, and, ultimately, for Divine Enlightenment. This greater process begins to flower in the fourth stage of life on the basis of a profound conversion to love.

Stage Four—Spiritualization: Even while still maturing in the first three stages of life, many people devote themselves to religious practices, submitting to an ordered life of discipline and devotion. This is the beginning of establishing the disposition of the fourth stage of life, but it is only the beginning. The real leap involved in the fourth stage of life is a transition that very few ever make. It is nothing less than the breakthrough to a Spiritually-illumined life of Divine contemplation and selfless service. How does such a life become possible? Only on the basis of a heart-awakening so profound that the common human goals—to be fulfilled through bodily and mental pleasures—lose their force.

The purpose of existence for one established in the fourth stage of life is devotion—moment to moment intimacy with the Spiritual Reality, an intimacy that is real and ecstatic, and which changes one's vision of the world. Everything that appears, everything that occurs is now seen as a process full of Spirit-Presence. This new vision of existence is given through Spirit-Baptism, an infilling of Spirit-Power (usually granted by a Spiritually Awakened Master), which is described in many different religious and Spiritual traditions.

For the devotee in the Way of the Heart, Da Avabhasa's Spirit-Baptism is first felt as a Current of energy descending from above the head, down through the front of the body to the perineum, or bodily base. This descent is forceful, sublime, and very effective in purifying and Spiritualizing the human personality, bringing forth the signs of radiance, peace, and universal love that characterize a Spiritually Awakened being. By the time the fourth stage of life is complete, not only has the Spirit-Current descended fully down the front of the body but It has turned about at the bodily base and ascended up the spine to a place deep behind the eyes (called the "ajna chakra", or sometimes the "third eye"), where It is felt to rest.

The fourth stage of life, though it represents a profound and auspicious advance beyond the foundation stages, is only the beginning of truly Spiritual growth. Da Avabhasa points out that the primary presumption of one in the fourth stage of life is that God and the individual personality are inherently separate from one another. God is the Sublime "Other" with Whom one Communes and in Whom one may become ecstatically absorbed at times, even to the point of apparent union. Nevertheless, such raptures pass, and one is left with the continuing urge for union with the Divine Beloved. The individual being is still a separate ego, still searching, even though the goal of seeking is Spiritual in nature.

Stage Five—Higher Spiritual Evolution: The fifth stage of life could be described as the domain of accomplished Yogis—individuals involved in the pursuit of Enlightenment through mystical experience, such as the vision of the "blue pearl" and through the attainment of psychic powers. But it is important to note that just as exceedingly few religious practitioners fully Awaken to the Spiritual Reality in the fourth stage of life, exceedingly few would-be Yogis become fifth stage Realizers.

The important difference between the fifth stage of life and all the stages of life that precede it is that awareness on the gross physical plane is no longer the normal mode of existence. Rather, attention is constantly attracted into subtle realms—dreamlike or visionary regions of mind.

The phenomena of the fifth stage of life arise as a result of the further movement of the Spirit-Current, now in the higher regions of the brain. In the fifth stage of life the Spirit-Current moves from the ajna chakra through and beyond the crown of the head. At its point of highest ascent, the Spirit-Current triggers the Yogic meditative state traditionally called "Nirvikalpa Samadhi" ("formless ecstasy") in which all awareness of body and mind is temporarily dissolved in the Divine Self-Condition. (Da Avabhasa describes this Realization as "fifth stage conditional Nirvikalpa Samadhi".) Such an experience marks an enduring change in one's being. It is now clear that the individuated self has no eternal existence or significance. Only the Divine Condition of absolute Freedom and Happiness truly exists. Once this Divine Condition has been glimpsed in the state of "formless ecstasy", one's relationship to embodied existence is entirely different—one begins to see the body as an arbitrary, even humorous phenomenon.

Even so, a limit remains. This great Samadhi, the culminating achievement of the fifth stage of life, is fleeting. At some point bodily consciousness returns, and so does the ache to renew that boundless, disembodied Bliss. Fifth stage conditional Nirvikalpa Samadhi, for all its profundity, is achieved on the basis of a subtle stress. It is the ultimate fruit of the Yogic strategy to escape the body by directing one's awareness upward into infinite Light.

In His description of the Way of the Heart, Da Avabhasa Reveals that higher mystical experience and the achievement of profound trance states in the maturity of the fourth stage of life and in the fifth stage of life are not prerequisites for ultimate Divine Enlightenment. In the Way of the Heart, the whole tour of the subtle planes can be bypassed, because of Da Avabhasa's unique Transmission of the Love-Blissful Power of the Divine Itself. When, in the fourth stage of life, the devotee in the Way of the Heart is mature enough to be responsible for constantly receiving and "conducting" Da Avabhasa's Spirit-Current, a most extraordinary process begins to take place in the body-mind. The Infusion of His Spirit-Current purifies and quickens the body-mind in every cell from the crown of the head to the very toes. Every knot in the body-mind is opened up in this ecstatic reception of Him.

When this Sublime Infusion has completed its Work, a great conversion has occurred in the body-mind. One is not susceptible to the fascinations of visionary experience, even when such experiences arise. Neither is one moved to direct one's attention up and out of the body into the infinitely ascended state of "formless ecstasy". Rather, the "tour" of mystical experience is revealed to be simply more of the futile search to be completely Happy and fulfilled. And so that whole pursuit of mystical satisfaction relaxes, and the devotee may be easily drawn beyond all habits of identification with bodily states and even beyond the subtle mind states of the fifth stage of life into a pristine understanding of Reality as Consciousness Itself.

Stage Six—Awakening to the Transcendental Self: In the sixth stage of life, one is no longer perceiving and interpreting everything from the point of view of the individuated body-mind with its desires and goals. One stands in a Transcendental Position, Awake as the Very Consciousness that is the Ground of all that exists. In that Position, one stands as the "Witness" of all that arises, even while continuing to participate in the play of life. While life goes on like a movie on a screen, one sees the greater import of Existence and the non-necessity of all that arises. This is the beginning of what Da Avabhasa calls "the ultimate stages of life", or the stages of Identification with Consciousness Itself.

The sixth stage of life may include the experience of Jnana Samadhi, which, like fifth stage conditional Nirvikalpa Samadhi, is a form of temporary and conditional Realization of the Divine Self. However, fifth stage conditional Nirvikalpa Samadhi comes about through the strategy of ascent, the urge to move attention up and beyond the body-mind; in Jnana Samadhi, on the other hand, awareness of gross and subtle states is excluded by concentration in Transcendental Self-Consciousness.

Most prominent among the great sixth stage Realizers, historically, have been the Hindu and Buddhist, and in some cases Taoist, Sages who eschewed the fascinations of experience from the beginning. These great Realizers turned away from the enticements of "money, food, and sex" in the first three stages of life, as well as from the attractions of devotional (fourth stage) rapture and of Yogic (fifth stage) mysticism. Instead, the Sages of the sixth stage of life have traditionally contemplated the freedom and purity of Consciousness—to the degree of Realizing that Consciousness Itself, eternal and Prior to any mortal form or temporary experience, is our True Condition, or True Self.

But even deep resting in the freedom of Transcendental Consciousness is not Most Perfect Enlightenment. Why not? Because there is still a stress involved. Sixth stage Realizers have one last barrier to Divine Self-Realization that must be penetrated. Sixth stage practice and Realization is expressed by turning within, away from all conditional objects and experiences (including the energies and the movements of attention of one's own body-mind), and concentrating upon What is felt to be the Source of individual consciousness. Thus, the root of egoity is still alive. The search still remains, in its most primitive form. The sixth stage of life is the search to identify with Pure Consciousness Prior to and exclusive of phenomena.

Stage Seven—Divine Enlightenment: The Realization of the seventh stage of life is uniquely Revealed and Given by Da Avabhasa. It is release from all the egoic limitations of the previous stages of life. Remarkably, the seventh stage Awakening, which is Da Avabhasa's Gift to His devotees, is <u>not</u> an <u>experience</u> at <u>all</u>. The true Nature of everything is simply obvious. Now the Understanding arises that every apparent "thing" is Eternally, Perfectly the <u>same</u> as Reality, Consciousness, Happiness, Truth, or God. And that Understanding is Supreme Love-Bliss.

Da Avabhasa calls this Divine Awakeness "Open Eyes" and also "seventh stage Sahaj Samadhi" ("Sahaj" meaning "natural", or inherent, and "Samadhi" meaning exalted State). No longer is there any need to seek meditative seclusion in order to Realize perpetual Identification with the One Divine Reality. The Ecstatic and world-embracing Confession "There is <u>Only</u> God" is native to one who enjoys the State of "Open Eyes". Consciousness is no longer felt to be divorced from the world of forms, but Consciousness Itself is understood and seen to be the very Nature, Source, and Substance of that world. And so the life of the seventh stage Realizer, Most Perfectly Awake by Grace of Da Avabhasa, becomes the Love-Blissful process of Divinely Recognizing, or intuitively acknowledging, whatever arises to be only a modification of Consciousness Itself.

The Divinely Self-Realized Being is literally "Enlightened". The Light of Divine Being Flows in him or her in a continuous circuitry of Love-Bliss that rises in an S-shaped curve from the right side of the heart to a Matrix of Light above and Beyond the crown of the head. This is Amrita Nadi, the "Nerve of Immortal Bliss", mentioned in the esoteric Hindu Spiritual tradition, but fully described for the first time by Da Avabhasa Himself. After His Divine Re-Awakening in 1970, Da Avabhasa experienced the "Regeneration" of this Current of Love-Bliss, and He came to understand Amrita Nadi as the Original Form of the Divine Self-Radiance in the human body-mind (and in all conditional beings and forms).

In the seventh stage of life, or the context of Divine Enlightenment, the evolutionary process (which is now the Divine Yoga of Amrita Nadi) continues. Da Avabhasa, the first to Realize the seventh stage of life, is also the first to describe this most profoundly esoteric aspect of our Divine potential. He describes the seventh stage of life as having four phases: Divine Transfiguration, Divine Transformation, Divine Indifference, and Divine Translation.

In the stage of Divine Transfiguration, the Realizer's whole body is Infused by Love-Bliss, and he or she Radiantly Demonstrates active Love, serving the Awakening of others.

In the following phase of Divine Transformation, the subtle or psychic dimension of the body-mind is fully Illumined, which may result in extraordinary Powers of healing, longevity, and the ability to release obstacles from the world and from the lives of others.

Eventually, Divine Indifference ensues, which is spontaneous and profound Resting in the "Deep" of Consciousness Itself, Blessing the world directly from the Heart-Place, rather than Working outwardly to effect benign changes.

Divine Translation is the ultimate "Event" of the entire process of Awakening—the Outshining of all noticing of objective conditions through the infinitely magnified Force of Consciousness Itself. Divine Translation is the Destiny beyond all destinies, from Which there is no return to the realms.

The experience of being so overwhelmed by the Divine Radiance that all appearances fade away may occur <u>temporarily</u> from time to time during the seventh stage of life. But when that Most Love-Blissful Swoon (or Moksha-Bhava Samadhi) becomes permanent, Divine Translation occurs and the body-mind is inevitably relinquished in death. Then there is only Eternal Inherence in the Divine Domain of unqualified Happiness and Joy.

Da Avabhasa once described the unfolding Mystery of the seventh stage of life through the homely image of crocks baking in a furnace:

SRI DA AVABHASA: When you place newly made clay crocks in a furnace of great heat to dry and harden the crockery, at first the crocks become red-hot and seem to be surrounded and pervaded by a reddish glow, but they are still defined. Eventually the fire becomes white-hot, and its radiation becomes so pervasive, so bright, that you can no longer make out the separate figures of the crocks.

This is the significance of Divine Translation. At first, conditions of existence are Transfigured by the inherent Radiance of Divine Being. Ultimately, through Self-Abiding and through Divinely Recognizing all forms, in effect all forms are Outshined by that Radiance. This is the Law of life. Life lived Lawfully is fulfilled in Outshining, or the transcendence of cosmic Nature. In the meantime, cosmic Nature is simply Divinely Transfigured, and relations are Divinely Transfigured, by the Power of the Divine Self-Position. [February 9, 1983]

* * *

Many religious and Spiritual traditions conceive of human life as a "Great Path of Return", a struggle to be reunited with the Divine Source of existence. From Da Avabhasa's viewpoint, this is an error. The Way of the Heart is founded in "radical" understanding, or constant restoration to the intuition of <u>present</u> Happiness, <u>present</u> God. Thus, although Da Avabhasa allows for and fully explains all the developmental signs or stages of life through which

His devotee may pass, the Way of the Heart is not purposed to "progress through" the stages of life. The entire process is founded in the Wisdom of the seventh stage from the very beginning—and thus is one of <u>release</u>, of surrendering, progressively, via heart-Communion with Da Avabhasa all obstructions in body, mind, and psyche that prevent that unqualified Enjoyment.

Because the ultimate non-necessity of the stages of life and our real, present Inherence in the Divine State of Happiness is always utterly obvious to Him, Da Avabhasa can speak Ecstatically of the seven stages of life as seven "jokes":

SRI DA AVABHASA: Living the stages of life, though a profound and necessary gesture, is ultimately foolishness. The seven stages of life are stages of laughter, each of which must, in its turn, become a great laugh to you. You must be able to feel the pleasure of self-forgetting in the face of each stage of experience before you can go on to complete the next stage. In your present level of realization, however, you have not yet laughed at any of the stages of life. You are still burdened by them, still carrying them around, still being tested by them.

Even the seventh stage of life, you will see, is a colossal lot of foolishness. The only way to move through the seventh stage is to laugh your head off. The seventh stage of life must become a laughing matter, along with all the rest of your body and its stages of growth. You must get the seventh joke, the last laugh. That joke is eternal, and its Humor is infinite Love-Bliss. [February 14, 1979]

An Invitation to Support
the Way of the Heart

D a Avabhasa's sole purpose is to act as a Source of continuous Divine Grace for everyone, everywhere. In that spirit, He is a Free Renunciate and He owns nothing. Those who have made gestures in support of Da Avabhasa's Work have found that their generosity is returned in many Blessings that are full of His healing, transforming, and Liberating Grace—and those Blessings flow not only directly to them as the beneficiaries of His Work, but to many others, even all others. At the same time, all tangible gifts of support help secure and nurture Da Avabhasa's Work in necessary and practical ways, again similarly benefiting the whole world. Because all this is so, supporting His Work is the most auspicious form of financial giving, and we happily extend to you an invitation to serve the Way of the Heart through your financial support.

You may make a financial contribution in support of the Work of Da Avabhasa at any time. You may also, if you choose, request that your contribution be used for one or more specific purposes of Free Daism. For example, you may be moved to help support and develop Sri Love-Anandashram, Da Avabhasa's Great Hermitage Ashram and Empowered Retreat Sanctuary in Fiji, and the circumstance provided there for Da Avabhasa and the other "free renunciates" who practice there (all of whom own nothing).

You may make a contribution for this specific purpose directly to the Sri Love-Anandashram (Naitauba) Trust, the charitable trust that is responsible for Sri Love-Anandashram. To make such a contribution, simply mail your check to the Sri Love-Anandashram (Naitauba) Trust, P.O. Box 4744, Samabula, Fiji.

If you would like to make such a contribution and you are a United States taxpayer, we recommend that you make your contribution to the Free Daist Communion, so as to secure a tax deduction for your contribution under United States tax laws. To do this, mail your contribution to the Advocacy Department of the Free Daist Communion, P.O. Box 3680, Clearlake, California 95422, USA, and indicate that you would like it to be used in support of Sri Love-Anandashram.

You may also request that your contribution, or a part of it, be used for one or more of the other purposes of Free Daism. For example, you may request that your contribution be used to help publish the sacred Literature of Da Avabhasa, or to support either of the other two Sanctuaries He has Empowered, or to maintain the Sacred Archives that preserve Da Avabhasa's recorded Talks and Writings, or to publish audio and video recordings of Da Avabhasa.

If you would like your contribution to benefit one or more of these specific purposes, please mail your contribution to the Advocacy Department of the Free Daist Communion at the above address, and indicate how you would like your gift to be used.

If you would like more information about these and other gifting options, or if you would like assistance in describing or making a contribution, please contact the Advocacy Department of the Free Daist Communion, either by writing to the address shown above or by telephoning (707) 928-4096, FAX (707) 928-4062.

Planned Giving

We also invite you to consider making a planned gift in support of the Work of Da Avabhasa. Many have found that through planned giving they can make a far more significant gesture of support than they would otherwise be able to make. Many have also found that by making a planned gift they are able to realize substantial tax advantages.

There are numerous ways to make a planned gift, including making a gift in your Will, or in your life insurance, or in a charitable trust.

If you would like to make a gift in your Will in support of Sri Love-Anandashram, simply include in your Will the statement "I give the Sri Love-Anandashram (Naitauba) Trust, an Australian charitable trust, P.O. Box 4744, Samabula, Fiji, _____" [inserting in the blank the amount or description of your contribution].

If you would like to make a gift in your Will to benefit other purposes of Free Daism, simply include in your Will the statement "I give the Free Daist Communion, a California nonprofit corporation, 12040 Seigler Road North, Middletown, California 95461, USA, _____" [inserting in the blank the amount or description of your contribution]. You may, if you choose, also describe in your Will the specific Free Daist purpose or purposes you would like your gift to support. If you are a United States taxpayer, gifts made in your Will to the Free Daist Communion will be free of estate taxes and will also reduce any estate taxes payable on the remainder of your estate.

To make a gift in your life insurance, simply name as the beneficiary (or one of the beneficiaries) of your life insurance policy the Free Daist organization of your choice, according to the foregoing descriptions and addresses. If you are a United States taxpayer, you may receive significant tax benefits if you make a contribution to the Free Daist Communion through your life insurance.

We also invite you to consider establishing or participating in a charitable trust for the benefit of Free Daism. If you are a United States taxpayer, you may find that such a trust will provide you with immediate tax savings and assured income for life, while at the same time enabling you to provide for your family, for your other heirs, and for the Work of Da Avabhasa as well.

The Advocacy Department of the Free Daist Communion will be happy to provide you with further information about these and other planned gifting options, and happy to provide you or your attorney with assistance in describing or making a planned gift in support of the Work of Da Avabhasa.

Further Notes to the Reader

AN INVITATION TO RESPONSIBILITY

The Way of the Heart that Da Avabhasa has Revealed is an invitation to everyone to assume real responsibility for his or her life. As Da Avabhasa has Said in *The Dawn Horse Testament,* "If any one Is Interested In The Realization Of The Heart, Let him or her First Submit (Formally, and By Heart) To Me, and (Thereby) Commence The Ordeal Of self-Observation, self-Understanding, and self-Transcendence." Therefore, participation in the Way of the Heart requires a real struggle with oneself, and not at all a struggle with Da Avabhasa, or with others.

All who study the Way of the Heart or take up its practice should remember that they are responding to a Call to become responsible for themselves. They should understand that they, not Da Avabhasa or others, are responsible for any decision they may make or action they take in the course of their lives of study or practice. This has always been true, and it is true whatever the individual's involvement in the Way of the Heart, be it as one who studies Da Avabhasa's Wisdom-Teaching, or as a Friend of or a participant in Da Avabhasa International, or as a formally acknowledged member of the Free Daist Communion.

HONORING AND PROTECTING THE SACRED WORD THROUGH PERPETUAL COPYRIGHT

Since ancient times, practitioners of true religion and Spirituality have valued, above all, time spent in the Company of the Sat-Guru, or one who has, to any degree, Realized God, Truth, or Reality, and who thus Serves the awakening process in others. Such practitioners understand that the Sat-Guru literally Transmits his or her (Realized) State to every one (and every thing) with which he or she comes in contact. Through this Transmission, objects, environments, and rightly prepared individuals with which the Sat-Guru has contact can become Empowered, or Imbued with the Sat-Guru's Transforming Power. It is by this process of Empowerment that things and beings are made truly and literally sacred, and things so sanctified thereafter function as a Source of the Sat-Guru's Blessing for all who understand how to make right and sacred use of them.

Sat-Gurus of any degree of Realization and all that they Empower are, therefore, truly Sacred Treasures, for they help draw the practitioner more quickly into the process of Realization. Cultures of true Wisdom have always understood that such Sacred Treasures are precious (and fragile) Gifts to humanity, and that they should be honored, protected, and reserved for right sacred use. Indeed, the word "sacred" means "set apart", and thus protected, from the secular world. Da Avabhasa has Conformed His body-mind most Perfectly to the Divine Self, and He is thus the most Potent Source of Blessing-Transmission of God, Truth, or Reality, the ultimate Sat-Guru. He has for many years Empowered, or made sacred, special places and things, and these now Serve as His Divine Agents, or as literal expressions and extensions of His Blessing-Transmission. Among these Empowered Sacred Treasures is His Wisdom-Teaching, which is Full of His Transforming Power. This Blessed and Blessing Wisdom-Teaching has Mantric Force, or the literal Power to Serve God-Realization in those who are Graced to receive it.

Therefore, Da Avabhasa's Wisdom-Teaching must be perpetually honored and protected, "set apart" from all possible interference and wrong use. The Free Daist Communion, which is the fellowship of devotees of Da Avabhasa, is committed to the perpetual preservation and right honoring of the sacred Wisdom-Teaching of the Way of the Heart. But it is also true that in order to fully accomplish this we must find support in the world-society in which we live and from the laws under which we live. Thus, we call for a world-society and for laws that acknowledge the Sacred, and that permanently protect It from insensitive, secular interference and wrong use of any kind. We call for, among other things, a system of law that acknowledges that the Wisdom-Teaching of the Way of the Heart, in all Its forms, is, because of Its sacred nature, protected by perpetual copyright.

We invite others who respect the Sacred to join with us in this call and in working toward its realization. And, even in the meantime, we claim that all copyrights to the Wisdom-Teaching of Da Avabhasa and the other sacred literature and recordings of the Way of the Heart are of perpetual duration.

We make this claim on behalf of Sri Love-Anandashram (Naitauba) Pty Ltd, which, acting as trustee of the Sri Love-Anandashram (Naitauba) Trust, is the holder of all such copyrights.

DA AVABHASA AND THE SACRED TREASURES OF FREE DAISM

Those who Realize God to any degree bring great Blessing and Divine Possibility for the world. Such Realizers Accomplish universal Blessing Work that benefits everything and everyone. They also Work very specifically and intentionally with individuals who approach them as their devotees, and with those places where they reside, and to which they Direct their specific Regard for the sake of perpetual Spiritual Empowerment. This was understood in traditional Spiritual cultures, and those cultures therefore found ways to honor Realizers, to provide circumstances for them where they were free to do their Spiritual Work without obstruction or interference.

Those who value Da Avabhasa's Realization and Service have always endeavored to appropriately honor Him in this traditional way, to provide a circumstance where He is completely Free to do His Divine Work. Since 1983, Da Avabhasa has resided principally on the Island of Naitauba, Fiji, also known as Sri Love-Anandashram. This island has been set aside by Free Daists world-wide as a Place for Da Avabhasa to do His universal Blessing Work for the sake of everyone and His specific Work with those who pilgrimage to Sri Love-Anandashram to receive the special Blessing of coming into His physical Company.

Da Avabhasa is a legal renunciate. He owns nothing and He has no secular or religious institutional function. He Functions only in Freedom. He, and the other members of the Naitauba (Free Daist) Order of Renunciates, the senior renunciate order of Free Daism, are provided for by the Sri Love-Anandashram (Naitauba) Trust, which also provides for Sri Love-Anandashram altogether and ensures the permanent integrity of Da Avabhasa's Wisdom-Teaching, both in its archival and in its published forms. This Trust, which functions only in Fiji, exists exclusively to provide for these Sacred Treasures of Free Daism.

Outside Fiji, the institution which has developed in response to Da Avabhasa's Wisdom-Teaching and universal Blessing is known as "The Free Daist Communion". The Free Daist Communion is active worldwide in making Da Avabhasa's Wisdom-Teaching available to all, in offering guidance to all who are moved to respond to His Offering, and in providing for the other Sacred Treasures of Free Daism, including the Mountain Of Attention Sanctuary (in California) and Tumomama Sanctuary (in Hawaii). In addition to the central corporate entity of the Free Daist Communion, which is based in California, there are numerous regional entities which serve congregations of Da Avabhasa's devotees in various places throughout the world.

Free Daists worldwide have also established numerous community organizations, through which they provide for many of their common and cooperative community needs, including needs relating to housing, food, businesses, medical care, schools, and death and dying. By attending to these and all other ordinary human concerns and affairs via self-transcending cooperation and mutual effort, Da Avabhasa's devotees constantly free their energy and attention, both personally and collectively, for practice of the Way of the Heart and for service to Da Avabhasa, to Sri Love-Anandashram, to the other Sacred Treasures of Free Daism, and to the Free Daist Communion.

All of the organizations that have evolved in response to Da Avabhasa and His Offering are legally separate from one another, and each has its own purpose and function. He neither directs, nor bears responsibility for, the activities of these organizations. Again, He Functions only in Freedom. These organizations represent the collective intention of Free Daists worldwide not only to provide for the Sacred Treasures of Free Daism, but also to make Da Avabhasa's Offering of the Way of the Heart universally available to all.

A Selection of the Sacred Literature of Da Avabhasa

NEW EXPANDED EDITION
The Knee of Listening
The Early-Life Ordeal and The "Radical" Spiritual Realization of The Divine World-Teacher and True Heart-Master, Da Avabhasa (The "Bright")

This new, unabridged edition of Da Avabhasa's autobiography (which sold over 100,000 copies in its previous edition) has been called the greatest Spiritual autobiography ever written. Since its first publication in 1972, *The Knee of Listening* has become an acknowledged classic of modern Spiritual literature—essential reading for anyone interested in Spiritual life.

In Part I, Da Avabhasa recounts His first 31 years—the poignant, often hilarious, always astonishing story of a Being who was absolutely determined to discover the Truth of our existence, and did. He describes His Illumined birth and infancy, His experiments with every kind of possible human experience—from the Western pursuits of "money, food, and sex" to the mystical experiences of the East—and His Transcendence of all of it.

Parts II and III feature Da Avabhasa's earliest Essays on the process of "radical" understanding He Offers to everyone, and the final section of the book tells the remarkable Story of His Life and Work over the two decades since *The Knee of Listening* was originally published.

$18.95, * quality paperback; **$39.95,** cloth
605 pages

NEW EXPANDED EDITION
The Method of the Siddhas
Talks on the Spiritual Technique of the Saviors of Mankind

In these provocative dialogues, Da Avabhasa discusses the sublime import of Spiritual life and Reveals the secret of the profound and transforming relationship that He Offers everyone.

Self-help is not the ultimate answer. At best, it produces a better-adjusted, more functional ego. How could it produce anything else?

As *The Method of the Siddhas* makes clear, the sacred relationship with an Awakened Being (a "Siddha") has always been the most effective means for Spiritual growth. But few have been daring enough to engage such a relationship. The conversations in *The Method of the Siddhas* are unique glimpses into how that relationship is conducted.

I first read The Method of the Siddhas *twenty years ago and it changed everything. It presented something new to my awareness: One who understood, who was clearly awake, who had penetrated fear and death, who spoke English (eloquently!), and who was alive and available!*

Ray Lynch
composer, *Deep Breakfast,*
No Blue Thing, and *The Sky of Mind*

$14.95, quality paperback, 420 pages

* All prices are in U.S. dollars

Easy Death

Spiritual Discourses and Essays on the Inherent and Ultimate Transcendence of Death and Everything Else

In this major revision of the popular first edition of His Talks and Essays on death, Da Avabhasa Reveals the esoteric secrets of the death process and Offers a wealth of practical instruction.

- Near-death experiences
- How to prepare for an "easy" death
- How to serve the dying
- Where do we go when we die?
- Our Ultimate Destiny
- The truth about reincarnation
- How to participate consciously in the dying (and living) process

An exciting, stimulating, and thought-provoking book that adds immensely to the literature on the phenomena of life and death. Thank you for this masterpiece.

Elisabeth Kübler-Ross, M.D.
author, *On Death and Dying*

$14.95, quality paperback
432 pages

Free Daism

THE ETERNAL, ANCIENT, AND NEW RELIGION OF GOD-REALIZATION
An Introduction to the God-Realizing Way of Life Revealed by The Divine World-Teacher and True Heart-Master, Da Avabhasa (The "Bright")

Addressed to new readers and written in a highly accessible style, *Free Daism* is an introduction to Da Avabhasa's Life and Work, the fundamentals of His Wisdom-Teaching, the Guru-devotee relationship in His Blessing Company, the principles and practices of the Way of the Heart, and life in the community of His devotees. This book is a comprehensive and engaging introduction to all aspects of the religion of Free Daism, the Liberating Way that Da Avabhasa has made available for all.

$17.95, quality paperback
376 pages

The Love-Ananda Gita (The Wisdom-Song Of Non-Separateness)

*The "Simple" Revelation-Book Of
Da Kalki, The Divine World-Teacher
and True Heart-Master,
Da Love-Ananda Hridayam*

In 108 verses of incredible beauty and simplicity, *The Love-Ananda Gita* reveals the very essence of the Way of the Heart—Contemplation of Da Avabhasa as the Realizer and Revealer of the Divinely Awakened Condition. Then, in an extensive section of commentary following the verses, Da Avabhasa leads us into a full understanding of the details of this Contemplative practice. Finally, in a collection of inspiring stories from His devotees, the effectiveness of this practice is demonstrated.

Therefore, because of My always constant, Full, and Perfect Blessing Grace, it is possible for any one to practice the Way of the Heart, and that practice readily (and more and more constantly) Realizes pleasurable oneness (or inherently Love-Blissful Unity) with whatever and all that presently arises. . . .

Da Avabhasa
The Love-Ananda Gita, verse 78

This is the birth of fundamental and radical Scripture.

Richard Grossinger
author, *Planet Medicine, The Night Sky,*
and *Waiting for the Martian Express*

[Future editions of *The Love-Ananda Gita* will be titled *The Da Love-Ananda Gita* and will be published with the following attribution: The Simple Revelation-Book Of The Divine World-Teacher and True Heart-Master, Da Avabhasa (The "Bright").]

$19.95, quality paperback
818 pages

The Dawn Horse Testament

*The Testament Of Secrets Of
The Divine World-Teacher and
True Heart-Master,
Da Avabhasa (The "Bright")*

This monumental volume is the most comprehensive description of the Spiritual process ever written. It is also the most detailed summary of the Way of the Heart. *The Dawn Horse Testament* is an astounding, challenging, and breathtaking Window to the Divine Reality.

The Dawn Horse Testament *is the most ecstatic, most profound, most complete, most radical, most comprehensive single spiritual text ever to be penned and confessed by the Human-Transcendental Spirit.*

Ken Wilber
author, *Up from Eden*
and *A Sociable God*

$24.95, quality paperback
$45.00, cloth
8-1/2" x 11" format, 820 pages

The Hymn Of The True Heart-Master

(The New Revelation-Book Of The Ancient and Eternal Religion Of Devotion To The God-Realized Adept)

This book is Da Avabhasa's passionate proclamation of the human Guru as the supreme means of Enlightenment. In 108 poetic verses, freely evolved from the traditional *Guru Gita*, Da Avabhasa extols the great virtues of worship of and service and devotion to one's chosen Guru. This central Hymn is followed by a selection of Da Avabhasa's most potent Talks and Essays on the nature, primacy, and laws of the Guru-devotee relationship. The book concludes with moving stories and confessions by His devotees about the

sacred trial of growth and awakening in Da Avabhasa's Company. A most beautiful and inspirational text for anyone interested in Spiritual growth.

I do feel this Hymn will be of immense help to aspirants for a divine life. I am thankful that I had an opportunity to read and benefit by it.
M. P. Pandit
author, *The Upanishads: Gateways of Knowledge* and *Studies in the Tantras and the Veda*

$19.95, quality paperback
$27.95, cloth
450 pages

The Da Upanishad
The Short Discourses on self-Renunciation, God-Realization, and the Illusion of Relatedness

In this sublime collection of Essays, Da Avabhasa Offers an unsurpassed description of both the precise mechanism of egoic delusion and the nature, process, and ultimate fulfillment of the Sacred Ordeal of Divine Self-Realization.

The Da Upanishad *is a work of great linguistic beauty, as well as a remarkable description of the "before" of self and existence. It is a book about the* direct realization of Consciousness, *characterized by intellectual precision, but also with a depth of feeling that works away beneath the surface of the words.*
Robert E. Carter
author, *The Nothingness Beyond God*

[Future editions of this book will be titled *The Da Avabhasa Upanishad*]

$19.95, quality paperback
$39.95, cloth
514 pages

The ego-"I" is the Illusion of Relatedness

Published here in book form, this central Essay from *The Da Upanishad* is an indispensable introduction to the esoteric Wisdom-Instruction of Da Avabhasa. It includes His unique commentaries on dietary and sexual Yoga, His Divinely Enlightened secrets on how to responsibly master and transcend all dimensions of our existence, and passages of sublime beauty in which He Gives us glimpses of the absolute Divine Condition.

$8.95, quality paperback
192 pages

The Basket of Tolerance
A Guide to Perfect Understanding of the One and Great Tradition of Mankind

A unique gift to the world—an overview of the traditions of humanity from the viewpoint of the Divinely Enlightened Adept! This comprehensive bibliography (listing more than 2,500 publications) of the world's historical traditions of truly human culture, practical self-discipline, perennial religion, universal religious mysticism, "esoteric" (but now openly communicated) Spirituality, Transcendental Wisdom, and Perfect (or Divine) Enlightenment, is compiled, presented, and extensively annotated by Da Avabhasa. The summary of His Instruction on the Great Tradition of human Wisdom and the sacred ordeal of Spiritual practice and Realization.
(forthcoming)

The Perfect Practice

This book is Da Avabhasa's summary distillation of the Wisdom and Process of practice in the ultimate stages of life in the Way of the Heart. In it, Da Avabhasa wields His Great Sword of Most Perfectly self-transcending God-Realization, dispatching the dragons of egoic delusion, and all limited truths. He Calls us, and Draws us, to Realize the Very Divine Consciousness that is Radiantly Free, beyond all bondage to the limited states of the body, mind, and world.

The Perfect Practice includes the text of *The Lion Sutra*, Da Avabhasa's poetic Revelation of the esoteric technicalities and Liberated Freedom of the "Perfect Practice", and the text of *The Liberator (Eleutherios)*, in which He Epitomizes, in beautiful prose, the simpler approach to that same ultimate, or "Perfect", Practice leading most directly to Divine Awakening.
(forthcoming)

Scientific Proof of the Existence of God Will Soon Be Announced by the White House!
Prophetic Wisdom about the Myths and Idols of mass culture and popular religious cultism, the new priesthood of scientific and political materialism, and the secrets of Enlightenment hidden in the body of Man

Speaking as a modern Prophet, Da Avabhasa combines His urgent critique of present-day society with a challenge to create true sacred community based on God-Communion and a Spiritual Vision of human destiny. A masterpiece of prophetic and groundbreaking commentary!

A powerfully effective "de-hypnotizer" . . . that will not let you rest until you see clearly—and so seeing, choose to act. In modern society's time of troubles, this is a much needed book.
Willis Harman, president
The Institute of Noetic Sciences

$12.95, quality paperback
430 pages

294

The Transmission of Doubt

Talks and Essays on the
Transcendence of Scientific
Materialism through "Radical"
Understanding

Da Avabhasa's "radical" alternative to scientific materialism, the ideology of our time. The discourses in this book help each of us to grow beyond the linear, left-brained point of view so prevalent in today's society.

The Transmission of Doubt *is the most profound examination of the scientific enterprise from a spiritual point of view that I have ever read.*

Charles T. Tart
author, *Waking Up*
editor, *Altered States of Consciousness*

$10.95, quality paperback
484 pages

The Eating Gorilla Comes in Peace

The Transcendental Principle of Life
Applied to Diet and the Regenerative
Discipline of True Health

In this book, the result of years of experimentation by His devotees, Da Avabhasa Offers Enlightened Wisdom on diet, health, healing, and the sacred approach to birthing and dying. The book discusses:

• The true principle of health as Love, or the feeling-connection to Infinite Life
• The root of many food obsessions and common health failures
• How to compensate for physical and emotional imbalances through right diet and health practices
• How right diet affects your ability to have a pleasurable, mature, and regenerative sex-life
• Fasting, herbal remedies, and dietary modifications to purify and regenerate the body
• And much, much more

$16.95, quality paperback
565 pages

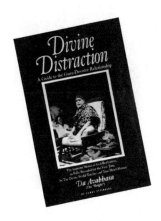

Divine Distraction

*A Guide to the Guru-Devotee
Relationship, The Supreme Means of
God-Realization, as Fully Revealed for
the First Time by the Divine World-
Teacher and True Heart-Master,
Da Avabhasa (The "Bright")*
by James Steinberg

In this wonderful book, a long-
time devotee of Da Avabhasa discusses the joys and challenges, the lore
and laws, of the most potent form of
Spiritual practice: the love relationship
with the God-Man. Along with many
illuminating passages from the
Wisdom-Teaching of Da Avabhasa,
Divine Distraction includes humorous, insightful, and heart-moving
stories from His devotees, as well as
other Teachings and stories from the
world's Great Tradition of religion
and Spirituality. Essential for anybody
who wants to know first-hand about
the time-honored liberating relationship between Guru and devotee.

$12.95, quality paperback
288 pages

Feeling Without Limitation

*AWAKENING TO THE TRUTH
BEYOND FEAR, SORROW,
AND ANGER
A Spiritual Discourse by The Divine
World-Teacher and True Heart-Master,
Da Avabhasa (The "Bright")*

A woman once confessed to Da
Avabhasa that she often felt emotionally frozen, unable to allow herself to
really feel and release anger, sorrow
and fear. Da Avabhasa's response to
her is illuminating to us all.

In the very direct and simple
Discourse contained in this book, Da
Avabhasa presents His fundamental
insight into human suffering, seeking,
and the nature of Liberation. Also
included in this brief introductory volume are three remarkable personal
testimonies about Da Avabhasa's life-
transforming Divine Influence.

$4.95, paper
112 pages

The books listed on these pages are only a selection from the titles by and about Da Avabhasa that are currently available. For a complete listing of books and periodicals, as well as audiotaped and videotaped Discourses by Da Avabhasa, please send for your free Dawn Horse Press Catalogue.

The Heart's Shout
THE LIBERATING WISDOM OF DA AVABHASA
Essential Talks and Essays by The Divine World-Teacher and True Heart-Master, Da Avabhasa (The "Bright")

The Heart's Shout is a powerful and illuminating introduction to Da Avabhasa's Wisdom-Teaching on such topics as the sacred relationship to Da Avabhasa; the awakening of self-understanding; the Nature of the Divine Reality; the Great Tradition of religion, Spirituality, and practical wisdom; human politics; truly human culture; cooperative community; science and scientific materialism; death and the purpose of life; the secrets of love and sex; the foundations of practice in the Way of the Heart; Da Avabhasa's "Crazy Wisdom"; and Divine Self-Realization.

$14.95, quality paperback
360 pages

Ordering the Books of Da Avabhasa

To order books, or to receive your free Dawn Horse Press Catalogue, send your order to:

THE DAWN HORSE PRESS
P.O. Box 3680, Department IL-B
Clearlake, CA 95422, USA
or
Call TOLL FREE (800) 524-4941
Outside the USA call
(707) 928-4936

We accept Visa, MasterCard, personal check, and money order. In the USA, please add $4.00 for the first book and $1.00 for each additional book. California residents add 7-1/4% sales tax. Outside the USA, please add $7.00 for the first book and $3.00 for each additional book. Checks and money orders should be made payable to the Dawn Horse Press.

GLOSSARY

advanced and ultimate

Da Avabhasa uses the term "advanced" to describe practice of the Way of the Heart in the context of the fourth stage of life and the fifth stage of life. He reserves the term "ultimate" for practice of the Way of the Heart in the context of the sixth stage of life and the seventh stage of life.

Agent

When Sri Da Avabhasa Speaks and Writes of "Agents" of His Divine Blessing Work, He is referring to the various Mechanisms He has Empowered to serve as unobstructed Vehicles of His Divine Grace and Awakening Power. The first of His Agents to be fully established by Him are His Wisdom-Teaching, the three Retreat Sanctuaries He has Empowered, and the many sacred Objects and Articles He has Empowered for the sake of His devotees' Remembrance of Him and reception of His Heart-Blessing.

Heart-Master Da also uses the word "Agent" to indicate any formally Acknowledged and specially chosen Divinely Self-Realized "free renunciate" devotee who will, in the future beyond His physical Lifetime Transmit His Spiritual, Transcendental, and Divine Heart-Blessing to others and the world, and to provide authoritative present-time commentary on His Word and His Leela, or His Play with His devotees. For more information on such human Agents, please see the description of "Murti-Gurus" in *The Dawn Horse Testament.*

Circle

The Circle is the primary circuit, or passageway, of the Living Spirit-Current and natural bodily energy as they flow through the body-mind. The Circle is composed of two arcs: the descending Current associated with the frontal line, or the more physically oriented dimension, of the body-mind; and the ascending Current associated with the spinal line, or the more mentally and subtly oriented dimension, of the body-mind.

"conductivity"

Da Avabhasa's technical term for the intentional exercises of feeling and breathing that He Gives His devotees, to "conduct", or freely circulate, the natural energies of the body-mind and, in the event of Spiritual maturity, His Spirit-Current. "Conductivity" is a support for the "conscious process".

"conscious process"

Da Avabhasa's technical term for those practices in the Way of the Heart through which attention, or the mind of self-involvement, is surrendered to feeling-Contemplation of Him. The "conscious process" is the senior discipline and responsibility of all practitioners in the Way of the Heart.

"consideration"

Sri Da Avabhasa's technical term for the "process of one-pointed but ultimately thoughtless concentration and exhaustive contemplation of a particular object, function, person, process, or condition, until the essence or ultimate obviousness of that subject is clear". As engaged in the Way of the Heart, "consideration" is not merely an intellectual investigation. It is the participatory investment of one's whole being. If one "considers" something fully in the context of one's practice of feeling-Contemplation of Sat-Guru Da, this concentration results in "both the highest intuition and the most practical grasp of the Lawful and Divine necessities of human existence".

Darshan

"Darshan" is a Sanskrit term that literally means "seeing", "sight of", or "vision of". To receive Darshan of Sri Da Avabhasa is to receive the spontaneous Blessing He Grants Freely by Revealing His bodily (human) Form (and, thereby,

His Spiritual, and Always Blessing, Presence and His Very, and Inherently Perfect, State). In the Way of the Heart, Darshan of Sri Da Avabhasa is the very essence of all practice.

Practitioners of the Way of the Heart may enjoy Darshan of Sri Da Avabhasa through each of the following means: sighting of Him in formal occasions of sitting with Him personally (when rightly prepared, and formally invited, to do so), or in apparently less formal occasions when He makes Himself physically visible to those of His devotees who are rightly prepared; and association with Him through His books, photographs, videotapes, and recorded Talks, through the Leelas (or Stories) of His Teaching Work and Blessing Work, through places or objects He has Blessed for His devotees, and through simple, heart-felt Remembrance of Him and visualization of His bodily (human) Form in the mind.

Divine Ignorance

Sri Da Avabhasa's term for the fundamental awareness of Existence Itself, prior to all sense of separation from or knowledge about anything that arises. As He Proposes, "No matter what arises, you do not know what a single thing is." By "Ignorance" He means heart-felt participation in the universal Condition of inherent Mystery, not mental dullness or the fear-based wonder or awe felt by the subjective ego in relation to unknown objects. Divine Ignorance is the intuition of Consciousness Itself, transcending all knowledge that is cognized and all experience that is perceived by the self-contracted ego-"I".

Divine Transfiguration, Divine Transformation, Divine Indifference, Divine Translation

In the context of Divine Enlightenment in the seventh stage of life (which is Revealed and Given only by Sri Da Avabhasa) the Spiritual process continues. Da Avabhasa has described

this most profoundly esoteric aspect of our ultimate evolutionary potential as having four phases: Divine Transfiguration, Divine Transformation, Divine Indifference, and Divine Translation.

In the phase of Divine Transfiguration, the Realizer's body-mind is Infused by Da Avabhasa's Love-Bliss, and he or she Radiantly Demonstrates active Love, serving the Awakening of others.

In the phase of Divine Transformation, the subtle or psychic dimension of the body-mind is fully Illumined, which may result in extraordinary Divine Powers of healing, longevity, and the ability to release obstacles from the world and from the lives of others.

Eventually, Divine Indifference ensues, which is spontaneous and profound Resting in the "Deep" of Consciousness, Blessing the world directly from the Heart-Place rather than Working outwardly to effect benign changes.

Divine Translation is the ultimate "Event" of the entire process of Divine Awakening. Da Avabhasa describes Divine Translation as the Outshining of all noticing of objective conditions through the infinitely magnified Force of Consciousness Itself. Divine Translation is the Destiny beyond all destinies, from Which there is no return to the conditional realms.

The experience of being so overwhelmed by the Divine Radiance that all appearances fade away may occur temporarily from time to time during the seventh stage of life. But when that Most Love-Blissful Swoon becomes permanent, Divine Translation occurs and the body-mind is inevitably relinquished in death. Then there is only Eternal Inherence in the Divine Self-Domain of unqualified Happiness and Joy.

Dreaded Gom-Boo

Da Avabhasa's humorous term for the illusory "dis-ease" of egoity, which conventional religion tries to cure. He uses the term to point to humanity's erroneous relationship to the ego. We act as if the ego is something happening to us—something outside ourselves that can be "cured" through the search—rather than understanding egoity as an <u>activity</u> that we are always presently performing.

Great Tradition

Da Avabhasa's term for the total inheritance of human, cultural, religious, magical, mystical, Spiritual, Transcendental, and Divine paths, philosophies, and testimonies from all the eras and cultures of humanity, which has (in the present era of worldwide communication) become the common legacy of humankind.

Gurudev, Gurudeva

Sanskrit for "Divine Guru". A loving and intimate way of addressing or referring to one's Guru.

hearing. (See listening, hearing, seeing)

Heart

When spelled with a capital "H" in Da Avabhasa's Wisdom-Teaching, "Heart" refers to the Divine Being, Truth, and Reality.

Ishta-Guru-Bhakti Yoga

A compound of traditional Sanskrit terms that denotes the principal Gift, Calling, and Discipline Sat-Guru Da Avabhasa Offers to all who would practice the Way of the Heart.

"Ishta" literally means "chosen", or "most beloved". "Guru", in the reference "Ishta-Guru", means specifically the Sat-Guru, the Revealer of Truth Itself (or of Being Itself). "Bhakti" means, literally, "devotion".

Ishta-Guru-Bhakti, then, is devotion to the Supreme Divine Being in the Form and through the Means of Da Avabhasa, the human Sat-Guru.

"Yoga", from a Sanskrit root meaning "to yoke", "to bind together", is a path, or way, of achieving Unity with (or Realizing one's Prior Identity with) the Divine.

kali yuga

In the Hindu tradition, the kali yuga is the final, and most ignorant and degenerate, period, or the dark (kali) epoch (yuga), of mankind, when the Spiritual Way of life is almost entirely forgotten.

Lesson of life

Sri Da Avabhasa's term for the fundamental understanding that no conditional seeking can achieve Happiness but that Happiness is inherent in Existence Itself. As Sri Da Avabhasa has succinctly summarized it: "You cannot <u>become</u> Happy. You can only <u>be</u> Happy."

listening, hearing, seeing

Technical terms by which Da Avabhasa indicates three stages in the progress of the Way of the Heart, each of which takes place in the context of a heart-felt devotional relationship to Him. Listening, the foundation practice, takes place in the context of profound study of Da Avabhasa's Wisdom-Teaching, and it is a process of self-observation, or the observation of one's activity of self-contraction. Hearing is the crisis through which listening is fulfilled in most fundamental self-understanding. It is the stable capability to consistently transcend, or feel beyond, the activity of the ego. When hearing is truly established there is intuitive awakening to the Divine Condition that is always Prior to egoity. Seeing, which becomes possible on the basis of true hearing, is fundamentally an emotional conversion to love that is characterized by the stable capability to Commune with Da Avabhasa as All-Pervading Spirit-Presence.

niyamas (See yamas and niyamas)

Outshining

Sri Da Avabhasa uses the word "Outshining" to describe Divine Translation, the final phase of the seventh stage of life, which He Reveals and Gives. In the event of Divine Translation, or Outshining, body, mind, and world are no longer noticed, not because the Divine Consciousness has withdrawn or dissociated from manifested phenomena, but because the Ecstatic Divine Recognition of all arising phenomena (by the Divine Self, and As only modifications of Itself) has become so intense that the "Bright" Self-Radiance of Consciousness Itself now Outshines all phenomena.

"peculiar" (See "solid", "peculiar", and "vital")

"Perfect Practice"

The "Perfect Practice" is Sri Da Avabhasa's technical term for the discipline of the sixth stage of life and the seventh stage of life in the Way of the Heart.

Devotees who have mastered (and thus transcended the point of view of) the body-mind by fulfilling the preparatory processes of the Way of the Heart, may, by Grace, be Awakened to practice in the Domain of Consciousness Itself, in the sixth and seventh, or ultimate, stages of life.

The three parts of the "Perfect Practice" are summarized by Sri Da Avabhasa in chapter 43 of *The Dawn Horse Testament.*

Prayer of Changes

A form of Divine Invocation and Divine Communion Given by Da Avabhasa to His devotees so that they may bring about positive changes in their lives and in the psycho-physical world. It is not a plea to the Divine for results. Rather, it is principally a form of Heart-Communion with Sri Da Avabhasa and, secondarily, a relinquishment of negative or problematic states of mind and emotion. Thus, practice of the Prayer of Changes releases identification with all negative conditions and affirms a wholly right and new condition, which is fully assumed, felt, breathed, and lived.

Puja

"Puja" is any form of sacred ceremonial worship.

"radical"

The term "radical" derives from the Latin "radix", meaning "root", and thus it principally means "irreducible", "fundamental", or "relating to the origin". Because Da Avabhasa uses "radical" in this literal sense, it appears in quotation marks in His Wisdom-Teaching to distinguish His usage from the popular reference to an extreme (often political) position or view. Da Avabhasa characterizes the entire Way of the Heart as "radical".

rajas (see tamas)

sadhana

Self-transcending religious or Spiritual practice.

sannyasa

Sanskrit for "to throw down completely", or "to renounce".

Traditionally in India, sannyasa was seen as the fourth of four stages of human life: student ("brahmacharya"), householder ("grihastha"), philosophical recluse or ascetic "forest dweller" ("vanaprastha") and finally "sannyasa"— the stage of one (sannyasin) who is free of all bondage and able to give himself or herself completely to the God-Realizing or God-Realized life.

Sat-Guru-Seva

In Sanskrit, "seva" means "service". Service to the Sat-Guru (a title meaning "true Guru" that is applied to Da Avabhasa) is traditionally treasured as one of the great Secrets of Realization.

In the Way of the Heart, Sat-Guru-Seva is the remarkable opportunity to live every action and, indeed, one's entire life, as direct service and responsive obedience (or sympathetic conformity) to Sri Da Avabhasa in every possible and appropriate way.

Satsang

Sanskrit for "true or right relationship", "the company of Truth, or of Being". In the Way of the Heart, Satsang is the eternal relationship of mutual sacred commitment between Da Avabhasa and each true and formally acknowledged practitioner of the Way of the Heart.

sattva (See tamas)

seeing (See listening, hearing, seeing)

self-Enquiry

Self-Enquiry is a form of practice Given by Da Avabhasa that expresses and deepens the process of self-observation and self-understanding in the Way of the Heart. In self-Enquiry, one asks oneself the question "Avoiding relationship?" as a means of transcending the self-contraction. It is the practice spontaneously developed by Da Avabhasa in the course of His own Ordeal of Divine Self-Awakening. Self-Enquiry is the principal technical practice chosen by some who practice the Way of the Heart—Da Avabhasa has also provided other forms of the "conscious process" that similarly serve and support self-understanding.

Siddha

Sanskrit for "a completed, fulfilled, or perfected one", or "one of perfect accomplishment, or power". In Sri Da Avabhasa's usage, a Siddha is a Transmission-Master who is a Realizer, to any significant degree, of God, Truth, or Reality.

Siddhi

Sanskrit for "power", or "accomplishment". When capitalized in Da Avabhasa's Wisdom-Teaching, "Siddhi" is the Divine Awakening-Power that He spontaneously and effortlessly Transmits to all.

sila

A Pali term meaning "habit", "behavior", "conduct". It connotes the restraint of outgoing energy and attention, the disposition of equanimity, or free energy and attention for the Spiritual process.

"solid", "peculiar", and "vital"

Sri Da Avabhasa has observed and Described three distinct character types or patterns—ways individuals tend to dramatize egoity in the first three stages of life—which He calls "solid", "peculiar", and "vital". These correspond, respectively, to the reactive and self-protective egoic strategies of a characteristically mental (or chronically mentally conceptual), a characteristically emotional (and even hysterical), and a characteristically vital (or physically self-indulgent) kind.

For further discussion, see *The Dawn Horse Testament.*

Spirit-Baptism

The tangible communication of Spiritual Energy, or Blessing, from a Spiritual Adept to his or her devotee. Da Avabhasa's Spiritual Transmission is often felt as a Current of Spirit-Energy descending in the front of the body and ascending in the spinal line. Nevertheless, Sri Da Avabhasa's Spirit-Baptism is fundamentally and primarily the moveless Transmission of the Heart Itself, whereby He Rests His devotee in the Heart-Source of His Baptizing Spiritual Current and Awakens the intuition of Consciousness Itself. As a secondary effect, the Spirit-Current Transmitted through His Great Baptism serves to purify, balance, and energize the entire body-mind of the devotee who is prepared to receive it.

tamas

The principle or power of inertia. The Hindu texts declare that manifested existence is a complex variable of three qualities, or "gunas". These are "tamas", "rajas", and "sattva". "Rajas", or the "rajasic" quality, is the principle or power of action, or motivation. "Sattva", or the "sattvic" quality, is the principle or power of equilibrium, or harmony.

tapas

"Tapas" literally means "heat". The fire of self-frustrating discipline generates a heat that purifies the body-mind, transforms loveless habits, and liberates the practitioner from the consolations of ordinary egoic existence.

Tcha

"Tcha" is the sacred sound that Sri Da Avabhasa characteristically makes as a form of Blessing in Acknowledgement of a devotee's response to Him.

vital (see **"solid"**, **"peculiar"**, and **"vital"**)

vital shock

Da Avabhasa uses the term "vital shock" to describe the primal recoil of every individual from the experience of being born—and, throughout the course of egoic life, from the vulnerable condition of bodily existence and of relationship itself.

yamas and niyamas

Yamas are restraints, or the things one must not do. Niyamas are disciplines, or the things one must do. The practice of yamas and niyamas is the foundation stage of traditional Yoga. In the Way of the Heart these disciplines support the practice of feeling-Contemplation of Sri Da Avabhasa.

INDEX

A

action
- change of, 33-34, 67, 68, 75, 78-79
- conducting life-energy in, 173
- as feeling-Contemplation, 37, 68, 173
- as sacrifice, 172-173

adaptations, changing, 78-79

adolescents, dramatization in, 60

agreements, honoring, 170-171

American Indians, balanced culture of, 153

anger, 58-60
- appropriateness, 87, 88-92
- breathing and, 73-74
- cause and effect, 52
- communication of, 39-42, 138-139
- feeling-Contemplation and, 64, 88
- freedom from, 223
- love more than, 91-92
- overcome by Happiness, 138-139
- from sex-suppressive orientation, 230-231
- "vital" character and, 58-59
- *See also* emotions, negative

animals, Da Avabhasa's Compassion for, 224-227, 241-249

associations, transitory nature of, 218

attachment
- grieving and, 211-212
- love compared with, 207-212, 214-215
- Outshined in God-Realization, 229-230
- to Undying Beloved, 220

attention
- discipline of, 75-76, 155-156
- *See also* feeling-Contemplation; feeling-surrender

authority, in community, 187

avoidance of relationship. *See* "Narcissus"; self-contraction

B

Basket of Tolerance, The, 178

beatitude of surrender, 238-240

beauty, creating environment of, 196

betrayal
- dramatization of, 112
- freedom from, 110

birth, fear and, 51, 54

blame
- error of assuming, 106-109
- victim mentality and, 107-108

Blessing. *See* Heart-Transmission

blessing all others, 181-183

body-mind
- affected by energy field, 157
- emotions and, 56, 59-60, 80-81
- feeling-Contemplation and, 28, 75-76, 100
- humor about, 76
- Life-Current and, 59-60
- as limitation, 25, 109
- Real Condition of, 66
- self-contraction and, 25, 26, 63, 235-238
- transforming chemistry of, 191

breathing, conscious, 73-74

Brihadaranyaka Upanishad, xiii

bringing energy. *See* life-energy, giving

C

challenge, and nurture, 151-153

change
- community role in, 186-188, 196
- how to, 67, 75, 78-79, 181-183
- inevitability of, 217-223
- necessity of, 33-34, 114, 120-121
- responsibility necessary for, 156-157

character types, 54, 57, 58-59, 235-238

childhood issues, relieved through Satsang, 82-83

children
- bringing into relationship, 161
- Da Avabhasa's service to, 252
- dramatization in, 60
- letting go of, 209-210
- responsibility for life-energy in, 154-155
- sex-positive orientation and, 230-231
- staying Happy with, 65-66
- as what is to be preserved, 250-251

communication
- arising from feeling-Contemplation, 172, 174
- assuming relationship in, 104-105
- changing agreements with, 170
- conserving, 172-173
- of displeasure, 39-42, 138-139
- energy field as medium of, 154-157, 173
- of Happiness, 131, 139
- life difficulties as common topic, 173
- of love, 135-136, 139
- as sacrifice, 172-173

community. *See* cooperative community

compassion, 167, 175-180
- *See also* forgiveness; love (human)

concern, letting go of, 67-68, 75-79

conflict
- avoidance, 44-45
- transformation, 67, 114, 159-160

confrontation. *See* conflict

Consciousness Itself
- Da Avabhasa as, 101, 103
- dependence-independence presumptions and, 214-217
- described, 216
- ego-death and, 229
- everything only a modification of, 24, 216, 222
- feeling without limitation, 6
- as Force of the Heart, 18
- Freedom of, 6, 81, 215
- identifying with qualities, 77-78, 98
- Inherent Perfection, 167-169, 216

negative emotions and, 84, 95-96
as Undying Beloved, 220, 221-222
as Witness-Position, 84, 94-96
See also Happiness; Love (Divine)
consolation, 48-49
fear and, 55, 61-62
no truth in, 141, 219
visions as, 46, 48
contraction. *See* "Narcissus"; self-contraction
control, 159-160
convention, as desensitization, 142
conventional religion. *See* religion, exoteric
conversion, of negative emotions, 52-53, 66-67
cooperation, 177, 178
cooperative community
as discipline, 188-189, 193
experiments in, 187
government, 187, 198-200
life-business and, 193, 194
living arrangements, 194-195
as meditation, 190
Mulund, India, as inspiration for, 195-196
necessary for true religion, 186, 188, 190, 192
as opportunity for self-transcendence, 192, 193, 194
as power for change, 186-188, 196
renunciation and, 193-195
responsibility in, 69, 190
sacred nature, 187-188
as sanctuary for growth, 188, 191, 195
Satsang central, 188-189
self-contraction and, 197
wound of love and, 140-141
cooperative democracy, 198, 199
correcting others
appropriateness of, 40-41, 174
in Happiness, 42, 65-66, 115, 138-139, 252
See also criticalness
counseling, unnecessary for devotee, 82-83
crisis, in Spiritual life, 69-70
criticalness
as barrier to relationships, 39-42, 168
overcome through self-understanding, 177-178
See also correcting others
culture
of "inspiration and expectation", 200
renunciates and, 200
of tolerance, 177-180
of wisdom, 65
cursing others, refraining from, 116-118
cycle of patterns, 77-78

D

Da Avabhasa
Acts to serve Awakening, 9
Compassion for all beings, 224-227, 241-249
Consciousness Itself, 101, 103
Demand of, 132, 152
Embraces all devotees, 164, 165, 167
Father-Force of, 152

His Love, x-xi, xv-xvi, xix-xxi, 10, 91
import of Appearance, 10, 78, 101, 173, 249
Mother-Force of, 152
Object of meditation, xv-xvi
Offers transforming relationship, xv-xvi, 10
provokes crisis, 70
relieves complications, 99, 101
in service to children, 252
suffering of, 34, 245-248, 250
Darshan, Heart-Transmission magnified in, 85
death, and sorrow, 57-58
demand
for competence, 39-42
of Da Avabhasa for transcendence, 132, 152
for exchange of love, 14-15, 176
dependence, Consciousness Itself and, 214-217
Descending Spirit-Current, 230-231
desire
fear and, 55
in reaction to what is arising, 97, 98
relationship and, 218
detachment, as immunization against frustration, 5
devotion
allowing to humanize, 32
confession of Love-Bliss and, 29
means to Liberation, xix-xx, 11
relieves suffering, 82-83
See also Ishta-Guru-Bhakti
devotional exercises, as occasions of ecstasy, 134
devotional groups, 189
dietary discipline, 73
differentiation, from what is arising, 27, 96, 97, 98
difficulties, being served by, 112
dilemma
absence of, 18, 75-79
dissolution in self-understanding, 24
solving not reason for love, 24
discipline
feeling-Contemplation and, xviii-xix
Happiness as, 123-124
increased for dramatization, 68, 71-72
purpose, xviii-xix, 11, 23-24
secondary to Satsang, 253-254
See also relational disciplines
discipline of others. *See* correcting others
displeasure
communication of, 39-42, 138-139
See also anger; emotions, negative
dissociation
described, 146
inspecting, 147
transcending in God-Realization, 148
Divine Communion. *See* Satsang
Divine Ignorance, Happiness and, 131-132
Divine Person. *See* Consciousness Itself;
Happiness; Love (Divine)
Divine Purpose, 23-24

Divine Reality. *See* Consciousness Itself;
    Happiness; Love (Divine)
Divine Transfiguration, 140
Divine Transformation, 140
Divine Translation, 140
Divine Vision, 23-24, 245-246, 252
dominance, 159-160
doubt
    conscious breathing and, 74
    freedom from, 223
    See also emotions, negative
dramatization
    in children and adolescents, 60
    in conflict, 44-45
    culture of wisdom, 65
    feeling-surrender of, 49-50, 76, 84, 86, 87
    increased discipline for, 68, 71-72
    obstructs release of tendencies, 76
    responsibility for, 5-7, 32, 47, 60-61, 71
    self-understanding and, 107, 210-211
    in "Spiritual" people, 13
    victim mentality and, 106
"Dreaded Gom-Boo", 53
duty, and social obligations, 171
dying
    from exploitation of the life-force, 173
    in Happiness, 15, 245-246
    from love, 14
    as our reality, 218-223, 242-247
    painfully, 242-245
    as transition, 211-212
    from Truth, 34
    while living, 221

E

economics, and women, 198
ecstasy, 132-134
    defined, 25
    in free-falling, 219
    in Satsang, 214
    and Spiritual life, 134
    while dying, 245-246
ego. *See* "Narcissus"; self-contraction
ego transcendence. *See* self-transcendence
ego-collapse, symptoms of, 229
ego-death, and Consciousness Itself, 229
emotion
    appropriateness of, 40-42, 86, 87-92
    central to God-Realization, 147
    See also emotions, negative; *individual
        emotions*
emotional dissociation. *See* dissociation
emotional-sexual relationships
    fasting of, 71-72
    relation to parents and, 126-129
    as sacrifice, 172-173
    as Yoga, 129
    See also relationships
emotions, negative
    affected by energy field, 157
    breathing and, 73-74

conversion of, 52-53, 66-67
culture of wisdom and, 65
defined, 51
expressing, 39-42, 138-139, 173
feeling-Contemplation and, 64, 66-67, 75, 157
freedom from, 110, 223
outshined by love, 62, 91-92
patterned in infancy, 80-81
in relation to parents, 2-4, 126-129
relinquishing, 83-86, 100, 123-124, 157, 182
responsibility for, 60-61, 80-81, 154-157
as secondary symptom, 66
self-contraction and, 51-52, 115
self-understanding and, 54-57, 63-64, 115
Spiritual crisis and, 69-70
unconcern about, 75-79
from "Viewpoint" of Consciousness Itself,
    84, 95-96
See also emotion; *individual emotions*
emptiness
    guilt and, 51
    repentance of, 52
energy. *See* life-energy, giving
energy field, 154-157, 173
equality, 166-167
    in Satsang, 164-165
    sexual, 198
equanimity, as a discipline, 155-156
evolution, human, love necessary for, 15, 31-32
existence
    dependent upon others, 14-15
    threatened, 176-177, 191-192, 218-223,
        242-247
expectations, love not dependent upon meeting,
    3-5, 7-8
experience, three qualities of, 77-78

F

face-losing, 164-165
fasting, in difficult times, 71-72
father. *See* parents
father-force
    of Da Avabhasa, 152
    described, 151-153
    role of, 68
fear, 54-57
    appropriateness of, 87-88, 90-92
    arising from "otherness", xiii, 26, 54-56
    avoidance of, 61-62
    conscious breathing and, 74
    consolation and, 55, 61-62
    conversion of, 52-53, 56-57
    desire and, 55
    feeling-Contemplation and, 54-55, 57
    freedom from, 62, 223
    of love, 143
    love more than, 91-92
    manipulation of others and, 159-160
    shame and, 51
    See also emotions, negative

feeling
  central to practice, 146-148
  suppression of, 6-8, 42, 80, 88-90, 208
feeling of relatedness, transcending, 27-28, 216
Feeling without limit, 90-91, 141
feeling-Contemplation
  in actions, 21, 37, 47
  as basic principle, xviii, 21, 49
  blessing others through, 118, 181-183, 215
  communication arising from, 172, 174
  discipline and, xviii-xx
  as ecstasy, 134
  fear and, 54-55, 57
  Liberation and, 11, 49
  lived in relations, 12, 20, 47, 181, 215
  love made possible by, ix-x, xix-xxi, 17-18,
    21
  negative emotions and, 66-67, 75, 157
  passion and, 91-92
  Prayer of Changes and, 181-183
  rather than struggle, 29, 63-64
  relationships and, 12, 17, 21
  release of self-contraction through, xv-xvi,
    11, 82-24, 232
  self-observation and, 28, 123-124, 232
  stages of maturing in, 97
  unconcern and, 67-68, 75-79
  and the Wisdom-Teaching, 49
  See also feeling-surrender; Satsang
feeling-surrender, 26
  in absolute pain, 238-240
  beatitude in, 238-240
  essential for true relations, 21, 145
  release of dramatization and, 49-50, 71, 86
  relief of karmas and, 94, 123-124
  transformation of action and, 173
  See also feeling-Contemplation; Satsang
femininity, and relationship with mother,
    126-129
food
  love as, 14-15
  sacrifice and, 242-244
forgiveness
  as bringing great energy to, 116-118
  discipline of love and, 3-5, 119-120
  feeling-Contemplation and, 118
  as forgetting or ignoring offense, 116-118
  in Happiness, 223
  hearing and, 100
  of parents, 3-4, 126-129, 135
  ritual of, 3, 118-119
  Satsang and, 100-101, 124
  self-understanding and, 100
  ultimately unnecessary, 100-101, 119
  See also compassion; love (human)
freedom
  of Consciousness itself, 6-7, 81, 215
  of the heart, 6-7, 76, 81
  from negative emotions, 110, 223
  from others and things, 216
free-fall, life as a, 218-219

fulfillment
  an egoic goal, 3-5, 7-8, 168
  fear and, 55

G

giving. See life-energy, giving
global situation. See world situation
God-Realization
  by being love, 47
  emotional matter, 147
  Gift, not attribute, 164
  Great Work, 165-166
  Satsang and, 161, 164
  self-denial and, 229
  suffering and, 20, 142, 176
  as transcendence of dissociation, 148
  worship of Divine in all beings in, 181
  wound of love and, 140
"Good Company" of devotees, 82
  See also culture
gossip, not indulging, 174
government, of cooperative community, 198-200
Great Purpose, 23-24
Great Tradition, as basis for tolerance, 177-178
grieving, 211-212
guilt
  cause and effect of, 51-52
  over failure to love all, 118
  responsibility rather than, 123
  sorrow and, 51
  See also emotions, negative

H

habits, changing, 78-79
Happiness
  basis for morality, 166
  basis for renunciation, 217, 228
  communication of, 131, 139
  as discipline, 123-124
  Divine Ignorance and, 131-132
  Divine Nature of, 131
  forget all things in, 223
  giving life-energy and, 149-150
  Love as, 19, 132-133
  magnifying in relationships, 217
  making room for, 133
  not dependent upon perfection, 167-169
  our responsibility, 106, 109-110, 123-124
  our true Condition, 132, 216, 217
  redirection of attention and, 65-66
  release of self-contraction and, 24, 115, 132
  Remembering, 139
  service as, 36
  unreasonableness of, 131, 161, 166
  See also Consciousness Itself; Love (Divine)
hearing, and forgiveness, 100
Heart. See Consciousness Itself; Happiness;
    Love (Divine)
heart, freedom of, 6-7, 76, 81
Heart-Master
  as Unique Method of Awakening, 173
  See also Da Avabhasa

Heart-Transmission
  always available, 29
  egoic contents and, 28, 85-86
  as fundamental Means, xvi-xvii, 254
  giving to others and, 149-150
  Leela on, ix-xi
  magnified in community of devotees, 190
  magnified in Darshan, 85
  Non-Separateness and, 28
  undoing self-contraction through, xvi-xvii,
    91, 254
Heart-Vision, 23-24, 245-246, 252
hierarchy, in community, 187
"hole" in the universe, wound of love as, 140
holidays, rituals of feeling, 8
honesty, 174
householder life, and cooperative community,
  189
human, becoming
  foundation for Spiritual life, 31-34, 46
  through Satsang, 32
human existence. See existence
humility
  necessary for God-Realization, 165-166
  not self-doubt, 166-167
  sign of devotee, 163-164
humor
  about cranky body-mind, 76
  assuming relationship and, 104-105
  irony and, 174

I

"I love you"
  as Heart-Communication, 62
  importance of expressing, 135-137
  reluctance to say, 120, 136
  as superficial expression, 7, 120-121
identification
  with Consciousness Itself, 95-97
  with what is arising, 27, 95-97, 98, 99
Ignorance, and Happiness, 131-132
illusion of relatedness, transcending, 27-28, 216
independence
  Consciousness Itself and, 214-217
  false presumption, 46
inferiority. See superiority/inferiority
insult, not taking love-wound as, 111
intimacy, central to practice, 251-252, 253
intimate relationships. See emotional-sexual
  relationships
irony, 174
Ishta-Guru-Bhakti
  cooperative community and, 189
  ecstasy, 133
  intimate matter, 251-252, 253
  love manifested, 18
  not about superiority or inferiority, 163
  sensitivity to Da Avabhasa and, 24
  See also devotion

J

justice, love greater than, 3-4

K

Kali Yuga. See world situation
karma
  cause of, 98
  purification in Satsang, 78, 94, 123-124
transcendence of, 52-53
Knoblock, Barbara, Leela on self-observation,
  xvii

L

Law, as love, 11, 47, 110, 149
Leelas
  on caring for fish (Jeff Polson), 224-227
  on Da Avabhasa's Love (Meg McDonnell),
    x-xi
  on Gift of Love in relationships, ix-x
  on self-observation (Barbara Knoblock), xvii
  on service (Cathy Lewis), 201-203
Lesson of life, 106, 220
letting go, 206, 209-210
  in grieving, 211-212
  of this unnecessary realm, 221
Lewis, Cathy, Leela on service, 201-203
life-business
  handling as basis of Spiritual process, 31-34
  handling in cooperative community, 193, 194
  renunciation and, 229
life-conditions, primary and necessary, 32
Life-Current, 59-60
life-energy, giving
  to all beings, 68
  central to Happiness, 149-150
  and conducting in action, 173
  in conflictive relationships, 114
  forgiveness as, 116-118
  love as, 146
  in mutual interdependence, 14-15
  responsibility for quality of, 154-157
life-negative orientation, 191, 230-231
life-positive orientation, 191-192, 230-231
living arrangements, in community, 194-195
Love (Divine)
  basis for Spiritual life, 10, 17
  contraction from, xix, 45-46
  Da Avabhasa as, x-xi, xv-xvi, xix-xxi, 91
  described, 16, 91
  Happiness as, 19, 132-133
  makes human love possible, ix-x, 21-22
  "only cure for the loveless heart", xxi
  Power, 47, 91
  Realization of, 47
  Undying Beloved, 220, 221-222
  See also Consciousness Itself; Happiness
love (human)
  as action, 19
  attachment compared with, 7, 18, 207-212,
    214-215
  basic principle, 20

blessing all others in, 181-183
demand on others to, 14-15
dying from, 14
expectations limit, 3-5, 7-8
failure of, 113
feeling-Contemplation frees us to, ix-x,
    xix-xxi, 17-18, 21, 134
food, 14-15
forgiveness, 120
frees heart from bondage, 10
giving energy as, 146
greater than justice, 3-4
imperfections and, 167
to include animals, 224-227, 241-249
as Law, 11, 47, 110, 149
letting go in, 209-210
liberation through incarnation of, 10, 20
manifested as Ishta-Guru-Bhakti Yoga, 18
many forms of, 9
misconceptions about, 18-19
more than fear, sorrow, and anger, 91-92
necessary for human evolution, 15, 31-32
negative emotions and, 62
pain and suffering in, 19-20, 34, 142, 208
as Puja, 251
reluctance to, 143-144
requires transformation, 19
sacrifice, 18
self-understanding necessary for, xvi-xvii,
    5, 111, 142, 209-212
service and, xix, 4, 35
Spiritual life and, 12-13, 17, 20, 110
as true test, 13
unobstructed relationship, 18, 146
when feeling unloved, 44-45, 47-48
wound of, 88, 111-113, 140-142, 250
See also compassion; forgiveness
lust, not love, 18

M

McDonnell, Meg, Leela on Da Avabhasa's
    Love, x-xi
managing others, disposition while, 40-42
manhood, and relationship with father, 126-129
manipulation, 66, 159-160
martyrdom, and self-importance, 107
masculinity, and relationship with father, 126-129
mediocrity, as desensitization, 142
meditation
    cooperative community as, 190
    Da Avabhasa as Object of, xv-xvi
    occasion of ecstasy, 134
men, liberation presumed for, 198
mind
    as self-contraction, 235-238
    See also body-mind
morality
    based on Happiness, 166
    development of, 154
    human foundation of, 147
    love more than, 16

mother. *See* parents
mother-force
    of Da Avabhasa, 152
    described, 151-153
Mulund, India, inspiration for cooperative
    community, 195-196

N

"Narcissus"
    conversion of, 52, 137
    dissociation, 147
    metaphor for egoity, xii
    method of, 26-27, 48, 50
    mind as, 236
    observing patterns of, 72, 84
    order is Truth to, 160
    See also self-contraction
negative circumstances, being served by, 112
negativity. *See* dramatization; emotions, negative
news reports, on world situation, 191
Non-Separateness, and Heart-Transmission, 28
nurture, and challenge, 151-153

O

obligations, honoring, 170-171
offenses
    being served by, 112
    wound of love and, 111-113, 140-142
options, escapes from surrender, 238-240
order, and "Narcissus", 160
"otherness"
    fear arises from, xiii, 54
    Liberation from, 11

P

pain
    absolute, Grace, 238-240
    in life and death, 242-243
    in love, 19-20, 208, 219-220
parents
    disposition toward, 151-152
    doing some good for, 130
    and manhood or womanhood, 126-129
    overcoming reactions to, 2-6, 126-129, 135
    See also father-force; mother-force
passion
    appropriateness of, 88-90
    feeling-Contemplation and, 91-92
patterns
    of qualities, 77-78
    of seeking, 72, 84
"peculiar" character
    emotional separateness and, 235-238
    sorrow and, 57
"Perfect Practice", 97, 98, 102-103
perfection, an egoic goal, 167-169, 230, 232
Polson, Jeff, Leela on caring for fish, 224-227
practice
    basis of, 10-11, 30, 63-64, 158
    Great Purpose and, 23-24
    relationships context for, 10-12, 192-193,
        194, 197

praise
appropriate relationship to, 166-167
cure for emotional neurosis, 157
prayer, 181-183
Prayer of Changes, 181-183
pride, inappropriateness of, 163-164
Principles, Callings, and Agreements, Given by Da Avabhasa, 199
"problem" mentality. See dilemma
psychiatric viewpoint, limitations of, 64, 82
psychic state, keeping free, 154-156
psychotherapy, unnecessary for devotee, 82-83
Puja, love as, 251
purification
in context of ordinary life, 33, 34
in crises, 69-70
through Satsang, 76-77, 78, 82-86
through self-observation, 230
with Truth, 136
purity, an egoic goal, 169, 230, 232
Purpose, Great, 23-24

Q

qualities of experience, 77-78

R

rajasic quality, 77-78
reactivity. See emotions, negative
Reality. See Consciousness Itself; Happiness; Love (Divine)
"reality consideration", 9, 29
Realization. See God-Realization
receiving
Heart-Transmission, 85-86, 149-150
life-energy from others, 14-15, 149-150, 161
recoil. See "Narcissus"; self-contraction
regrets, having none, 79
rejection, 62, 112
relational disciplines, described, xviii-xiv, 136
relationship
all that exists is, 104-105, 218
assuming, 104-105
desire and, 218
illusion of, 27-28, 216
restoring to condition of, 161
source of humor, 104-105
relationship to Da Avabhasa. See feeling-Contemplation; feeling-surrender; Satsang
relationships
bringing energy to, 114, 116-118, 146
"considered" at beginning of practice, 31
as context for practice, 10-12, 192-193, 194, 197
criticalness and, 39-42, 168
dependence-independence in, 207-212, 214-217
different kinds of, 104-105
epitomized in relationship to Da Avabhasa, 10-11
failure of, 220

fasting if disturbed, 71-72
feeling-Contemplation and, 12, 17, 21
God-Realization and, 229-230
incarnating love in, 10
inevitability of dying and, 176-169, 218-223
magnifying Love in, 17, 217
parents' influence on, 126-129, 135, 151-153, 160
renunciation and, 218
self-observation in, xvii, 11
service as principle in, 36, 114, 163
suffering and, 218-220
test of self-understanding, 12
wound of love in, 88, 111-113, 140-142, 250
relaxation
of body-mind patterns, 162
into difficulties, 147
as obligation, 155
religion, esoteric
about ecstasy, 134
as intimacy, 251-252, 253
needs cooperative community, 188, 191
religion, exoteric
not about ecstasy, 133-134
social religiosity, 190
suppression of emotions in, 87
religions, respecting other, 177-178, 180
reluctance
to love, 143-144
to practice, 33
remorse
cause and effect of, 52
See also emotions, negative
renunciates, position in culture, 200
renunciation
to allow free-falling, 219
based on Happiness, 217, 228
cooperative community and, 193-195
here, in the body, 13
life-business and, 229
love as, 19
not dissociation, 228
reducing life to intimacy, 251
relationships and, 218
social obligations and, 171
responsibility
in community, 69
foundation "yamas" and "niyamas", 170
for Happiness, 106, 109-110, 123-124
for life-energy, 154-156, 173
for love, 11, 31-32
for presumption of separateness, 46
for primitive emotional life, 80-81
rather than guilt, 123
in self-position, 108-109
See also discipline; relational disciplines
retreat, in difficult times, 71
righteousness
overcome by Happiness, 138-139
See also emotions, negative

S

sacrifice
    action as, 172-173
    food chain and, 242-244
sadhana. *See* practice
sadness. *See* sorrow
sanctuary for growth, cooperative community
    as, 188, 191, 195
Satsang
    basis for Spiritual life, xix-xxi, 29, 253
    in context of community, 188-189, 190
    cure for lovelessness, 45, 50, 74
    in difficult circumstances, 147
    ecstasy in, 214
    epitome of relationship, 10-11, 110
    equal access to, 164-165
    experience transformed by, 215
    forgiveness and, 100-101, 124
    God-Realization and, 161
    incarnating love in, 32
    an intimacy, 251-252, 253
    not a consolation, 219
    purification of karma in, 78, 85, 94, 123-124
    "radical" Condition, 143
    release of tendencies in, 74, 76-77, 78-79,
        82-86, 101
    See also feeling-Contemplation; feeling-
        surrender
sattvic quality, 77-78
"Secret of How to Change, The", 78-79
seeking
    freedom from, 110
    only not to be destroyed, 116
    recurring patterns in, 72, 84
    and separateness, xv, 26-27, 168-169
self-contraction
    affected by energy field, 157
    body-mind and, 25, 26, 63, 235-238
    conflict and, 44-45
    dependence-independence rituals and,
        214-215
    dissolved by Heart-Transmission, 28
    fear and, 26, 56
    in field of relations, 12
    negative emotions and, 51-52, 115
    observing in body-mind, 25, 26
    painfulness of, 145
    penetrating, xiv, xvi-xvii, xix-xxi, 28, 60
    presuming un-love, xii, 6, 47-48, 110-112,
        166
    resistance to community as, 197
    root of difficulties, 115
    self-understanding and, 27
    suffering and, xii-xiv, 54, 145
    See also "Narcissus"
self-discipline. *See* discipline
self-doubt, unreality of, 166-167
self-imagery, hindrance to God-Realization,
    165-166
self-importance, through victim mentality, 107

self-manipulation, futility of, 66, 159
self-negation, mistake of, 166-167, 169, 183,
    229, 232
self-observation
    feeling-Contemplation and, 28, 123-124, 232
    negative emotions and, 63
    from Position of Consciousness Itself, 84,
        94-96
    purification through, 230
    in relationships, xvii, 11
    in service, 36
Self-Realization. *See* God-Realization
self-sacrifice, daily existence as, 92
self-transcendence
    central to practice, 23-24, 169
    cooperative community and, 192, 193, 194
    an emotional matter, 21
    human implications of, 12, 177
    "radical" orientation to, 232
    service and, 35-36
self-understanding
    beginnings in ordinary life, 6
    dissolving dilemma, 24
    dramatization and, 107, 210-211
    forgiveness and, 100
    Happiness and, 132
    necessary to become love, xvi-xvii, 5, 111,
        142, 209-212
    negative emotions and, 54-57, 63-64, 115
    practice based on, 30, 63-64
    psychiatric viewpoint contrasted with, 64
    self-contraction and, 27
    tested in relationship, 12
separateness, presumption of
    do not indulge in, 145
    in each character type, 235-238
    fear and, 26, 54
    "me" and, xiii
    painfulness of, 145
    seeking and, xv, 26-27, 168-169
separation
    birth as, 51
    unreality of, 218
service
    basic disciplines relative to, 35-36
    cooperative community and, 190
    to Da Avabhasa, xix-xx, 37, 38, 165
    an expression of self-transcendence, 35-36
    as feeling-Contemplation, 37
    forgiveness of parents as, 128, 130
    free attention and, 156
    Happiness as, 36
    Leela on, 201-203
    as love, xix, 4, 35
    in relationships, 36-37, 114, 163
    self-observation and, 36
    self-transcendence and, 35-36
    without discipline of love, 4-5
sexual equality, 198
sexual preferences, tolerance and, 180

sexuality
    ecstasy and, 133
    positive orientation toward, 230-231
shame, 51-52
    See also emotions, negative
sila, 155-156
smile, for the sake of others, 150
social development, a moral and feeling gesture, 154-155
social obligations, duty and, 171
society, not cooperating with negative features of, 89, 178, 186-188
"solid" character
    fear and, 54
    mental separateness and, 235-238
sorrow, 57-58
    appropriateness of, 87, 88, 90-92
    conscious breathing and, 74
    freedom from, 223
    guilt and, 51
    of love, 88
    love more than, 91-92
    "peculiar" character and, 57
    relinquishing, 85
    See also emotions, negative
speech. *See* communication
Spirit-Current, 230-231
Spiritual life
    a crisis, 69-70
    ecstasy and, 134
    fear fundamental to, 55
    human basis of, 31-34, 46
    Love as basis for, 10, 17
    love central to, 12-13, 17, 20, 110
    Satsang as basis for, xix-xxi, 29, 32
stages of life, the first three
    anger and, 58, 230-231
    "consideration" of relationships in, 31
    Descending Spirit-Current and, 230-231
    dramatizing the self-contraction in, 8
    fear and, 55
    learning how to change agreements in, 170
    practicing in, 34
    relation to parents in, 151, 160
    responsibility for life-energy in, 154-155
    sorrow and, 57
stages of life, ultimate, and Witness Position, 97, 98
struggle, 159-160
    See also conflict
subjectivity, change action to change, 67
suffering
    as caused by self-contraction, xii-xiv, 54, 145
    of Da Avabhasa, 34, 245-248, 250
    God-Realization and, 20, 142, 176
    in love, 19-20, 34, 142, 208
    relationships and, 218-220
    seeking relief from, 25
    Truth erases, 33-34

superficiality
    desensitization, 142
    in expressing love, 7, 120-121
superiority/inferiority
    not the practice, 163-164, 181
    unreality of, 166-167
suppression of feeling, 6-8, 42, 80, 88-90, 208

T

tamasic quality, 77-78
Teaching (of Da Avabhasa), essential Communication of, 49
tendencies
    allowing to become obsolete, 78-79
    arising in Satsang, 75-77
    relinquishing, 83-86, 123-124
    unconcern with, 67-68
thoughts
    affect on others, 155
    affected by energy field, 157
    fear and, 56
    self-contraction and, 235-238
    See also body-mind; mind
threatened existence, 176-177, 191-192, 218-223, 242-247
tolerance, 175-180
    Great Tradition and, 177-178
town meeting, 199
transcendence. *See* self-transcendence
Transfiguration. *See* Divine Transfiguration
Transformation. *See* Divine Transformation
Translation. *See* Divine Translation
Transmission. *See* Heart-Transmission
true religion. *See* religion, esoteric
truth, a discipline, 174

U

unconsciousness, a decision, 104
understanding. *See* self-understanding
Undying Beloved, 220, 221-222
    See also Consciousness Itself; Love (Divine)
un-love. *See* "Narcissus"; self-contraction

V

victim mentality, 106-107
victory
    must be yielded, 164
    not in world or inwardly, 161
    only in devotion, 162
Vision of the Heart, 23-24, 245-246, 252
visions, as consolation, 46, 48
"vital" character
    anger and, 58-59
    bodily separateness and, 235-238
vital shock, fear and, 51, 54
vow, word to have force of, 170
vulnerability, in love, 111, 140-142

W

will, in converting negative emotions, 52
Wisdom-Teaching (of Da Avabhasa), essential
Communication of, 49
withdrawal, from relationship, 145-146
Witness-Position
    already stand in, 94, 95-96, 99-100, 102
    Consciousness Itself as, 84, 94-96
    ultimate stages of life and, 97, 98
womanhood, and relationship with mother,
        126-129
women, liberation presumed for, 198
world situation
    darkness of, 177-178, 180, 186-188, 243-245
    news reports on, 191
    transforming, 178, 183, 186-188, 196
worship, Divine in all beings, 181
wound of love, 88, 111-113, 140-142, 250

Y

"yamas" and "niyamas", traditional foundation,
        170

An Invitation

Da Avabhasa Offers you the most profoundly transformative opportunity that you will ever encounter— the opportunity to enter into sacred relationship with Him. In that relationship, He will Serve your human and Spiritual growth and, ultimately, your Divine Self-Realization.

If you would like to receive a free introductory brochure or talk to someone about forms of participation in the Way of the Heart, please write to or call:

Correspondence Department, IL
The Free Daist Avabhasan Communion
12040 Seigler Canyon Road
Middletown, CA 95461, USA
Phone (707) 928-4936